Midnight in some Burning Town

BRITISH SPECIAL FORCES OPERATIONS
FROM BELGRADE TO BAGHDAD

CHRISTIAN JENNINGS

CASSELL

Cassell Military Paperbacks

Cassell
Wellington House, 125 Strand
London WC2R OBB

1 3 5 7 9 10 8 6 4 2

First published 2004
by Weidenfeld & Nicolson
This Cassell Military Paperback edition 2005

British Library Cataloguing-in-Publication Data. A catalogue record
for this book is available from the British Library.

ISBN 0 304 36708 7

Cartography by Peter Harper

Printed and bound in Great Britain by Cox & Wyman Ltd, Reading, Berks.

In a few cases in this book where it has been necessary to use the
names of SAS men they have been changed. I have attempted to make
the research and subsequent writing as accurate as possible, but any
mistakes or inaccuracies in this book stand as mine and mine alone.
CJ

www.orionbooks.co.uk

This is for M

Contents

Thanks and Acknowledgements

It is sometimes good to discover in our twenty-first-century world of instant gratification, high expectation and total availability of electronic knowledge that some things still remain secret, covert and largely inaccessible. British Special Forces operations are one such thing. So, for helping me to write and research this book, in different ways, in different places, thanks and acknowledgements are due to a lot of different people on several different continents.

Firstly, to all those former and serving members, men and women, of the British, American, Australian, Polish, French, Canadian and New Zealand Armed Forces, intelligence services and governments, who can't be named. Then to my professional colleagues: Elida Ramadani-Lawton, Tina Kraja, Fis Abrashi and Andrew and Laura Testa-Kajtazi in Pristina; Merita Dhimgjoka-Ilo in Toronto and Elena Becatoros in New York; Cecile Feuillatre and Claire Snegaroff in Paris, Sebastian Rhodes-Stampa in Baghdad and Dominique Larsimont in Cyprus. In Amman, thanks to Astrid van Genderen Stort; in Lagos, thanks to Dave Clarke; to James

Hider in Baghdad; to Jessie Grimond in London; to Peter Andrews in Warsaw; and to Jonah Hull in Johannesburg. At *The Economist* in London, thanks must go to Johnny Grimond, Bruce Clarke, Xan Smiley and Venetia Longin, while for great kindness for allowing me the space and facilities in which to work in London, thanks to Iona Joy.

London and Hereford, March 2003

UZBEKISTAN

Mazar-i-Sharif

Bagram Air Base

Kabul

Jalalabad

AFGHANISTAN

Kandahar

PAKISTAN

Margo Desert

X **'site of Operation Trent'**

HELMAND
PROVINCE

0   100   200   300 /km

Afghanistan

CHAPTER ONE

All the Way From Credenhill

Britain and Sierra Leone, 2000–2001

Credenhill is a quiet village on the outskirts of Hereford, a cathedral town just over three hours' drive north-west of London and some 32km short of the border with Wales, in the shadow of the Black Mountains. There is nothing much of note in Credenhill as you drive through: a pub, some shops and, on the right-hand side of the road, dozens of identical semi-detached houses sitting in a small, grassy estate. Further on, past these houses, there is a fork in the road where a large and distinctive oak tree is set in a patch of grass between the forks. Known by local bus and taxi drivers as 'the Credenhill Tree', this is supposedly the main point of reference in the village. Nothing else in the small hamlet advertises itself. Even as you drive past the former RAF base, for instance, there is only a red sign indicating the presence of a 'Works Access', and there is little to suggest that the houses on the right-hand side of the road were at one time married-quarters lodgings for the former RAF Credenhill.

Yet there is more to the village than meets the eye. A closer inspection reveals multiple signs of new construction around the old Air Force base and a 4.5m-high fence topped with razor wire now stretches around the perimeter. After the sign announcing the 'Works Access' there is an entrance on the left, with barriers across the road, a checkpoint and a guardhouse; three Ministry of Defence policemen wearing body armour and cradling Heckler & Koch MP5 sub-machine-guns are posted at the entrance. The RAF moved out of Credenhill some time ago. The new occupants are the soldiers of 22 Special Air Service Regiment, Britain's SAS. The former RAF base first became the unit's new home in the late 1990s when the SAS moved there from its previous home at Stirling Lines, formerly known as Bradbury Lines – a slouching sprawl of barrack blocks, HQ buildings, parade grounds and two-storey red-brick living quarters in another Hereford suburb that had housed the unit since the 1960s. Credenhill is a rather more purpose-built arrangement. Beyond the armed guards, a gate leads through the barbed-wire fence to a helicopter pad, a shooting-range and armouries. Many of the facilities, curiously, have been built not only with money from Britain's Ministry of Defence, but also with the aid of a multimillion-pound legacy bequeathed by John Paul Getty II, the cricket-loving philanthropist who developed a curious affection for British excellence in all its forms.

By mid-October 2001, 22 SAS had been in a state of massive operational expectation for more than a month, since the fateful events of 11 September. The Regimental Headquarters had learned of the attacks on the twin towers of the World Trade Centre in New York through a variety of means. Information about the attacks had filtered in from soldiers watching television reports, through direct information passed on by the Secret Intelligence Service (SIS) liaison officer attached to the unit, from the Ministry of Defence in London and from the small cell of British Special Forces liaison staff posted with US SOCOM, the United States Special Operations Command based in Florida and South Carolina.

In the days immediately following the attacks, the commanding officer of 22 SAS – a colonel on attachment from the Green Jackets – had briefed as many of the unit as possible who were in the United Kingdom. Everybody in the unit knew that the United States was going to take some form of active operational retribution, almost certainly involving an attack on Afghanistan. That there would be a role for the SAS to play in America's about-to-be-declared 'War on Terror' was not in dispute, and each operational squadron of 22 SAS was keen to find out which units the commanding officer would assign to which theatres of operation. As it became clear that Britain was, in the words of Prime Minister Tony Blair, ready to stand 'shoulder to shoulder' with the Americans in the coming conflict, so it began to become apparent that the global nature of the 'War on Terror' would comprehensively affect the way in which British Special Forces operated. The nature of the operations on which Britain's Special Forces would be deployed from that point forward was going to change radically – the geopolitical nature of their task was metamorphosing and, like Special Forces units worldwide, they were going to find themselves increasingly busy in the new world order. 11 September 2001 would mark a line in the sand for the men from Credenhill.

Hereford is a close-knit town, and the surrounding rural villages are even more so: people know each other, and there is a strong sense of community. The SAS has been based in the city for over forty years and is well embedded in local life. Hereford residents could have told you in early October 2001 that the war in Afghanistan would definitely start by the middle of that month. The men operating and training abroad in the Balkans and in Oman, in Asia and the United States, and also locally in Hereford had been reporting back to their wives and girlfriends, who were eager to see them return home. The jungle telegraph of Special Forces wives was nearly accurate. They got the start date of Operation Enduring Freedom, as the US-led deployment in Afghanistan was code-named, wrong by only ten days: cruise missiles and 900kg laser-guided 'smart' bombs actually started thundering into the heart of the Taliban regime in Afghanistan on 7 October, a little sooner than the Hereford network had anticipated.

22 Special Air Service Regiment – or 'twenty-two', 'two-two', 22 SAS, the SAS or the Regiment, as it is variously called – is made up of four operational or 'Sabre' squadrons: 'A', 'B', 'D' and 'G'. There used to

be a 'C' Squadron, which was the Rhodesian Special Air Service. 'G' Squadron is so named because it was originally formed from the Brigade of Guards Independent Parachute Company in 1965, after the unit's dissolution on its return from fighting in Borneo. 22 SAS also comprises an HQ Squadron, a Training Wing, a Counter-Revolutionary Warfare Wing known colloquially as 'the Wing', an attached Signals unit 22nd (SAS) Signals Squadron, a Royal Engineers detachment and a focal headquarters-based Intelligence Corps unit. For large-scale deployments, additional men can be drawn in from 'R' or Reserve Squadron, and from the Regiment's two Territorial Army units, 21 and 23 SAS. Each Sabre squadron, nominally seventy-two men strong, is made up of four sixteen-man troops (plus support personnel), each troop commanded by a captain; each troop is further broken down into four four-man patrols. Each troop in each squadron has a combat speciality in addition to the multiple military skills each soldier is expected to possess. There will typically be an Air Troop specialising in high-altitude low-opening (HALO) freefall parachuting, a Mountain Troop trained in arctic and mountain warfare, a Mobility Troop based on specially converted V8 Land Rover Defender 110s and a Boat Troop trained in amphibious warfare.

By mid-October 2001, some 120 British soldiers from 'A' and 'G' Squadrons of 22 SAS had been dispatched to the Middle East, much to the chagrin of the Regiment's 'B' and 'D' Squadrons. The choice of squadrons to be deployed had been made on the basis of existing assignment and availability. 'D' Squadron was already assigned to Special Projects duty – they were the anti-terrorist unit on permanent notice to respond to domestic terrorism or any incident involving British citizens arising abroad outside the remit of Operation Enduring Freedom – and 'B' Squadron was on standby. 'A' Squadron was on long-term training and 'G' Squadron had recently returned from a training exercise in desert warfare in Oman and a small-scale deployment to Macedonia, where they had participated in the NATO operation codenamed 'Essential Harvest'. This operation had been part of a seemingly endless peace process designed to bring to an end that year's war in the small Balkan state between Albanian rebels and Macedonian government forces. The SAS that deployed to Afghanistan between October and December 2001 was possibly as well trained as it had ever been in the unit's short yet eventful regimental history that had begun in 1941.

Following its inception in World War II and subsequent operations in North Africa, Italy and North-West Europe, the SAS had carried out counterinsurgency operations in Malaya and Borneo, fought against Communist-backed nationalists in Aden, the Radfan and Dhofar, operated undercover in Northern Ireland and carried the war to the enemy against the Argentinians in the Falklands. The story of Britain's separation from her former colonies is reflected in the history of the SAS. Once the Cold War had ended in 1989, operations carried out by 22 SAS in the 1990s had included tours of duty in Croatia, Bosnia, East Timor and South America. Lessons had been learned in every conceivable form of warfare in places as diverse as Albania, Sierra Leone and Kosovo. Prior to 11 September 2001, however, the role of the unit – and British Special Forces in general – was still confined to four distinctly defined and fairly 'traditional' areas.

Firstly, since the beginning of the 1990s they had supported the increasing number of international peacekeeping, peace-support and military- and humanitarian-intervention missions carried out by US, EU and NATO troops. Secondly, they had dealt with the continuing threat of domestic terrorism within the United Kingdom's borders, frequently operating as the executive enforcing arm of the Security Services. Thirdly, they had helped to train the armies of foreign countries deemed friendly to the United Kingdom. Fourthly, they had carried out hostage-rescue missions to free British nationals captured abroad.

A mission typical of the deployments of British Special Forces prior to 11 September 2001 took place in September 2000 in the West African country of Sierra Leone. In September 2000, a British Army peace-support mission was operating in Sierra Leone alongside a UN mission. The former British colony had undergone political and economic meltdown during the 1990s as a succession of rebel factions, including some from neighbouring Liberia and Guinea, had battled for control of Sierra Leone against the country's lacklustre government forces, which were backed on an intermittent basis by a variety of South African and British mercenaries. In addition to the tactical and strategic value of this West African state, its far more lucrative and attractive diamond industry was also at stake. Control of the capital, Freetown, had swung backwards and forwards and atrocity-prone rebels from the self-styled Revolutionary United Front (RUF), known for their proclivity for amputating the limbs and noses of their prisoners, controlled much of the country. When the RUF's latest offensive took them to Freetown in January 1999, an international intervention mission had followed.

Back in September 2000, 'D' Squadron of 22 SAS, accompanied by troops from the 1st Battalion, the Parachute Regiment, had deployed to Sierra Leone to rescue British military personnel from the Royal Irish Regiment who had been captured and were being held hostage by one of a myriad of Sierra Leonean rebel militias. The kidnappers in question called themselves the 'West Side Niggaz'. In some American newspapers, there was at the time such politically correct fear of calling this (black African) group by the name 'Niggaz' – which it had chosen for itself and which almost certainly derived from some gangsta rap tune or other – that they became known as the 'West Side Boys'. In Britain they were first referred to as the 'West Side Group', later as the 'West Side Boys'. But since West Side Niggaz is what they called themselves, so they shall remain – in this narrative, at least. A subsidiary breakaway sect of the Sierra Leonean government forces loosely allied with deserters from the rebel Revolutionary United Front (RUF), they were in reality a five-star, twenty-four-carat gang of West African ganja-smoking, tooled-up anarchic fetishists – men, women and teenage boys and girls for whom the Kalashnikov was everything from a weapon to a plaything to a wife. Wearing wigs, totemic charms made from human fingers and rolled-up pubic hair, wedding dresses and bikinis into battle, with multiple ammunition clips bound together on their Kalashnikov assault rifles with masking tape emblazoned with United Nations logos, their commanders boasted names like 'Big Slaughter', 'Bring Down Da House', 'Fatty Automatic' and 'Mega-Rapist'.

They existed in a manner perfectly befitting any self-respecting West African rebel, their lives being a sea of dope, drink and automatic weapons, with refugee women on hand as sex-slaves and occasional forays on to the roads and into the cities of the country for a spot of fighting. Consequently in August 2000, when eleven officers and men from the Royal Irish Regiment on their way back from visiting a UN peacekeeping battalion in nearby Masiaka found themselves kidnapped by the Niggaz, things weren't looking too good for the British Army. An air of twitchiness started to prevail in Whitehall.

The kidnap and subsequent events were just another tiny clause in an endless chapter of African madness, this one called 'Sierra Leone'. The British, despite being one of the two most astute Western nations when it comes to dealing with black African armies and rebels – the other being the French – found themselves in a tricky position. It would be shaming and humiliating in the extreme for the British Army to have their officers, NCOs and men humiliated, wounded, mutilated or, at worst, killed and eaten by a bunch of African rebels. The British were discovering that life in Sierra Leone was just a little bit different from life in Catterick. What seems known, certain, a given, an absolute, the only way of doing things in Europe, has a habit of turning to grains of meaningless river sand washed away by the rains when it comes to Africa. Typically, assuming that what prevails in London prevails in the rest of the world, the British government dispatched to Sierra Leone two Metropolitan Police hostage negotiators. The experience these men had of dealing with cockney armed robbers holding up sub-post offices in Hounslow would undoubtedly come in useful in West Africa for dealing with a bunch of cocaine- and rape-addled child soldiers whose idea of handling conflict and anger-management issues was amputating somebody's arm with a machete. Interestingly, one of the last demands the West Side Niggaz made through their hostage-negotiation team – before they slipped back into the more familiar and comfortable negotiation vernacular of mock executions – was to demand scholarships so that they could study abroad.

It was questionable how effective the Metropolitan Police techniques would be against the four squads of West Side Niggaz who were now loosely commanded by four senior fighters calling themselves Commanders Blood, Terminator, Savage and Cambodia. The rebels were armed with a combination of Kalashnikov assault rifles, 7.62mm self-loading rifles that had been issued to them via the British Army, when they were still part of the Sierra Leonean government forces, and RPG-7 rocket launchers. They also had some 7.62mm general-purpose machine guns (GPMGs), some heavier .50-calibre Brownings, one artillery piece and a double-barrelled anti-aircraft gun. It was unclear how frequently or regularly the West Side Niggaz cleaned their weapons; an SAS team dispatched into the jungle to carry out surveillance of their camp had not reported the occurrence of any such weapons maintenance. That did not mean, however, that a substantial fire fight would not be required to take the camp. Curiously, it was the West Side Niggaz' very unorthodox behaviour, their belief in magic, jujus, spirits, of being bulletproof through taking drugs, that made them a difficult foe. That and the fact that their base would require a logistically complex operation to attack it. The operation had a lot of potential for going badly wrong, and the British were worried that it could turn into a version of 'Black Hawk Down' in the jungle if the SAS or the Paras got stuck on the ground. When the British government decided that the humiliation of the British soldiers had gone on long enough, the call went out on 30 August 2000 to Hereford and to the 1st Battalion of the Parachute Regiment.

The Niggaz had located their camp deep in the Sierra Leonean jungle on a bend in a river called Rokel Creek, not far from the village of Magbeni in the Occra Hills. Their leader, self-styled Brigadier Foday Kallay, had at one point ordered the hostages to be tied to bamboo stakes stuck into the ground on the edge of the river, in an area known as the 'Dead Zone', and threatened to execute them. It was here that other unfortunate victims of the Niggaz had met their ends. Allegedly wracked with a large amount of cocaine, he eventually relented, and the Royal Irish Regiment prisoners were returned to their bamboo and mud huts. Although five of the hostages had been released during the early stages of the negotiations, it was now very clear that the remaining hostages were in real danger of being executed. An SAS reconnaissance party dispatched to assess possible rescue scenarios discovered that it would be extremely difficult to get upriver in boats, and that the surrounding countryside was covered with jungle too dense to allow an infiltration to the target on foot. For the week prior to the rescue mission launched on 10 September 2000, the SAS party laid-up in the jungle, reporting back on the movements within the camp.

The team of SAS, SBS and Paras tasked with Operation Barras went in on three CH-47 Chinook helicopters, accompanied by three Lynxes and an Mi-24 Hind gunship. The CO of 22 SAS at the time was the same colonel, a former OC 'D' Squadron, who would be commanding the Regiment just after 11 September 2001. One group of paratroopers was tasked with attacking the village of Magbeni on the south bank of the creek, while the second group took the Gberi Bana camp on the north side. As the Chinooks swept in just before the sun came up, landing in the centre of the village where the Royal Irish soldiers were being held hostage, the fighters and child-soldiers of the West Side Niggaz were at their lowest ebb. It was early on a Sunday morning, there had been a typical rebel Saturday night preceding it and the last thing a hung-over, tired, muddy and rather traumatised West African child-soldier needed to face first thing on a Sunday morning was thirty-two men from 'D' Squadron of 22 SAS, few of whom had been in a 'contact' before, all armed to the teeth, in possession of a satisfactorily broad set of rules of engagement and all keen to see some action before they flew back to Hereford. As if this wasn't bad enough, there was the best part of a company from the 1st Battalion of the Parachute Regiment coming in behind the SAS – again, men from a self-styled military elite just dying to put African-rebel notches on their assault rifles. In went the Paras and the SAS; an enormous fire fight ensued, the hostages were rescued and the

West Side Niggaz were either scattered or shot to death. For the British it was home in time for tea and a dramatic number of medals, including Military Crosses and Distinguished Service Orders.

One SAS trooper from 'D' Squadron, Brad Tinnion, was hit and died as a result of his wounds. Tinnion, who had just passed the SAS selection course, had come from 29 Commando Regiment, Royal Artillery. Ten Paras were also hit, including the company commander of 'A' Company, 1 Para, Major Matthew Lowe, who was wounded when a group of men he had led through a swamp came under enemy fire after entering the village. His Company Second-in-Command (2 IC) Captain Danny Matthews, who had been a platoon commander in Kosovo the year before, was awarded the Military Cross for his part in the action.

Officially, the West Side Niggaz body count was twenty-five, of whom three were women. After the battle, it was estimated that the final death toll resulting from the operation could have been up to 100 Sierra Leoneans killed as they fled the area surrounding the villages through concentric rings of Parachute Regiment ambushes, or as they were chased into the bush or shot while hiding in it by the Paras and the SAS. How many of these casualties were actually fighters and how many were unarmed camp followers press-ganged into service by the West Side Niggaz is not clear.

In addition to the traditional Special Forces role of hostage-rescue fulfilled by 22 SAS in Operation Barras, the soldiers of that unit began to find themselves, even pre-11 September 2001, on a variety of other rather more curious deployments in places such as Macedonia, Serbia, Chechnya, Columbia, Ecuador, the Democratic Republic of Congo, the Philippines and Uzbekistan. What had the men from Hereford been doing in these places? The answer lies in the development of military- and humanitarian-intervention missions carried out by the UN, NATO and the European Union, and in the rapid growth of peace-support, peace-enforcement and peacekeeping duties that were increasingly being undertaken by the so-called 'international community' since 1990. To the techniques and operational procedures learned by 22 SAS in Aden,

Oman, Borneo, Northern Ireland and the Falklands were to be added a completely new set of skills. Already accomplished in counter-revolutionary warfare, in missions of hostage-rescue and jungle warfare, in deployments that saw the unit bring their counterinsurgency skills to bear and their anti-terrorist training into play, 22 SAS found itself increasingly operating at the forefront of, and alongside, complex deployments where the main operators on the ground were not just the military.

During the 1990s, 22 SAS was increasingly deployed in the same theatres as non-governmental organisations (NGOs) – the UN's multifarious agencies, the European Commission's complicated post-conflict restructuring missions and every conceivable crossover between the different players in the international community. This *ad hoc*, constantly changing, constantly adapting, constantly growing international political-economic amoeba consisted of the loosely linked band of soldiers, politicians, aid workers, journalists, UN staff, governmental lobbyists and human rights activists that had become, in many cases, the operational consciousness of governments. By the early 1990s it was a multibillion-dollar industry in its own right.

There were four significant international intervention missions during the 1990s that, coupled with the events of 11 September 2001, would redefine the way in which the international community would operate in the new millennium. These missions redefined the international community's policies on military intervention and, consequently, how Britain's Special Forces would find themselves being deployed in the future. These transformative missions took place in Somalia, Rwanda, Bosnia and Kosovo. In order to understand how the soldiers of Britain's Special Forces found their operational arena changing after 11 September 2001, it is imperative to look at the way it had already been influenced by the milestone international interventions of the 1990s.

Faced with huge numbers of Somali deaths caused by famine in 1992, the United States and the UN sent in troops to protect food-relief convoys and to prevent Somali warlords and their gunmen from hijacking the convoys, stealing the grain and selling it for profit instead of giving it to their starving and penniless fellow Somalis. It was a good idea to start with and initially it worked well. Then the United States decided to undertake the ambitious task of wresting civic power in Somalia from armed clan warlords, and went into this insane mission backed up by a UN Security Council Resolution that authorised a 'Chapter Seven' intervention instead of a 'Chapter Six'. The difference was one of 'peacekeeping' rather than 'peace enforcement'. The American military and their political masters were simply not up to the task of confronting armed Somali civilians.

Led by US Admiral Jonathan Howe, a man described by one British analyst in Mogadishu as having 'the political savvy of a mollusc', the mission was a complete disaster. The one-sided representation of the mission's culmination in the film and book *Black Hawk Down* did the Somalis grave injustice. The Americans fiercely bungled an operation to try to arrest some of the leading lieutenants of warlord Mohamed Farah Aidid. The mission went wrong and two Black Hawk helicopters were shot down over central South Mogadishu. A combined team of US Army Rangers and Delta Force operators, some of whom had been involved in the bungled arrest operation and some of whom were subsequently tasked with rescuing the downed helicopter crews, became horribly bogged down in a massive fire fight that spread across the whole of South Mogadishu. Militarily speaking, the Americans fought well both individually and in small units. At fault were their planning and knowledge of the Somalis' operating techniques. The Americans claimed afterwards that they had, in fact, killed around 1,000 Somalis during that operation for the loss of only eighteen of their own men. Somali human rights groups and international journalists, however, have cast aspersions on this estimate.

Talking about the incident later, the Somali gunman who is creditably believed to have shot down Warrant Officer Michael Durant's Black Hawk helicopter with an RPG-7 antitank rocket described the experience of fighting the Americans in a typically elegiac Somali way. Dressed in a sarong, flip-flops, pink-rimmed sunglasses and a blue flak-jacket emblazoned with the logo of Worldwide Television News – for whom he was working as a bodyguard at the time, in 1995 – 'Little Ears', as he was known, cradled his signature RPG-7 rocket launcher as he sat on a ruined wall overlooking the K50 airstrip outside South Mogadishu. 'The Americans,' he said, 'will always crash into things around them.'

As the warm wind coming off the Indian Ocean blew sand around his feet, 'Little Ears' continued, making movements with his hands like cars crashing into each other: 'They do not know how to move with things, only against them.'

The Somali gunman's analysis of the shortcomings of the US Army's fire-and-manoeuvre techniques was to the point. Just less than a decade later in the Afghan mountains around Tora Bora, Kandahar and in the north of the country with the Northern Alliance, the Americans were still very much crashing into things – with some success, it has to be admitted – but the lack of operational subtlety that 'Little Ears' had noticed was still in evidence.

Back in Somalia, after the deaths of eighteen of their men in Mogadishu and the subsequent airing of TV pictures showing the naked bodies of dead soldiers being dragged through the streets by a Somali mob, the American Marines, Rangers and Delta Force pulled out of Somalia. The entire UN mission followed them. Consequently, when 6 April 1994 came around and Rwanda fell over a moral cliff and imploded in the swiftest genocide in the history of the planet, there was no way that President Clinton was going to commit American troops to stop it. Six weeks later, with the best part of three-quarters of a million mainly Tutsi corpses splattered across the eucalyptus groves and banana plantations of Rwanda, the words 'never again' uttered at Nuremburg started to sound a little hollow.

Meanwhile, thousands of kilometres to the north, the international community's willingness and capacity to intervene to stop another epic bout of mass death in a fragmenting sovereign state was being put to the test in Yugoslavia. By the time the Dayton Peace Accords were signed in 1995 – effectively an internationally agreed ceasefire – it had been estimated that between 200,000 and 250,000 people – Croats, Bosnians, Serbs and Muslims – had died. Lieutenant-General Sir Michael Rose, who had been the British commander of UN forces in Bosnia in 1994, came to the conclusion after the UN's vacillations in Africa and through assimilating the experiences of military colleagues who had commanded the mission in Bosnia that an effective means of gathering intelligence on the ground was needed in any future operations of this nature. He therefore tasked a number of men from his Regiment, 22 SAS, with the job of working as 'Joint Commission Observers' (JCOs). Rose, himself a recipient of a Distinguished Service Order and Queen's Gallantry Medal, had commanded 22 SAS during the operations in the Falklands, had commanded 'G' Squadron and had overseen 22 SAS's assault on the Iranian Embassy in London in 1980. His JCOs were to be his eyes and ears on the ground in Bosnia for the duration of the UN operation. In addition, up to a squadron of SAS were deployed from Hereford during 1994 and 1995 who had seen action in a variety of locations, mostly enclaves that included Goradze, Maglaj, Bihac and Srebrenica.

The bombing campaign and subsequent military occupation of Kosovo by NATO and the UN in 1999 was something of a turning point, intended to rectify the mistakes made in Somalia, Rwanda and Bosnia. Having learned in Bosnia and across Africa that operating under a frustratingly limited UN Security Council mandate was often a recipe for lack of military progress at best, or disaster at worst, NATO's military praetorian guard decided to take on the Serbs in Kosovo in 1999 without a UN Security Council mandate. In the case of Kosovo, the military- and humanitarian-intervention plan worked excellently, almost like a textbook example of how to react to incidences of vast human rights abuses being carried out by the agents of a foreign state – in this case Slobodan Milosevic's soldiers and paramilitaries – against an ethnic minority – the Albanian population of Kosovo.

If Kosovo was the intervention mission where the international community responded to and appeared to have learned some of the lessons of Rwanda, Somalia and Bosnia, then the United States' subsequent decisions to operate on a unilateral basis in Afghanistan and Iraq, with or without an international coalition, was partially dictated to it by the lessons it had learned in Kosovo. Kosovo was a vital milestone in international intervention missions: it marked a fulcrum, a mid-point, a crucial focus of lessons learned and those that remained to be learned, from Rwanda, Bosnia and Somalia before it, to Iraq and Afghanistan after it. Similarly, the two key international developments that changed the way in which Britain's Special Forces would operate, in which theatres and to what political ends were the NATO and interim UN administration in Kosovo and the events of 11 September 2001.

This, then, was the international environment in which 22 SAS was operating between 1993 and 2003. Their deployments increasingly reflected the rapidly changing *modus operandi* of the international community, the nature of which was itself constantly shifting and altering. Like the rest of the world, Britain's Special Forces had been deeply affected by the transformation of society by electronic and new media technology, by the advent of a global war against terrorism, the end of the Cold War, the enlargement of NATO and the EU and the evolving, escalating challenges posed to international security by religious fundamentalism and ethnic nationalism. For 22 SAS, the changing world picture meant combining more 'traditional' skills with new mission objectives not previously in their remit. Operations in Kosovo for 22 SAS centred on their usual business of guiding in air strikes, training members of the Kosovo Liberation Army (KLA), reconnaissance and arresting war criminals, but also involved supplying military muscle to a NATO peace-support operation. Prior to that, operations in Bosnia were partly about directing air strikes and partly about the new remit to gather intelligence for Lieutenant-General Sir Michael Rose.

It is worth noting, however, that although the political climate in which 22 SAS was being deployed and the military aims of their operations may have changed, quite often the manner in which they found themselves fighting altered little. In the mountains around Kandahar and Tora Bora in Afghanistan in November 2001, the SAS were back to the kind of war-fighting operation that had changed little for them since the days of the Western Desert in 1942. SAS patrols around Tora Bora and on the Pakistani border involved heavily laden soldiers operating at troop and squadron strength, walking up mountains carrying a very large amount of equipment and fighting an enemy dug into strong defensive positions. In effect, the fighting at Tora Bora was almost as conventional a form of small-scale counterinsurgency war-fighting as it is possible to imagine. Operation Trent, the attack on an al-Qaeda opium storage plant in Helmand Province in November 2001, was entirely based on columns of heavily armed Land Rovers, calling to mind distant memories of patrols of Willys jeeps armed with Vickers 'K' machine guns operating in the Western Desert and in mainland Europe during World War II. However, Operation Trent, as will be argued later, could have been implemented using line infantry. There is clearly a distinction to be drawn between context and action. While the international political situation has continued to change, in some cases Special Forces' operational methods have not – although they may find themselves more and more often in increasingly complex situations, working alongside more unconventional allies than they might have done a couple of decades earlier in their history.

The changing nature of British Special Forces deployments is reflected in the careers and military accomplishments of the British SAS officers who began their Special Forces careers in the early 1990s and who by 2003 were running the British Special Forces establishment. Subsequent to the US and coalition operations in Afghanistan and Iraq, in which Western Special Forces have played such a huge part, it is not an overstatement to say that the future nature of Special Forces warfare and covert missions within the mantle of land-war operations is being increasingly defined by a relatively small number of extremely capable British and American officers. The small size of 22 SAS means that not only do all the soldiers know each other, but also that the SAS network is entirely run by soldiers who have been commanded by, or have commanded, each other in action. The individuals who have commanded its units, fought its battles, dictated its policy, overseen its development and maintained its carefully developed traditions while constantly developing, innovating and modifying its methods of operation include a small group of officers from such units as the Parachute Regiment, the Brigade of Guards, the Light Infantry, the Green Jackets, the Black Watch, the King's Own Scottish Borderers and the Royal Scots.

A good example of how the careers of these SAS officers have also embodied and revealed the unit's evolving operational nature since the beginning of the 1990s would be a recent Director Special Forces. He was originally a Parachute Regiment brigadier, decorated with the Military Cross for bravery under fire and for outstanding leadership as a lieutenant commanding a platoon in the 3rd Battalion, the Parachute Regiment, during the battle for Mount Longdon in the Falklands in June 1982. Subsequently a troop commander and squadron commander in 22 SAS and a battalion commander in the 2nd Battalion, the Parachute Regiment, he became commanding officer (CO) of a British Mechanised Infantry Brigade in Kosovo and finally achieved the highest position within the SF community, that of Director Special Forces.

There are many other such examples. A recent CO of 22 SAS – a colonel from the Irish Guards – was an SAS troop commander during the fighting around the enclaves of Maglaj, Gorazde and Srebrenica in Bosnia in 1994. His brother, an SAS troop commander on attachment from the Green Jackets, was awarded the Military Cross for operations in and around a Serb enclave as a result of a citation written by his own brother. Prior to taking up the appointment as CO of 22 SAS, the colonel from the Irish Guards had served as a squadron commander and then as chief of staff of a Mechanised Brigade in Kosovo between 1999 and 2000. A CO of 16 Air Assault Brigade, Britain's quick-reaction helicopter-borne force, has split his career between the Parachute Regiment and the SAS, with a small diversion to a cavalry regiment, and is himself a former Director Special Forces and a former CO of 22 SAS. One of his infantry battalion commanders from the Royal Irish Regiment who served under him in the Gulf with distinction – and notoriety – is a former squadron commander of 22 SAS.

The Green Jackets have an established track record of providing officers for the SAS, and at least one CO of the Regiment in the last decade began his career there. Two squadron commanders and two troop commanders in 22 SAS, at least one of whom was on attachment from the Green Jackets, have seen action in Bosnia – at Gorazde, Maglaj and Srebrenica – and in Kosovo, Afghanistan and Northern Ireland. A former OC 'G' Squadron was a Parachute Regiment major on attachment from the 1st Battalion. After operations in Bosnia he attended Staff College, where he graduated top of his class; he then became chief of staff for an Armoured Brigade in Kosovo, then OC of 'G' Squadron before returning to lecture at the Higher Command Staff College.

Officers serving with 22 SAS spend three years on each of their attachments to the Regiment, firstly as a captain commanding a sixteen-man troop, then as a major commanding a seventy-two-strong squadron, then either as a lieutenant-colonel acting as 2 IC of the Regiment, or as full colonel commanding. Above and beyond the Regiment itself is the Directorate of UK Special Forces, normally commanded by a brigadier. Between 1993 and 2003, 22 SAS has been commanded by a Green Jacket, a Light Infantry officer, a Parachute Regiment officer, a Scots Guardsman, a Welsh Guardsman and an Irish Guardsman.

The last operational deployment of 22 SAS before the attacks on New York's twin towers was a perfect example of how tried and honed military skills – in this case reconnaissance – were being used in support of a rather more complex and wide-ranging international operation of preventive diplomacy. On 16 September 2001, just days after the attacks on the World Trade Centre, men from 'G' Squadron were sitting in Dal Met Fu, a popular terraced café in the Macedonian capital of Skopje. It had been the latest in a string of scorchingly hot days in the Balkan summer of 2001, just before the world was apparently to change for ever. Led by their squadron commander, a major attached from the Parachute Regiment, the SAS soldiers had been assisting in reconnaissance and disarmament operations involving the self-styled Albanian rebels of the National Liberation Army (NLA), who that year had been fighting heavily with Macedonian government forces across the cornfields and scorched mountains of the whole north and west of that southern Balkan state. The operation had been tricky, only partially successful and heavily covered in the media, and NATO's mediation efforts with the Albanian rebels had led to a perceived rebel victory over the Skopje government's forces, with resulting accusations that NATO was aligning itself with terrorism and Albanian nationalism.

As will be discussed, the war in Macedonia was a by-product of the war in Kosovo, itself a vital proving ground for the emerging new resolve of the international community. Macedonia stood between the agonies of the war in Bosnia, the birthing pains of the new international community and the military operations that would be carried out during the 'War on Terror' by Western nations experimenting with the establishment of a new kind of illiberal democracy. While NATO, the UN and the international community had found their truest, though still very flawed, expression in Kosovo and Macedonia, there is an argument that everything thereafter would smack of US-tainted anticlimax. Is this also true of British Special Forces operations? Was their world simpler and better understood before 11 September 2001? Did they have more operational leeway before the events of 11 September turned the whole globe into one vast intelligence operation, namely the 'War on Terror', in which British Special Forces troops play an executive part? Or have they changed little, simply evolving already existing skills to meet the same type of operational deployment as of old, except in new countries with new American political masters? The answers to these questions can perhaps be found in an in-depth examination and analysis of the pivotal conflicts that emerged at the turn of the millennium, beginning with the war in Kosovo.

CHAPTER TWO

Fighting Under the Banner of the Double-Headed Eagle

Kosovo, 1999

There was a full moon on the night of 11–12 June 1999, illuminating the mountains and the oak forests of the Albanian border with Kosovo, and even at midnight the outside temperature was close to 30°C. Aside from the soft glow of the moon, however, there were no landing lights on the rudimentary airstrip that had just been built by a construction company of soldiers from the United Arab Emirates. Perhaps they had thought that nobody would actually need to use the runway in the middle of the night, that the nearby temporary refugee camps of Kosovo Albanians would really only need aid supplies that could be flown in during the day. Whatever the reason, the murram airstrip made up of red gravel and grey granite chips overlaid with Tarmac had no lights. It sat just beyond the waving yellow stalks of a ripening cornfield outside the northern Albanian town of Kukes. A kilometre away, just to the far northern end of the cornfield, were the refugee camps that had been full of Kosovo Albanian refugees since the spring – old men, women and children cramped into sweltering tents, fleeing President Slobodan Milosevic's campaign of ethnic cleansing in neighbouring Kosovo.

The C-130 Hercules that lined up for take-off on the unlit airstrip that night had no markings apart from a small blue and red RAF roundel on its tail. The fuselage was painted silver-grey. It taxied to the middle of the runway and revved its engines. There were no other aircraft competing for take-off that night. It accelerated along the central line of the runway, engines roaring, and just before the point of no return it pulled back its nose and, with an effort, struggled off into the warm air of the Albanian night. Inside the aircraft were three long-wheelbase Land Rover V8 110s, each spray-painted in camouflage. Each vehicle was reported to be mounted with a combination of 7.62mm general-purpose machine guns (GPMGs), 40mm automatic grenade launchers, Milan antitank missile launchers and .50-calibre Browning heavy machine guns. Intelligence sources and SAS men say that there are two versions of the subsequent events, specifically involving the destination of the aircraft.

One version reports that SAS men from 'B' Squadron were aboard and, according to a report from an SAS commander, 'loaded for bear' and fully operational, heading into Kosovo to help capture Slatina Airport, located just outside Pristina. The lights inside the aircraft were set on muted red for night operations, and in this version of events the men would already have started to think about the flying time to Pristina Airport, 120km to the north-east. It was not going to be an easy operation. The men knew that they could well be going into an armed confrontation at best, a fire fight at worst, with the most unexpected of foes: Russians.

A second, less feasible, version of events has it that the men aboard the aircraft were from the Revolutionary Warfare Wing of 22 SAS and had just been exfiltrated from Kosovo after weeks spent covertly inside the province supplying NATO with intelligence and assisting the Kosovo Liberation Army (KLA). They were thus supposedly on their way back to Italy, although why an operational troop of 22 SAS men returning from a mission would be deploying with fully armed and equipped Land Rovers is not explained.

Regardless of the disputed destination of the aircraft, disaster struck on take-off. The aircraft had barely lifted its nose and cleared the airstrip when there was a violent jerk and the power seemed to diminish. Then the engines roared, the plane lurched, dropped suddenly and finally jarred furiously into the Albanian cornfield. Seen from a standpoint 1.5km away across the lake at Kukes, the Hercules ploughed nose-first into the cornfield. The pilot wrenched the screeching, slithering aircraft to a stop. The vehicles inside, which had been attached to the floor of the aircraft for transit, began to lurch and shift position. One SAS man is reported to have taken the terrible weight of a sliding Land Rover that fell across his leg, trapping him. The flight engineer opened the door leading from the cockpit to the interior of the aircraft, where he saw the air load-master struggling to manually open one of the sliding side-doors of the Hercules. There was an all-pervasive smell of Avtur – aviation turbine fuel – leaking everywhere. The Land Rovers and the SAS troops were loaded with ammunition, explosives and grenades. All it would take would be one spark – the pilot knew that the three-man crew and the twelve SAS troopers had seconds to get out of the aircraft before it exploded, taking them all with it. The SAS man whose reportedly badly broken leg was trapped under the Land Rover could not escape the aircraft without assistance. Heroically, one of his 22 SAS comrades is said to have risked his own life to lift the side of the fallen Land Rover, giving the trapped man just enough space to crawl free and allowing him to be dragged out and carried to safety just moments before the fuel and ammunition in the plane started to explode. The soldiers and the crew ran hard across the field on to a dirt track running through the corn, providing an access route to the refugee encampments further up the track. Behind them, the Hercules aircraft burst into flames, ammunition and explosives 'cooking off' as the heat inside the fuselage increased.

The aircraft was still burning fiercely nearly two hours later as NATO fighter aircraft and helicopters circled in the sky above the Kukes refugee camps. Firing bright white magnesium flares into the air around them to deflect any incoming ground-to-air missiles launched by the Serbs just over the nearby border with Kosovo, the SAS men were evacuated by helicopter into the warm summer night. On this night of 11–12 June 1999, the SAS were spearheading the deployment of NATO troops into Kosovo. It would be the largest military- and humanitarian-intervention operation since the Korean War, and British Special Forces were involved at every level.

Earlier that day, north-west of the town of Kukes inside Kosovo itself, the temperature had been nearly 32°C. Even under the shade of the scrubby oak trees, there was no wind to raise the dust on the narrow dirt track that led to the main road. The group of Kosovo Albanian guerrilla fighters gathered under the trees were silent, the only noises the metallic click of ammunition clips being settled into place on Kalashnikov assault rifles and the creak of webbing as one man or another shifted position. Most of the men were smoking, drawing deeply on counterfeited Albanian cigarettes pinched between dirt-stained fingers. Their commander was waiting. On the left shoulder of his dusty black combat shirt and on the camouflaged forage cap set on his head was a striking insignia coloured red, orange and black. It showed a double-headed black eagle set against a red background: the national flag of Albania. Surrounding the eagle was a semi-circular three-word inscription sewn on to the patch in orange letters. It read *'Ushtria Clirimtare e Kosoves'* – Kosovo Liberation Army – abbreviated by Kosovans to UCK and by English speakers to KLA. And it was for a group of Englishmen that one of the KLA commanders was waiting that day in the summer of 1999 outside the small town of Kacanik in southern Kosovo, on one side of the road that led from the Blace border crossing from Macedonia to the Kosovan capital of Pristina. His eyes moved swiftly backwards and forwards across the landscape in front of him, watching the clusters of Serb military vehicles crawling along the main road towards Pristina, 50km away. Hidden under the trees, his men were invisible to the Serb soldiers on their lorries and in their jeeps. But his eyes missed no detail of the Serbs. A typically Albanian sense of irony had given one of the KLA commanders present that day his nickname, his *nom de guerre*: *Commandante Qorri*. Commander Blind Man.

In the trees surrounding the waiting guerrillas, one man from the group slid a rucksack off his shoulders, laid it between his legs and loosened the drawstrings. Underneath a half-eaten loaf of bread wrapped in an old newspaper, a handful of onions, cucumbers and peppers, some medical dressings and a pair of black combat trousers almost dirtier than the ones the man was wearing, there was a package enclosed in bubble-wrap plastic. The guerrilla fighter pulled off the protective covering and laid the grey and black plastic rectangular object on the ground in front of him. Awaiting orders from his commander, he didn't move to open it. A few minutes later, the commander turned to him, sighed and waved. The fighter opened the hinged grey plastic tray that formed the cover, revealing the sleek, grey matt finish of the keypad inside. Unwinding a stretch of thin black cable, the Kosovan fighter positioned the grey lid, attached to one end of the wire, on a patch of grass just outside the shade of the trees and turned it to and fro until the miniature compass on the lid showed that it was angled towards a spot in the sky some 270 degrees from where the men were sitting. Returning to the shade, the man reached forward and pushed the 'power' button. The Nera satellite WorldPhone sprang to life with a small electronic *bleep* as the battery activated. The other men watched as the subordinate reached out and shifted the antenna backwards and forwards, tilting it until a continuous black bar stretched from left to right on the LCD panel next to the grey handset, indicating a signal strength of 420. The guerrilla fighter remembered what he had been taught about using the satellite phone: always try to get a signal strength of more than 400; that way the voice transmission is clearer and you have to stay on the line for less time, meaning that the MUP – the much-hated and feared Serb Interior Ministry Police, the *Ministarstvo Unutrasnjih Poslova* – would have less chance of tracking the signal. The Albanian man tapped in a fourteen-figure number written in pencil on a scrap of paper and then pressed the 'call' button. Fewer than 32km away, across the border in Macedonia in a sweltering khaki British Army tent, another satellite phone began to emit an electronic ringing tone.

Also earlier that day, somewhere on the Macedonian side of the hill between the Blace border crossing and the small village of Radusa, a small group of SAS men were waiting in two heavily camouflaged Land Rover 110s. They were dressed in the British Army's distinctive disruptive-pattern tropical camouflage and were each laden down with black, brown and green chest-webbing harnesses. Each vehicle carried a pair of Belgian-made 7.62mm GPMGs manufactured by Fabrique Nationale in Liege. One was set in front of the passenger seat of each Land Rover, the other on a swivel mount at the rear of each vehicle. Camouflage nets were stowed along the sides of the Land Rovers next to jerry cans of fuel. Bergen rucksacks and cases of mineral water filled the back areas of the Land Rovers. The men, believed to be two patrols – eight men in total – were armed with a variety of weapons. There was a PM Accuracy International sniper rifle, its stock and butt spray-painted brown, green and dusty grey, and a 5.56mm Minimi belt-fed machine gun with a retractable stock and a 200-round box magazine attached under the weapon. The remaining weapons were mostly US M-16A2 Armalite assault rifles, with a sprinkling of Heckler & Koch 7.62mm and 5.56mm assault rifles. One man had a 40mm M-203 grenade launcher slung beneath the barrel of his M-16. The sergeant in charge of the group was looking through binoculars – down the slope, across the border into Kosovo.

As far as the eye could see, the road from Skopje up towards the Blace border crossing was jammed with British Army Challenger II tanks, Warrior armoured personnel carriers, camouflaged Land Rovers, Bedford and Foden four-ton lorries, civilian cars and trucks, white Toyota Land Cruisers from the UN, Mitsubishi Pajero four-wheel drives from the Organisation for Security and Co-operation in Europe (OSCE), as well as hundreds and hundreds of British soldiers representing every element of the British armed forces from the Parachute Regiment and the Irish Guards to the Gurkhas. NATO and the international community were moving into Kosovo.

The eight-man SAS patrol carried on waiting.

There had been chaos and war in Eastern Europe for the better part of a decade. Since 1989, when President Slobodan Milosevic had stood in front of the historic Serb war memorial on the ancient battlefield of Kosovo Polje in the cornfields just outside Pristina and promised Kosovo's Serb population that the province was rightly and historically theirs and not the Albanians', the pace had been set for a vicious expulsion of the Albanian minority. In 1389, the Serbs had been defeated at the battle of Kosovo Polje – the name means 'field of blackbirds' – by Ottoman Turks. In the Balkans, memories are long, and since that defeat the Serbs had regarded Kosovo, with some justification, as their spiritual and historical homeland. The Orthodox patrimonial sites at Decane and Gracanica, with their ancient monasteries, were set in the heartland of Kosovo. The Albanians, with their Muslim faith, their refusal to bow to authority, their traditional culture based upon the lore of kidnapping, banditry and the blood feud so common in northern Albania, were seen as dark-skinned interlopers. Clannish, suspicious, insular and armed, they were everything the Serbs hated. Racism and ethnic hatred are easily fostered in an atmosphere of insular jealousy and insecurity, and Milosevic knew how to tug on the historical and nationalistic heart-strings of Kosovo's Serbs better than anyone. His argument was simple and powerful: these Albanians are here to try to steal your land, your traditional way of life and your God-fearing, Western-looking beliefs. By the beginning of the 1990s, a series of draconian edicts emanating from Belgrade had begun to make the lives of Albanians in Kosovo more and more difficult. Albanians were denied access to state-funded further education and places at university started to become impossible to obtain. Jobs in the public sector began to dry up. Before long, the Albanian community, long masters of organising parallel economic and political structures, were taking matters into their own hands. Not only did they set up a parallel presidency under the aegis of the veteran pacifist Ibrahim Rugova, they also devised ways of circumventing the Serb blocks on access to primary health care, education and jobs. Most crucially, in the Swiss coffee shops, German–Albanian tea-houses and Austrian bars in

Zurich, Graz and Munich, as well as in Washington and New York, there was fighting talk.

The Albanian and Kosovo Albanian diaspora that lives abroad, remitting money home to its relatives, is huge. Most households have at least one family member living and working outside of their home state. When a small coterie of ultra-nationalist Kosovo Albanians with revolution in their hearts and a vision of a Serb-free Kosovo in their minds started to plot and plan between 1994 and 1996, the Kosovo Liberation Army (KLA) was born. From the start, the KLA envisaged an armed fight against the Serbs for an independent Kosovo, where they, the hard men of the KLA, would control the political system, the organised criminal scene and the political and economic landscape. But how could they achieve this? When men like Hacim Thaci, Ramush Haradinaj and Fatmir Limaj, who were to become the future leaders of the KLA, sat down together in Switzerland, it seemed incomprehensible that a small rebel group would be able to face down the tanks, artillery and standing army of the Belgrade regime, not to mention its police force and the notorious, much-hated MUP. So, their thinking went, why not ally ourselves with the most powerful country on earth – the United States – and the most powerful military alliance on earth, in the form of NATO?

After that, things moved fast. By mid-1998, in a sweltering southern European summer in the Kosovan heartland of the Drenica Valley, *de facto* guerrilla war was raging. It was Serb village versus Albanian village, small bands of the KLA lightly armed with Kalashnikovs, RPG rocket launchers and Chinese belt-fed machine guns, against the might of the Serb forces. The fighting followed fairly conventional guerrilla patterns. The KLA would ambush a Serb military or MUP convoy on a road, kill all their targets and then melt away. They became masters of the rocket-launcher ambush. For their own protection, the Serbs travelled in wheeled armoured personnel carriers that could carry some ten men at a time inside their hot, cramped, diesel-reeking hulls. The MUP in particular favoured these vehicles. The KLA learned that one of the best ways of ambushing these APCs was to fire an RPG rocket through the tiny triangular side window next to the driver's seat. Given that this piece of thick armoured glass measures no more than 30.5cm by about 20cm, it required considerable accuracy to achieve a hit like this on a moving vehicle. But the results were lethal. In a ruined car park on a back road behind the town of Decane in far-western Kosovo, the Serbs left behind some of their destroyed vehicles. One APC, hit by an RPG-7 antitank rocket through this little window, illustrates all to well what happened when a rocket exploded inside its confined interior. Rusty dried blood is sprayed around the inside, along with scraps of body tissue, crisp shards of bone matter and burned fragments of the black and blue camouflage uniforms that were MUP standard issue. Any Serb troops who survived the initial blast would have been forced to evacuate the vehicle through a small door, straight into the machine-gun fire of the Albanian fighters. The Serb reactions to such ambushes were predictable: reprisals were taken against villages known to harbour KLA fighters. The Albanian civilian population was terrorised, houses were burned, women were raped and large chunks of the population were displaced from their homes, forced to go and live in the wooded mountains under the watchful eye of the KLA. The Serbs, unwittingly, were pushing the extremist armed Albanians into the bosom of NATO and the international community by creating an incipient humanitarian crisis to which Western countries would have no choice but to react.

In March 1998, when Serb soldiers massacred twenty-three men, women and children of the family of Adem Jashari, a prominent KLA leader and criminal from the rural village of Prekaz in the heart of central Kosovo's Drenica Valley, the pace of the fighting increased. No matter that some said that Jashari had been set up to be killed by Albanian rivals from within the KLA. The movement had its martyr. And already, within Kosovo, Special Forces from Britain, Canada, Germany and the United States were at work. After the huge body counts of Bosnia, the innumerable foreign interventions that did nothing to stop the blood and misery of the break-up of Yugoslavia, the massacre at Srebrenica, the failures of the UN, the Dayton Peace Accords, three different wars,

200,000 people killed and egg all over the face of the international community, the last thing anybody in NATO, the UN, the US or the EU wanted was another carve-up in the Balkans. Simply put, the removal of Milosevic from power and to a courtroom in The Hague was divinely to be wished. Problematic though it was bound to be, Serb forces had to be removed from Kosovo to avoid another war, another vast humanitarian crisis, another round of Serb paramilitary blood-madness, of TV images of Balkan roads crowded with streams of pitiful refugees fleeing burning towns, of mosques blown apart by Serb tanks and women and girls telling of the terrible night when the drunken paramilitaries came and committed atrocities consisting of violations of every chapter, paragraph, clause and sub-clause in the human rights lexicon. The problem in Kosovo had to be contained. Milosevic had to go. After Bosnia, the international community could not stand by once again and watch Balkan history repeat itself.

The US Defence Intelligence Service (US DIS) fielded the first plan to back the KLA in their fight against Milosevic. The Central Intelligence Agency (CIA) came in with a second, larger one. Both were straightforward schemes: a combination of British and American Special Forces would be infiltrated into Kosovo – by means to be decided – and would give the nascent guerrilla army a helping hand in matters pertaining to guerrilla warfare. They would also work as an 'eyes and ears' intelligence-gathering network, ascertaining the intentions of the KLA, reining them in from committing atrocities and using them as reconnaissance troops and spotters on the ground should NATO air strikes against the Serbs become the order of the day. The Special Forces operatives would hopefully also be able to find out who was funding and financing the Kosovan guerrillas and supplying them with weapons.

The CIA and the US DIS presented the plan; the British Secret Intelligence Service, or MI6, was asked to provide assistance. What the Americans wanted from the Brits was their assets from Hereford: SAS soldiers. Given that aspects of the operation would almost certainly need to be deniable and that the Special Forces teams would be operating in tiny

Kosovo – a third of the size of Belgium – in front of the entire international humanitarian, journalistic and human rights community, the men would have to assume another perfectly legitimate role under which to conduct their activities. In other words, they would have to work 'double-hatted', in intelligence speak. The commanding officer of 22 SAS in Hereford and Britain's Director Special Forces were half-hearted in their enthusiasm for the scheme. In spring 1998, the bombing campaign of Kosovo that was to take place in spring 1999 was a long way off. Hopes were that it would still be possible for a workable ceasefire to prevail, that the KLA would curtail their activities and that the Serbs would withdraw from Kosovo. The idea of having precious SAS assets sitting in Kosovo indefinitely did not appeal. So MI6, at Hereford's suggestion, went recruiting for ex-SAS men who could fit the bill. Regular, serving soldiers could always be sent in once fighting intensified and bombing became inevitable.

A solution appeared from an unexpected angle. The Organisation for Security and Co-operation in Europe (OSCE) is a Vienna-based international organisation made up primarily of staff attached on secondment from the foreign offices of their host European governments, whose role is to promote, provide, lecture in, train in and logistically and financially facilitate the promotion of democracy and, thus, security and co-operation in Europe. To them fell the task of organising free and fair elections in places like Poland, and of teaching aspirant democratic politicians in places such as Macedonia what human rights actually meant. In Kosovo in the summer of 1998, their role was becoming somewhat more hardcore. The Kosovo Democratic Observation Mission, or K-DOM as it was popularly known, existed to provide some form of verification process whereby the various activities of the Serb forces and Kosovan guerrillas could be, if not directly influenced, then at least witnessed and reported on. What that meant, in reality, was that a group of KLA guerrillas would carry out an ambush and kill a number of Serb soldiers or policemen. The Serbs would be bound to carry out a reprisal operation, which eight times out of ten would result in Albanian civilian casualties. Increasingly, the Serbs had taken to attacking, killing, raping and robbing Albanians from any village suspected of being sympathetic to the KLA, or whose menfolk were fighting with it. The OSCE would then be among those bodies tasked with reporting such activities.

On 23 September 1998, the UN Security Council passed Security Council Resolution 1199. Its message and meaning were unambiguous: it called for an immediate cessation of all actions by Yugoslav and Serb security forces against civilians in Kosovo. Out in the early autumn wheatfields and in the oak forests of the Drenica Valley, however, the Serbs were not listening – particularly not two units of the Serb Ministry of the Interior or Internal Affairs, the *Specijalna Antiterorističeku Jedinica* or SAJ and the *Jedinica za Specijalne Operacije* or JSO, both special-operations and anti-terrorist units. The Serbian Ministry of the Interior or Internal Affairs – the *Ministarstvo Unutrasnjih Poslova* – was run from April 1997 to October 2000 by Vlajko Stojiljkovic, nicknamed '*Deda*' or 'Grandpa'. The Ministry's security arrangements were split into three different sections, namely Public Security, State Security and Educational Institutions such as police academies.

Public Security was run by Colonel-General Vlastimir Djordjevic – nicknamed '*Rodja*' or 'Cousin' – and was further split into three separate police departments: the Special Forces anti-terrorist police or SAJ, mentioned above, the Regular Police, commanded by MUP General Sreten Lukic – the *de facto* senior Ministry official in Kosovo, and the blue and black-uniformed *Posebne Jedinice Policije* or PJP, whose 13,000 Special Police members were generally known simply as the 'MUP'.

The State Security Department was the *Sluzba Drzavne Bezbednosti* or SDB; the special-operations troops of this department were the JSO, commanded by Milorad 'Legija' Lukovic, and were almost certainly the brainchild of former Yugoslav Army intelligence officer Franko 'Frenki' Simatovic. Known as 'Frenki's Boys', the JSO were just one of a number of Serb paramilitary, police and military groups at whose feet much of the killing of Kosovo Albanians can be laid.

Frenki Simatovic from the JSO was an Interior Ministry official with widespread connections in the Belgrade underworld. When Operation Horseshoe – the Serb plan to force the Albanian population out of Kosovo that was to begin in March 1999 – was conceived, it was Frenki Simatovic who recruited from prisons in Serbia many of the former Serb special-operations police, JSO and Serb paramilitaries who would carry out much of the worst of the killing. Serving sentences for murder, rape and other ultra-violent crimes, 'Frenki's Boys' were a byword in Kosovo for violence and cruelty. The deal was simple: in return for assistance in ethnically cleansing Kosovo, by whatever means it took, their prison sentences would be annulled. In June 1999, one Kosovo Albanian old man recounted how 'Frenki's Boys', wearing their trademark black Stetsons, had in March of that year arrived in the small village where he lived, outside the western Kosovan town of Ishtok. The old man had pleaded to be allowed to flee to Albania with his aged wife. Sure, said the Serb paramilitaries, the deal was simple: give us the equivalent of 20,000 Deutschmarks in cash – about £7,000 sterling – and we'll let you go. The farmer had pleaded poverty. The Serbs had insisted. Neighbours were begged for money. The farmer's meagre hoard of cash was offered up. Gold and jewellery were produced. Nearly three-quarters of the sum of money was somehow accumulated, a fortune for such an impoverished pair of peasants in the western Balkans. It was handed to the Serbs, who were drunk on cheap brandy and dead-eyed from smoking heroin. The old man was allowed to depart. The farmer was assured that his wife would be coming with him. Just before they left the house, the Serbs cut her head off with a bread knife and passed it to the old man to take with him on his flight across the border.

Six months before these events, just days after the UN Security Council Resolution was passed on 23 September 1998, the Serbs had struck again. Fighting had been going on all summer between the KLA and the Serbs for control of the Drenica Valley, which runs in a north-east to south-west diagonal line across the centre of Kosovo. In the third week of September 1998, there had been heavy fighting for the village of Gornje Obrinje and fourteen Serb policemen had been killed by the KLA.

When the fighting intensified and Serb artillery fire began to land close by, civilian families from the village left their farms and went to hide in the woods and forests surrounding them. The Delijaj family, an extended Albanian clan, were just some of those who grabbed a few possessions – mattresses, plastic sheeting, food, clothes – and hid in the woods, leaving the older people at home in the compound. When the Serb Special Police found fourteen of the family members hiding in the trees, including five children between the ages of eighteen months and nine years old and six women, they were each machine-gunned on the spot. Two of the girls, Antigona and Mihane, were led further away into the trees and gang raped. Their rotting, mutilated bodies were not found until several weeks later. At the family compound, seven of the menfolk were killed. Ninety-four-year-old Fazli Delijaj was burned to death inside his house. Habib and Hysen Delijaj were executed in front of Hysen's wife and children. Adem Delijaj had his throat cut. Up and down the Drenica Valley, as the autumn clouds gathered, the story was the same. It was becoming increasingly apparent that the Serbs were not listening to the international community. Outside Kosovo, in the international Special Forces and intelligence communities, thoughts began to turn to what would happen if it did prove necessary to initiate a NATO bombing campaign and, possibly, unleash an all-out NATO troop deployment into the province.

The OSCE chose this moment – mid-autumn 1998 – to change the nature of its observer mission. K-DOM was transformed into the Kosovo Verification Mission, or KVM. Headed up by a lugubrious and charmless American career diplomat called William Walker, the mission took on a much keener, almost covert military-intelligence-gathering role. William Walker was hated by the Serbs in Belgrade and his suitability to run the KVM was questioned by many of the Western diplomats in Kosovo's capital, Pristina. Walker had formerly served as US ambassador in El Salvador. To many of his critics both in the international community and in Belgrade, his real job was actually straightforward: he was an American intelligence officer heading up an intelligence-gathering mission masquerading as a humanitarian one. Many of the staff recruited to the mission, which numbered around 1,300, came from military backgrounds or were simply detached from their home countries' intelligence or Special Forces communities. A British SAS officer and three non-commissioned officers (NCOs) from Hereford were among the first of the British detachment to arrive. Later that autumn, a separate SAS training team was flown into the Albanian capital, Tirana, ostensibly to provide a 'liaison' facility at the British Embassy there. In fact, their mission was to infiltrate, as trainers, the KLA bases and training camps being set up around the lawless bandit town of Bajram Curri, high in the northern Albanian mountains near the border with Kosovo. As the fighting in Kosovo intensified between the Serbs and the Albanians of the KLA during that frozen winter of 1998, so international intelligence penetration of the Albanian guerrilla operation grew. Every time the fighting was at its most intense or the ethnic cleansing at its most savage, two of the SAS men would attempt to travel to the area, observe the Serbs in action and report back both to OSCE headquarters in Pristina and to the British Embassy in Tirana.

By January 1999, final battle lines were being drawn. Massive international condemnation of Slobodan Milosevic's regime was the order of the day after forty-five Kosovo Albanians were machine-gunned to death by the Serb MUP on 15 January in the small village of Racak, half an hour's drive south of Pristina. The Serbs claimed that KLA fighters had been hiding in the village, that some of the men killed had been rebels and that the dead bodies had been moved by the KLA to make the operation look like a planned Serb execution. The international community was swift to condemn the killing. Western intelligence telephone intercepts had picked up conversations between the Yugoslav Deputy Prime Minister Nikola Sainovic and MUP General Sreten Lukic, who commanded the Interior Ministry Regular Police in Kosovo. They had been overheard saying that troops should be ordered to 'go in hard' at Racak, and after the event more conversations were intercepted during which they discussed ways to cover up the massacre. The leader of the

KLA, Hacim Thaci, commented later that 'after Racak, there was no going back'. As war in Kosovo drew closer, and as the NATO bombing campaign of the province began to seem more like a reality than a mere empty threat used against Milosevic, teams of Special Forces soldiers – British, American, German and French – began to deploy covertly into Kosovo.

An increasingly concerned international community had tried every threat and bargaining ploy with Slobodan Milosevic in Belgrade, without success. Promises of ceasefires had been broken; troop withdrawals had not been respected; clauses of peace deals had been violated. Finally, in March 1999, NATO decided enough was very much enough. Without the backing of a UN Security Council Resolution, NATO Secretary-General Javier Solana, US President Bill Clinton, British Prime Minister Tony Blair and NATO's Supreme Commander in Europe, General Wesley Clark, had taken a huge step and put into action a plan to force Milosevic to withdraw his soldiers, policemen and paramilitaries from Kosovo and to bomb him to the negotiating table. Their option of last resort would be to fight their way from town to town, village by village, street after street, until the Serb forces withdrew, the atrocities against Albanians ceased and Kosovo's citizens could return to their homes from the refugee camps in neighbouring Macedonia and Albania. Such was the plan.

The first phase – bombing Milosevic back to the Stone Age or the negotiating table – began on 24 March 1999. Day and night for seventy-eight days, NATO aircraft launched thousands of air strikes against targets inside Kosovo and Serbia. Day after day and night after night, from air bases on the Italian seaboard such as Gioia del Colle, Falconara, Vicenza and Aviano, and from US and British aircraft carriers standing offshore in the Adriatic and the Mediterranean, jets screamed off the Tarmac and carrier steam catapults propelled fighter-bombers skywards on their missions to bomb the will to fight out of the Serb regime. Each evening the sky over the Adriatic was a crisscross of vapour trails. To the fury of local residents, returning US pilots were reported to be occasionally dumping unlaunched missiles and bombs in the lagoon outside

Venice. The summer of 1999 was furiously hot. From Albania in the south to Italy in the west, across Kosovo, Serbia and the western Balkans and right up to NATO's headquarters in Belgium and London's corridors of government, the energy of war consumed the planning time of Europe. Would Milosevic pull out of Kosovo without a fight? Would the bombing campaign work? Would a ground invasion of the province prove necessary? Would the Serbs cease their ethnocidal rampage across Kosovo without insisting on fighting to the bloody end in the face of the bayonets and superlative urban warfare skills of Britain's Parachute Regiment and Irish Guards on the dusty plains and in the ruined backstreets of Kosovo?

Britain, at least, was planning for this endgame. A plan known as Operation Bravo Minus had been formulated, under which some 56,000 British troops – much of the standing regular army – backed up by French and American air power would physically invade Kosovo and fight the Serbs out of the province, using hand-to-hand combat if necessary. Knowledge of how the Serbs were likely to react to the proposed invasion was vital to NATO's military planners, as was feedback on how Serb forces inside Kosovo were reacting to the bombing campaign. Consequently it became the job of NATO's Special Forces to provide effective 'eyes and ears' on the ground inside the province for NATO's planners, and also to prepare the ground for the coming invasion by curtailing the worst excesses of the KLA and by training the rebels in order to maximise their potential as allies.

Consequently, by the time the bombing campaign was drawing to a close in June 1999, there were Special Forces teams from Britain, France, America, Canada and Germany inside Kosovo. In May 1999, British Special Forces teams from 22 SAS were operating alongside the Albanian rebels of the KLA in their struggle against Serbs. In the west of Kosovo, near the Montenegrin border, a team of four SAS men under the command of a sergeant were attached to the Dukagjin Brigade of the KLA, commanded by Albanian rebel leader Ramush Haradinaj. However, their mission objective to utilise the KLA as NATO allies was far from straightforward. They not only had to physically infiltrate themselves into hostile territory held by the Serbs, they had to try and coordinate with the KLA once they got there. The situation on the ground was complex. Ramush Haradinaj was the effective KLA commander in this key region, which bordered Montenegro to the west and Albania to the south. He was in charge of the so-called Dukagjin Brigade, made up of Albanian fighters mostly drawn from the area around the towns of Peja and Djakova. Operating alongside Haradinaj's brigade was another unit led by a rival commander, Tahir Zemaj. This situation highlighted one of the challenges facing pre-invasion Special Forces on the ground in the province. It was not just the alleged mistreatment of Serb prisoners that gave the SAS men cause to worry about the KLA men: some were alleged to be just as interested in beating and mistreating Albanians from Zemaj's rival unit, who were accused of being collaborators.

There were special forces units from several different NATO nationalities operating in the different regions of Kosovo. Each regional KLA unit could have a complicated series of local political agendas which confused things further on the ground. Early in May 1999 a group of KLA men and the British Special Forces troopers had returned just before dawn to a ruined house somewhere on the mountain slopes above the village of Junik, near the Montenegrin border, where they had made their base. The previous night had been spent in an observation post on the hills above Junik, towards Mount Pastrik, and further down towards the road, trying to guide in NATO air strikes against a column of Serb tanks that was taking advantage of the hours of darkness to move positions on the roads below. They were also trying to guide in NATO strikes against Serb troops deploying to attack KLA positions on the mountainous border. Circling in the sky some 2,400m above had been American A-10 tank-busting aircraft and British Harriers, all operating out of the NATO air base at Gioia del Colle in southern Italy. The joint KLA–SAS patrol had spent a frustrating six hours trying to approach close enough to the column of Serb tanks to be able to 'paint' them with a target-indicating laser designation device that would allow the aircraft circling above either to deploy their bombs or enable the A-10s to attempt a nocturnal ground-attack run with their nose-mounted 30mm Gatling guns.

As if it wasn't a sufficient challenge to move close enough to get a clear line of sight on the column of Serb vehicles, the Special Forces soldiers had two KLA fighters with them who had come along to interpret if the patrol was compromised in any way by local Albanian villagers. The SAS men were divided into two pairs and the two KLA fighters had reportedly been left behind the SAS men's positions, told to keep absolutely silent and only move or, worse, open fire with their Kalashnikovs if they were directly compromised by Serb forces. At their disposal, the sergeant and his three colleagues from Hereford had three M-16 assault rifles, one with an M-203 40mm grenade launcher attached, and a Heckler & Koch 5.56mm assault rifle. That night on the Montenegrin border was extremely dark. The circling NATO aircraft could be heard above the clouds and the growling and rumbling of the Serbian T-55 and T-72 tanks rose up from the road in front of their positions as the armoured vehicles moved slowly along the Tarmac.

It was possible, reports say, that the patrol would have been able to perform their target-marking task and withdraw unseen had it not been for the two Kosovo Albanian fighters behind them. As it became clear that the heavy cloud cover was adversely affecting the British Special Forces soldiers' ability to mark their targets effectively, the SAS men decided that it would be expedient to withdraw from their positions, extricate the patrol and pull back towards the KLA forward base outside Junik. At this point a Serb vehicle, possibly a tank or a Praga armoured car, is reported to have spotted the Kosovo Albanians, moved towards them and opened fire. The patrol was compromised and forced to withdraw.

Back at the Kosovo–Macedonia border on 11 June, across the border from the SAS men in their heavily armed Land Rovers outside the village of Radusa, their colleagues from 22 SAS – two troops of 'G' Squadron – were waiting to hook up with Commander *Qorri*'s KLA guerrillas, as well as another unit of KLA fighters. Their mission was simple: to secure NATO's entry point into Kosovo. Any NATO force trying to drive from the Blace border crossing out of Macedonia into Kosovo and up to the capital Pristina had to take the single main road that led from Blace up to the small town of Kacanik, through the Kacanik Gorge. Three main bridges carried the road across this gorge and three tunnels carried the road under the mountains. The Serbs had placed explosive charges on, in and under all six installations. Simply put, if these charges were not removed, defused and the road through the tunnels and across the bridges secured, then NATO's vast main force of some 30,000 men waiting in Macedonia with all their tanks and armoured vehicles and support systems was not going to get more than 8 or 9km into Kosovo. Access into the province through Serbia – which rings Kosovo on three sides – was obviously out of the question. Access through northern Albania was possible, but the road conditions and logistics of funnelling the entire NATO force along one narrow, badly maintained road in northern Albania and then through one narrow point of entry into Kosovo was militarily unacceptable. Macedonia it had to be. Consequently the bridges and tunnels of the Kacanik Gorge had to be taken.

Less than 16km behind the village of Radusa, where the SAS men were standing on 11 June on the hillside overlooking Kosovo, the headquarters of the British element of Operation Allied Force was installed in a sprawl of baking hot khaki tents set up across a series of cornfields beside a motorway, just outside the Macedonian capital, Skopje. Britain had deployed its paratroopers and reconnaissance units of 5 Airborne Brigade and its tanks and infantrymen of 4 Armoured Brigade to Macedonia between April and June 1999. Both the British force and the whole NATO deployment were under the command of Lieutenant-General Michael Jackson, a veteran Parachute Regiment officer with a hangdog face, a tactical and strategic command of soldiering that made him one of the foremost military practitioners in the British Army and a close fondness for Scotch malt whisky. Known also as 'Wacko', 'the Prince of Darkness' and 'Darth Vader', he was immensely popular with his officers and men.

It was his job to get NATO's Kosovo Force, K-FOR, into the province and installed as an occupying and liberating military force. The first step for him was to secure the route to Pristina, and the second to secure the province's main airport, located outside the small village of Slatina some 15km west of the capital. For both tasks he turned to the men from the SAS and the Parachute Regiment.

From the moment Commander Ogrri and his men were in operational contact with the British headquarters outside Skopje, the plan to seize the bridges and tunnels crossing the Kacanik Gorge went into action. The task was allocated to three separate teams of SAS men from 'G' Squadron. The half-troop of eight men in their two Land Rovers who had been scouting out the border between Kosovo and Macedonia were to join up with another eight men who would infiltrate the province via the oak-covered hills rising to the east of the Skopje–Pristina road. A small team of six men from 'G' Squadron was already in place inside Kosovo observing the Serb traffic passing through the Kacanik Gorge. They had been dug into covert observation positions on the steep slopes overlooking the road for three days, unable to move from their camouflaged hides concealed at the foot of the scrub oak trees. The Serb military, they reported, had indeed mined the bridges and tunnels. Any operation to seize these key features would depend on whether the Serbs chose, in the words of one paratrooper, the 'fight' or 'flight' option.

Jackson and his staff envisaged a pincer movement against the bridges and tunnels, involving deployments by Puma helicopter of Paras from 5 Airborne's elite Pathfinder Platoon, as well as the specialist Reconnaissance and Patrols Platoons of the 1st Battalion, the Parachute Regiment. Along with the KLA fighters who, with a handful of SAS men, would block any Serb counterattack coming down the hillsides above the roads on either side – an unlikely event, since the woods and mountains above the Kacanik Gorge had been firmly in the hands of the KLA for four days – this deployment of some eighty British soldiers and over 100 Albanian fighters was estimated to be equal to the task.

D-Day for the 'ACTORD' or Activation Order for the British entry into

Kosovo was to be the morning of Saturday 12 June. It was hoped that by the morning of Monday 14 June, some 14,000 NATO troops would be inside the province. It was on the night of 10–11 June, Thursday night into Friday morning, that a potential new enemy blindsided Major-General Jackson and the rest of NATO, an enemy far more threatening and potentially dangerous than the Serbs in terms both immediately strategic and more broadly geopolitical: the Russians showed their hand.

As NATO troops prepared to enter Kosovo, as Commander *Qorri* waited to hook up with the SAS teams and as the troopers and NCOs from Hereford started to infiltrate across the Macedonian border towards the Kacanik Gorge, US Deputy Secretary of State Strobe Talbott was in Moscow. The chief Russian negotiator on Kosovo, General Leonid Ivashov, made his position clear: 'Russia is not going to beg NATO to give us a specific sector [of Kosovo].'

Given that the Russian troops that were about to enter Kosovo had never been under NATO command, simply working alongside NATO under an 'agreement' between the Russian Department of Defence and the Pentagon, NATO had never had much actual, physical control over what the Russian soldiers might decide to do once they were in the province. But nobody had expected the Russians' latest move.

On 10 June, NATO intelligence at their air-operations centre at Vicenza in north-eastern Italy picked up a report from Bosnia that over 2,000 Russian airborne troops based with NATO's Stability Force (S-FOR) detachment – based in Bosnia-Herzegovina to monitor and oversee the implementation of the Dayton Peace Accords – along with their light-armoured vehicles, were *en route* both by road and air to Kosovo. Their intention was to drive across the border from Serbia and head straight for Slatina Airport. Major-General Jackson, backed up by NATO, British Prime Minister Tony Blair and Washington, decided they had to be stopped. Access to Slatina Airport was crucial to NATO – it was the only functioning airstrip in the whole of Kosovo. It was also feared that the Russians were trying to hide, destroy or ship out of the province much technical equipment that they had given to the Serbs. And Pristina was bang in the middle of the proposed British zone of control. Jackson decided to get to Slatina Airport before the Russians did. The SAS and the elite Pathfinder Platoon of 5 Airborne Brigade were put on imme-diate standby to move early on the morning of Friday 11 June.

The main difference between the soldiers of the SAS and the Pathfinder Platoon of 5 Airborne Brigade is one of role. The Pathfind-ers are the lead reconnaissance unit of the Brigade; their main role dates back to World War II, when it had been their job to mark out drop zones ahead of an airborne landing. In Macedonia that June, the platoon consisted of some forty men under the command of a major. Based on adapted Land Rover Defender V8 110s mounted with pairs of 7.62mm GPMGs similar in design to those used by the SAS, the Pathfinders were drawn from all branches of the British Army and had been selected via a gruelling series of qualifying tests. The first of these is pre-parachute selection, the notorious 'P' Company physical test designed to single out those soldiers considered fit to wear the maroon beret of the airborne forces. Then comes parachute training at RAF Brize Norton in Oxford-shire, followed by the Pathfinder selection process, modelled closely after that of the SAS. After passing out into the platoon, the men return to RAF Brize Norton to complete their free-fall parachute training in HALO techniques.

In June 1999, 5 Airborne Brigade was commanded by Brigadier Adrian Freer, a Parachute Regiment veteran who had fought on Mount Longdon in the Falklands with the Regiment's 3rd Battalion. Freer's advice to Major-General Jackson was that the Pathfinders should drive straight to Pristina and confront the Russians at Slatina Airport. Conflicting reports kept coming in from NATO in Italy as operatives tried to ascertain from available intelligence the number of Russian troops on their way to Kosovo and their true intentions. Major-General Jackson and Brigadier Freer formulated a plan: the Pathfinders in their Land Rovers would storm across the border into Kosovo at the Blace border crossing and head straight to Pristina, driving through the Kacanik Gorge during the night of Friday 11 June. They would pick up the SAS men from the units of 'G' Squadron as they went through the gorge and leave units of the 1st Battalion, the Parachute Regiment, to be helicoptered in to hold the tunnels and bridges the following day, Saturday 12 June, at dawn. Simultaneously, some reports said, a team of SAS soldiers would be flown into Kosovo by a C-130 Hercules from the RAF's Special Forces Squadron, which would take off from a runway in Albania and land directly on the Tarmac at Slatina Airport, where the SAS would race their Land Rovers down the tail ramp of the aircraft and join the fray.

On the evening of 11 June, the atmosphere at the British headquarters in Macedonia was tense. The plan was a go. One officer who was present said, 'It was like a scene from that Alistair MacLean thriller, *Ice Station Zebra*. We knew we could be at war with the Russians in seconds.' As the Pathfinders stormed up through the Kacanik Gorge that night, heading at 80mph for Pristina, Commander *Qorri*'s men engaged the retreating Serbs in a heavy fire fight. From where the British soldiers sat waiting in their vehicles to cross the border into Kosovo, the red *whiz* of tracer rounds and the stuttering of automatic weapons fire rolled across the hills in front of them. It was just after midnight when Major-General Jackson, trying to track the progress of the Russians towards Kosovo, received some further devastating news: the Hercules aircraft carrying the SAS mobile patrols from Albania to Slatina had crashed on a remote airstrip in northern Albania. For now, at 1.00 a.m. on the hot summer night of 12 June, that left everything in the hands of the Pathfinders.

CHAPTER THREE

Turn Left at the Dead Horse

Kosovo, 1999–2001

By the time the Pathfinders got to Slatina Airport, it was too late: the Russians had already arrived. The contingent that the Russians had sent to grab the airport was not several thousand strong, as NATO had feared. In the summer heat, some 200 Russian paratroopers lounged around on top of their armoured personnel carriers, the vehicles positioned so that they blocked the entrance to the airport. There was little that the handful of British soldiers could do: the Paras were reportedly keen to use force to get rid of the Russians, but Lieutenant-General Jackson was aware of the potential political repercussions in Macedonia if the Pathfinders opened fire. As he reportedly said to American General Wesley Clark, he was keen 'not to start World War Three'. Consequently, Brigadier Adrian Freer's men were told to stay put and to wait for the arrival of the rest of the British forces.

Later on that Saturday, 12 June 1999, in a pouring rainstorm, Jackson arrived at Slatina to give a press conference. The British continued to occupy their area of operations in the centre of Kosovo, while the Russians kept the airport. A thorn in NATO's side, they remained outside the control of either NATO or UN mandates; they were to become effectively uncontrollable and refused to relinquish *de facto* control of the airport. By early 2003, they were still there. The Kosovo Albanians were quick to allege that the Russians, whose semi-Slavic culture and identity tied them closely to the Serbs, were only holding on to the airport because a variety of Russian-supplied military equipment had been hidden there by the Serbs in underground hangars. Other Albanians believed that many of their relatives, missing since the Serb rampages through Kosovo in 1998 and 1999, were being held there in a secret underground concentration camp. Regardless, the Russians stayed put at the airport for more than two years, their military routine and camp life rather different from those of the Western armies based around them in Kosovo. In late 1999, a British engineer working on flight-guidance systems at the airport reported watching a Russian soldier, bare-chested in the freezing winter snow, being flogged by an officer on the runway.

The UN had issued Security Council Resolution 1244 on 9 June, authorising the UN to set up an interim administration in Kosovo until elections could be held and provisional self-governing institutions put into place. NATO troops were to provide security. '1244', as it became known, effectively mandated the entrance of the UN and NATO into the province. For the soldiers of Britain's Special Forces detachments operating in and around Kosovo, the arrival of the international community signalled a downscaling and shift in focus of their operations. Prior to June, the activities of the SAS in support of the international community's 'intervention-to-end-all-interventions' had ranged from the purely military to the almost humanitarian. Some of these were operations that the Regiment had frequently carried out before; others were new.

Firstly, they had resorted to skills of old to operate in a covert environment to train, oversee and assist the KLA. Having a presence on the ground with the KLA meant that the British could gain vital intelligence and, where necessary, be in a position to guide in air strikes. The British Secret Intelligence Service (SIS) was very keen to find out exactly who was funding the KLA, where their weapons were coming from and what their exact intentions were towards the Serbs. The answer to the first question was relatively straightforward: monies raised by the enormous Albanian and Kosovo Albanian diaspora based in Europe and the United States were going a long way to funding the guerrilla fighters. Some of this cash was obtained from legitimate sources; some of it was procured via Albanian criminal activity, mainly from drug trafficking and prostitution rackets. In late April 1999, Italian customs officers from the *Guardia di Finanza* had searched three articulated lorries attempting to leave the port of Ancona on Italy's eastern seaboard for Albania. Marked with the logos of the 'Caritas' aid organisation, the trailers of the thirty ton vehicles were found to contain false floors, under which were hidden tonnes of weapons. There were sniper rifles, multi-barrelled 40mm grenade launchers, silenced pistols, hand grenades, ammunition and ground-to-air missiles – everything, in fact, that a guerrilla army would need to operate in the field. The Italians had worked out that the weapons had travelled a circuitous route from Germany to Sarajevo to Italy, and were destined for a priest working in a hospital in the Albanian town of Scutari. One of the lorry drivers was also discovered to be working as an intelligence agent for the German Foreign Intelligence Service. Clearly, all of NATO's members were keen to find out who, apart from themselves, was arming the KLA.

Secondly, having members of the SAS on the ground with the guerrillas made possible attempts to impose a restraining hand on the KLA should they decide to attack Serb civilians or to ambush Serb forces in a way that their British instructors thought would provoke a hefty reprisal from the Serbs against Kosovo Albanian civilians. The SAS were also in a position, by being inside the province, to attempt to observe and record the nature of the atrocities and war crimes carried out by the Serbs and, if possible, to mark the sites of mass graves, particularly where Serb forces had tried to disguise the evidence.

Special Forces had been involved at every level of the preparations for the international community's arrival in Kosovo, and as the maroonbereted soldiers of the Parachute Regiment fanned out on to the streets of Pristina and the first hesitant UN officials started scouting out their new operating environment, the nature of the workload for the SAS and Special Forces of other nationalities began to alter. From that point forward, their activities would be loosely regulated by the international agreements that had mandated the entry of the international community into Kosovo.

When the NATO bombing campaign stopped on 8 June 1999, President Slobodan Milosevic's Serbs agreed to meet NATO at the negotiating table. In a vast sweltering tent set up outside the Macedonian town of Kumanovo, Lieutenant-General Michael Jackson hammered out a deal with the Serb military general staff. After three days of negotiation, the so-called 'Kumanovo Accord' or 'Military Technical Agreement' (MTA) was signed. It detailed the provisions and terms under which NATO would enter Kosovo and the Serb armed forces would leave. The Special Forces teams from Britain, France, Germany and America, hitherto the only NATO troops inside the province, would be joined by up to 35,000 regular troops. The Serbs would stream north back into Serbia proper, the best part of a million Kosovo Albanian refugees would return from abroad and from camps in Macedonia and Albania and Kosovo would become a UN-administered protectorate, with NATO riding shotgun for security. The extent to which the Serbs would fight or flee was still unclear, but the agreement formulated by Jackson allowed them to pull out of Kosovo with their weapons, and theoretically their honour, intact. Gone, hopefully, was that huge and awesome worry that NATO would have to fight its way from village to village, house to house, taking heavy casualties, in order to evict the Serbs from Kosovo.

As it turned out, things moved faster and more peacefully than anyone could possibly have predicted. Between 11 and 14 June, NATO roared into Kosovo from Albania and Macedonia. In Pristina, the British Parachute Regiment wasted no time in stamping their authority on their turf. A drunken Serb policeman outside a shop in downtown Pristina began waving his gun and yelling at a patrol of men from the Paras' 1st

Battalion; cautioned to drop the weapon several times without result, a young member of the patrol opened fire with his SA-80 assault rifle, blowing the recalcitrant Serb backwards, his head and chest fragmented, into the window of a shop. On the road from the Macedonian border crossing at Blace, a platoon of Gurkhas stopped a bus loaded with members of the feared Serb Interior Ministry Police, the MUP, and demanded that they relinquish their weapons. Sweating in the boiling heat of the Balkan summer, many of them drunk, all of them humiliated, defeated and fleeing, the Serb police squad informed the Gurkha officer that they were not accustomed to being disarmed by a group of 'monkeys'. It was quietly and forcefully pointed out to the Serbs that the group of 'monkeys' would be perfectly happy to kill all of them, using either their assault rifles or, preferably, their *kukri* knives, if they did not co-operate. The Serbs were given a minute to disarm. All of them did.

Into the southern city of Prizren, Kosovo's beautiful Ottoman town, on Sunday 13 June, Lieutenant-General Fritz von Korff led a German armoured brigade accompanied by a battalion of paratroopers that had poured up the road from the Morine border crossing on the Albanian–Kosovan border. The column came to a halt outside the Hotel Theranda in the centre of Prizren. The city was in mayhem. Kosovo Albanians who hadn't fled their houses but rather had hidden from the Serbs in their cellars and basements, living on bread, stale onions, fear and hope that the 'steel falcons' of NATO's air force would chase the Serbs away, now emerged. For three months since the beginning of the bombing campaign on 24 March of that year, the Albanians of Prizren, like every Albanian who had stayed behind rather than fleeing as a refugee, had lived in constant terror of the rampaging, drunken, murdering, burning, raping Serb soldiers, paramilitaries and policemen. Now NATO had arrived, and the boot was very firmly on the other foot. On the road from the Morine border crossing, the worm had turned. Up to only a week previously, the road had been the preserve of columns of Serb policemen and soldiers heading down towards the Albanian border, and columns of Albanian refugees trudging, terrified, into exile. Now

Lieutenant-General von Korff's Leopard tanks thundered up the road, the grey summer dust raised by their whirling tracks settling on the leaves of the lime and elm trees that lined the road. In the ditches and on the verges were scattered the detritus of the hundreds of thousands of refugees who had fled along this route towards safety. Here was an old mattress, one of a pair of black rubber galoshes, some blankets, grey and red, one covered with vomit and the dark rust of dried blood. There was a shopping trolley, a suitcase that had burst open scattering a collection of striped shirts and old, black flannel trousers into the grey mud of the ditch, and a tin of peas with a bayonet hole in the side. There were soggy husks of stale bread, endless empty plastic mineral water bottles, a child's shoe, a red corduroy hat, a quilt wrapped around a dozen framed photographs of an Albanian family, taut and formal in their best clothes. Kalashnikov cartridge cases and burned-out Yugoslav Army and Chinese-manufactured smoke grenades, stained purple, vermillion and green by their contents, lay alongside each other in the dried mud of the ditch and on the gravel-strewn verge. From somewhere hidden in the bushes and the dark furrowed earth of the field behind, where corn waved unharvested that summer, came a wafting stench of sweet decay and putrid flesh from a refugee who hadn't made it to Albania. Along the road under the lime trees a grey dappled horse lay dead on the verge, stomach gases swelling its body. German tank crews passing the spot wrinkled their noses before the stink was lost on the hot summer wind behind them.

Arriving on the outskirts of Prizren, the German soldiers, the journalists accompanying them and the few aid workers who had ventured this far into Kosovo were bombarded with flowers by the Albanian population emerging from their houses. German armoured personnel carriers and tanks, stencilled with nicknames like 'Pit Bull', 'Iron Horse' and 'Joker', were suddenly strewn with gladioli, carnations, roses and marigolds. German paratroopers, some with up to five ammunition clips fixed back to back on their Heckler & Koch 36S assault rifles, walked alongside the roaring armoured vehicles, exhausted eyes rimmed with grey dust, metre-long gladioli protruding from their dusty camouflaged body armour.

Around 6.00 p.m. that afternoon there were some six or seven Marder armoured personnel carriers parked up in front of the Hotel Theranda, bang in the centre of Prizren, just on the north side of the river. A huge crowd of Albanians were milling around the edges of a vast convoy of Serb cars, tractors, trucks and lorries, packed and ready to flee northwards to Serbia. On the roofs of the little Ladas and Zastavas, the Serbs had put their washing machines and refrigerators, their precious 'white goods'. There was a hierarchical method for loading each car: the black-clad grandmother went in the back seat, her crabbed, aged fingers clicking furiously through her rosary as the hot, sun-scorched faces of Albanians peered in through the car windows, drawing fingers across their throats in unmistakable signs. Occupying the rest of the back seat would be the children and the grandchildren, while mother was in the front seat with father beside her, driving.

German soldiers edged along the sides of the Serb convoy, discouraging Albanians from getting too close, even prising stones out of their hands. The television crews that had accompanied the German advance had already set up their cameras inside the Theranda Hotel, overlooking the square in front, the river behind it, the cheering crowds, the Serb convoy and the celebrating Albanians. They were perfectly placed to film any trouble the moment it occurred. When it did, it happened so fast, so furiously and so suddenly that people not 10m away who had happened to be looking the other way missed it. It was many things: it was a flagrantly demonstrative piece of Serbian bravado in the face of the invading foreigner; it was a suicidal action, given the huge and overwhelming superiority of the German military. However, the incident was most important, most newsworthy and most interesting because it was the first time that the German's post-war new-model army known as the *Bundeswehr* had opened fire in action. It was in fact the first time that the German Army had opened fire since 1945, since the dying breaths of World War II.

As the scorching heat of that afternoon started to subside, as one of the longest days in Europe's recent history began to draw towards night and as a freshly liberated Kosovo looked around and wondered what to do next, a small, yellow Zastava saloon car emerged from a turning opposite the hotel. There were two men inside it; in the boot were a .50-calibre Browning machine gun, a jerry can of petrol, some assorted rounds of ammunition and a sandbag. The car headed slowly down the road towards the river, its progress slowed by the press of the crowds. As it drew level with the hotel and a group of German soldiers standing outside it, one of the men leaned out of the car window with a Bulgarian copy of a Kalashnikov assault rifle and opened fire.

The dancing heat of the dusty late afternoon seemed to slow down to treacle-like sloth. Crowds of Albanians and Serbs were diving for cover anywhere they could find it – behind the pillars of the hotel's entrance, behind the trees that lined the river, on the pavement, crouched flat behind cars, anywhere to escape the tearing *crack* of the Kalashnikov as it worked its way through the thirty-odd 7.62mm short rounds in its curved magazine. A German soldier twisted and spun on the heels of his boots as a bullet hit him. Somebody screamed that Serb snipers were firing from the old fort set high on the hill above Prizren. As the yellow car slowed to a halt, the Serb man realised that he had leaned too far out of the window with the weapon to be able to change magazines quickly, and then the Germans opened fire. First were three *Fallschirmjager,* or paratroopers, firing high-speed bursts into the car with their HK 36s; then an NCO lying sideways on top of an armoured car emptied the magazine of his 9mm Glock pistol at the two Serb men; then one of the turret-mounted 7.62mm MG56 machine guns opened fire, closely followed by two more. The machine-gun fire sounded like a sodden bed sheet being torn in half by a massive carpet-beater, and was joined by the single *crack-cracking* stutter of assault rifles and the *thump, thump* of pistols. The two Serbs in the car were going nowhere.

Television footage of the incident recorded by Associated Press TV News shows the small car taking such a volume of fire that it is almost moving backwards. As it was being hit and the Serb triggerman was dropping his Kalashnikov, the injured German soldier was being lifted into the back of an armoured vehicle, a Kosovo Albanian teenager carrying one of the four corners of the stretcher. The firing crackled on for ten minutes. Then two German paratroopers shouting to each other from the side of the street pumped another high-speed burst of Heckler & Koch fire through the windscreen and approached the vehicle. There were more than forty-five bullet entry holes in the bonnet and windscreen alone. A German soldier was trying to give immediate first aid to the passenger. The driver was slumped over the wheel, the front of his chest sliced open by machine-gun fire, the blood of jellied tissue and foamy, frayed muscle mass ripped out from a hole under one of his shoulder blades. The front of his head was trickling oozing brain; the dashboard was splattered red, his neck a bloodied cutlet. Silence sat on the boiling street outside the hotel. The crowds pressed forwards. The spent brass of cartridge cases tinkled and rolled on the dusty Tarmac. The air smelt of tank diesel and roses.

It was 13 June 1999 and Kosovo had been liberated.

Six months later, the tiny province was being run under international tutelage as a *de facto* UN protectorate. In Pristina, the UN Interim Administration in Kosovo or UN Mission in Kosovo, known as UNMIK, was at the helm, its effective proconsul the French humanitarian veteran Doctor Bernard Kouchner. To him and to UNMIK fell the task of implementing UN Security Council Resolution 1244, which had mandated the UN's entry into the province and empowered it to act as an interim administration until such time as local and self-governing institutions – democratic and multi-ethnic ones, of course – could be established.

The Organisation for Security and Co-operation in Europe (OSCE) was in charge of overseeing the process of Kosovo's first free and fair elections, which were to take place in October 2000. In Belgrade, President Slobodan Milosevic still clung to power and on three sides the internationally overseen island of aspirant nation-statehood that was

Kosovo was surrounded by the Serb armed forces. To the south was the border with Macedonia, to the south-west Albania, to the west Monte-negro and to the north and east Serbia, effectively part of the Federal Republic of Yugoslavia.

NATO had divided Kosovo up into five separate Multinational Brigade Areas: the Americans had the east, the Germans the south, the Italians the west, the British the centre and the French the north. Alongside these 'lead' nations, a host of additional armies from NATO and a variety of UN countries participated in the provision of what UN Security Council Resolution 1244 euphemistically called 'a safe and secure environment'.

The KLA guerrilla fighters who had been trained and assisted by the British SAS, the German Foreign Intelligence Service and the French and American Special Forces had been formally disbanded and disarmed under the terms of Lieutenant-General Jackson's Military Technical Agreement (MTA). The black-uniformed fighters of the KLA who had fought against the Serbs and ambushed the vehicles of the Serb Interior Ministry Special Police, the *Posebne Jedinice Policije*, had been turned into a civil defence force known as the Kosovo Protection Corps (KPC). Inter-nationally funded by the EU, the Americans and the UN, it was meant to provide a role and an identity for the former KLA fighters by giving them a uniform and a job to do. By late 1999, however, they were doing little more than clearing ice from the streets and training as firemen. Their members were quick to disappear back into the armed Albanian clan fraternity from which they had sprung: members of the KPC were to be responsible for large numbers of attacks on ethnic minorities, and for a large percentage of organised crime and politically motivated killings. One international official summed them up when he described them as 'a perfectly average terrorist organisation masquerading as a not very good fire brigade'.

Across Kosovo, in hundreds of villages destroyed by Serb forces, some 350,000 Kosovo Albanians were spending Christmas either in tents, communal buildings or in the one room of their burned-out houses that they had had time to repair before winter hit. Heavy snow blocked roads, traffic accidents rocketed and at Slatina Airport outside Pristina, RAF meteorologists recorded temperatures as low as -17°C. Traffic and supplies coming in and out of Kosovo were blocked at the Blace border-crossing point with Macedonia after Macedonian officials had shut the border in the face of traffic jams. The roads were covered with black ice, blocked by deserted vehicles abandoned in snow drifts and 10km-long queues of lorries, cars and NATO vehicles. By Christmas Eve 1999, it was taking up to twenty hours to cross the border out of Kosovo and into Macedonia. On the frozen streets of Pristina and in the restaurants, shops and bars, a feeling of winter siege set in as the city struggled to cope in the face of repeated power cuts, inter-mittent water supply and very limited deliveries of fresh food. By the morning of Boxing Day, anything that had to be brought into the city from outside rocketed in price as availability plummeted. Holidays in Pristina had in the past been marked by children throwing thousands and thousands of firecrackers, whose reports were markedly similiar to the sound of automatic weapons fire. During the Flag Day celebrations in November 1999, however, a Serb family had been attacked; one man had been murdered by the Albanian crowd and his wife and mother-in-law violently beaten. Firecrackers had been stuffed into their mouths by Albanian teenagers. Consequently, this holiday period, the British Army clamped down on the possession, sale or use of the small card-board-encased explosives.

Britain's Special Forces teams in Kosovo were now based in the British Brigade headquarters set on a hill above Pristina. The Regiment followed its standard procedure of leaving one squadron in Hereford on anti-terrorism alert, one on standby and one on longer-term projects abroad, with half a squadron reportedly in Kosovo. They spent part of their time in the 'Ground Safety Zone' or GSZ, a 5km-wide strip of land between Kosovo and Serbia that had been cordoned off to form a barrier between the international community and the Serbs, and Belgrade-controlled armed forces were strictly limited in the amount of weaponry they could bring into the GSZ. To ensure that the Serb forces did not try to return to Kosovo, NATO's commanders deployed teams of Special Forces observers in the snowy scrub and oak forests of the GSZ; lying up in observation posts, they reportedly carried out patrols that took them into Serbia itself. Six months into the largest intervention mission ever carried out by the international community, the role of Britain's Special Forces was beginning to diverge from the traditional gamut of hostage-rescue missions, guiding in air strikes and training friendly guerrilla armies to include long-range reconnaissance and even such new tasks as identifying the sites of war crimes, as they had done during the bombing campaign. The SAS were also to find themselves employed in a capacity where they were effectively observing and spying on a NATO ally, in the form of the French Army.

By mid-February 2000, Kosovo was still in the grip of a zero winter. The K-FOR peacekeeping mission was at the centre of a furore after accusations were made by UN policemen serving in the province, as well as by Serbs and Albanians, that French troops serving with K-FOR had stood by, withdrawn or otherwise failed to prevent mobs of rampaging Serbs from hunting down and killing ethnic Albanians in the town of Mitrovica in the first week of February. Eight Albanians and Serbs had died and up to forty people had been injured, including NATO peace-keepers and UN policemen, when a mob of Serbs estimated to be some 300–500 strong had attacked Albanian apartments in an ethnically motivated wave of violence in the divided town. The scruffy former mining town of Mitrovica was the headquarters of the NATO Multi-national Brigade Area that was controlled by 4,600 French troops, with additional support from Danish soldiers and Italian *Carabinieri*.

On Thursday 3 February, when the violence started, a detachment of mainly American UN policemen had also been on duty. News had come through that on Wednesday 2 February two elderly Serbs had been killed by Albanian guerrillas in a rocket attack on a coach belonging to the UN High Commission for Refugees (UNHCR), which had been transporting the beleaguered Serbs from one isolated enclave to another. By this point in the international intervention in Kosovo, revenge attacks on the 100,000 Serbs who had chosen to remain in Kosovo had become so intense that all Serbs lived in enclaves protected by NATO troops. The large white coach, clearly marked with the blue UNHCR logo, was hit by RPG-7 rockets on a road in northern Kosovo. One of the rockets only failed to explode because the warhead, the size of a litre bottle of water, embedded itself in the soft abdominal tissue of an old Serb man.

The isolated and hardline Serb community in Mitrovica was fast to react. Forty-seven-year-old Albanian Gani Gjaka was in his flat in north Mitrovica, on the far side of the River Ibar, on the night of 3 February. He was with ten other people when seven or eight Serbs started shooting through the door, then throwing in grenades. His wife Nerimane was killed in the attack. Gani picked up the telephone at 10.10 p.m. and got through to both the UN police and to French NATO troops. Four and a half hours later, seven UN policemen arrived. They said that the French troops had refused to come to help the Albanians. A UN police investigator, J.D. Luckie, on attachment from Midland, Texas, said that he had asked for but received absolutely no help from the French troops. An experienced policeman, Luckie had also served in Vietnam, but he said afterwards that that night in Mitrovica had been the worst of his life. He had carried a pregnant Albanian woman down the stairs from her flat after she had been shot, then fought through crowds of Serbs with only a sidearm for protection. The Serb woman had died, and French soldiers present on the far side of the screaming mob of Serbs had simply watched what was happening, turned their backs and walked away to their armoured vehicles.

'Duty logs show that repeated calls for backup were made to French NATO troops,' said one international official after the incident. 'From the UN officers on the ground it was clear that French troops in several incidents either refused to help, or withdrew from the area of violence altogether.'

One of K-FOR's endless stream of press spokesmen, the well-meaning Canadian Lieutenant-Commander Philip Anido, was saddled with the task of standing by the official NATO string of propaganda in Pristina.

NATO was happy with the French, he said. A report would be issued. That was that. However, another American UN police officer commented that Mitrovica had gone mad that night. It was clear from the radio traffic what was happening. The UN police did not have enough weapons, vehicles or radios. They had received no help from the French. Subsequently, both the Albanian and international press were filled with reports on the incidents and over a dozen experienced international UN police officers had complained bitterly about how the French inaction resulted in the injuries and deaths of Albanians.

French Brigade Commander General Pierre de Saqui de Sannes defended his soldiers' performance by saying that the troops present that Thursday night were newly arrived from France and were not 'trained in anti-riot procedures'. A French K-FOR spokesman, Commander Nicolas Naudin, denied that French troops had a pro-Serb agenda, adding that it was 'commendable' that French troops had not used their weapons. The French Ministry of Defence and the French military were infuriated by the reports to the contrary, but there was little they could say or do: K-FOR officers of other nationalities claimed that not only were the French displaying an utter operational bias towards the Serbs, but that they had also, by their refusal to protect Albanians being evicted from their flats and by their refusal to prevent Serb crowds from attacking Albanians, at best been complicit in the ethnic attacks in northern Mitrovica in February 2000. At worst, they had actively co-operated with it. Even given a situation where the French military were allegedly tactically so lacklustre in their ability to control crowd disorder and so operationally ill-prepared for Kosovo, there was no get-out clause for them. As the situation in Mitrovica continued to deteriorate, and as the day in April came closer when the Americans would finally be sent in to help – the British, including a half-troop of 22 SAS, were by late February already on standby – various lead NATO nations in Kosovo expressed the opinion that the French should have tactical control of the north of Kosovo taken away from them. Several senior officers – German, British, American, Dutch and Canadian – concluded that the French were incapable of handling ethnically sensitive situations. It was time, a variety of British voices said, to go in, take Mitrovica, shoot as many paramilitary thugs as necessary and then simply restore multi-ethnic order.

There was evidence of the existence of French pro-Serb bias in the months leading up to the events of early February. For instance, they had done nothing to clamp down on a bunch of Serb paramilitary thugs who hung around the northern end of the Mitrovica Bridge, their openly stated aim being to prevent Albanians from crossing over from the south. 'The Bridgewatchers', as this gang became known, had been the ringleaders of the Serbs responsible for the violence in the first week of February. Armed, leather-jacketed bruisers originally recruited from a local karate class and a nearby gym, they hung around a grim, depressing, smoky coffee house and bar called the Dolce Vita that stood on the corner near the north end of the Mitrovica Bridge. After almost ten days of rioting on the Mitrovica Bridge as a result of the violence on both sides of it, the area around the bar and the bridge itself were by now a sea of broken bottles, bricks, chunks of rock, wooden planks, empty tear-gas canisters, cigarette ends, stones, brass cartridge cases, barbed wire and tin cans. At eight in the morning, fat Serb men with alcohol-scorched faces, orange smokers' fingers and the red, intolerant eyes of the ethnically marginalised would arrive at the Dolce Vita to drink brandy, the butts of their illegal Makarov and CZ pistols sticking out over the rolls of scarred and tattooed flesh that hung over the waistbands of their cheaply made tracksuit trousers. The air in the bar smelt of damp Kalashnikovs, frustration, cheap cigarettes and boiled poverty. Despite the fact that it was illegal under every UN and NATO regulation for almost all Serb and Albanian civilians to carry any sort of weapons in Kosovo – particularly the 'Bridgewatchers' – the French military turned an utterly blind eye towards them. The gang would become a real problem for K-FOR, and the French refusal to do anything effective about them for the next two or three years would be at least partially responsible for the coming split in national military unity in Kosovo. In the Dolce Vita and elsewhere in northern Mitrovica, in many cases Serb paramilitaries and French troops drank together, swapping glasses of *rakiya* or *slivovitz* and bemoaning the lot of the Serbs.

The problem was compounded when, by mid-February, it became apparent that there was also some fairly advanced Albanian complicity in the violence in northern Mitrovica. The French shot dead a number of alleged Albanian gunmen in the north of the town, and it transpired that they may have been former KLA men infiltrated into the town to instigate violence. Twelve months before, thirty-four-year-old Avni Haradinaj had been a rebel with the KLA fighting for an independent Kosovo, armed, trained and supported by NATO countries such as Britain the US and France. In mid-February 2000 he became the first KLA fighter to be killed by his former allies and was buried on a muddy, snowy hillside 5km outside Mitrovica, allegedly shot to death by French troops. NATO, the French, the Albanians and the Serbs all had their own versions of the events surrounding Avni's death, but one thing was clear: the Kosovo Albanian rebel fighters that NATO had backed the year before in their struggle to halt the Serb campaign of ethnic cleansing in Kosovo were now finding themselves under fire by troops from the very countries that had once supported them. In the mud and snow of the bitterly divided town of Mitrovica in mid-February 2000, NATO and the UN announced swingeing security measures and troop reinforcements designed to combat a massive upsurge in violence in the town, partly attributed to former KLA fighters.

'When NATO came into Kosovo,' said German General Klaus Reinhardt that week, 'we were only supposed to fight the Yugoslav Army if they came back uninvited. Now we're finding we have to fight the Albanians.'

Reinhardt, a well-meaning German general with a good grasp of operational planning but absolutely no tactical or operational experience to speak of, was now in command of the 43,000-strong K-FOR, which was by that time drawn from twenty-nine countries. He was described by one truthful though ungracious critic as 'a uniformed social worker'. Reinhardt and his fellow Germans wanted the French out of Mitrovica, as did the British and the Americans. The British estimated that it would take one battalion some thirty-six hours to occupy northern Mitrovica, shoot or arrest the 'Bridgewatchers', pacify the town and then hold it. In Pristina, the 2nd Battalion of the Royal Green Jackets, backed up by a small contingent from the SAS, were on standby. The French commander, General Pierre de Saqui de Sannes, secretly agreed with Reinhardt and the British that he and his men could not control Mitrovica, and that outside help was needed. Reinhardt told the French and NATO that he was considering sending a British task force into the north of the town.

The French Ministry of Defence went apoplectic at the thought of the crushed Gallic military pride that would result and started muttering threats about their intention to pull their soldiers out of Kosovo entirely if the British action went ahead. Meanwhile, the British themselves were plotting. There was increasing international criticism that the NATO and UN mission in Kosovo was teetering on the edge of failure, with Mitrovica the focal point of the instability.

'We have let Mitrovica fester for too long as a wound, it's not working,' said Ambassador Daan Everts of the OSCE later that week in Pristina. 'It's time we did some real surgery. Band-Aids don't work.'

By 18 February, twelve Serbs and Albanians had been killed in the town, more than fifty people had been injured or wounded, including thirteen French soldiers, while homes had been looted, properties and cars burned and over half of the city's 3,000-strong Albanian population had been terrorised from their homes and forced to flee to the Albanian-dominated south of the city. Former KLA fighters had been smuggling weapons into northern Mitrovica over the preceding weeks in order to hit French NATO troops and to increase violent pressure on Serb extremists in the north of the city, who they blamed for the expulsions of Albanians. Several weeks after the violence began, when NATO troops searched a Kosovan ambulance on the road to Mitrovica from Pristina after the Albanian driver and his colleague had crashed it into a ploughed field and promptly fled, it was found to contain fourteen RPG antitank rocket launchers, 260 rockets and Kalashnikov assault rifles and ammunition.

Meanwhile, outside Mitrovica, Avni Haradinaj's body went into the frozen, muddy ground in front of an estimated 4,000 mourners, including his seven crying sisters and a uniformed honour guard from the Kosovo Protection Corps (KPC). Several former KLA commanders stood nearby. The earth was churned to mud. Heavily made-up Kosovo Albanian teenage girls stood shivering on the windy hillside, their tight trousers, stack-heeled boots and cocktail-party faces at odds with the mud that clung to the mourners' feet as they stood on the slope. On the back of one Albanian man's fake leather jacket was a triumphant logo of international vocabulary: 'High Explosive Drop-Out Duty-Free Wear Back to the Adventure Zone-Always Authentic'.

Sulejman Selimi, a former KLA commander, stood impassively in the wind. A NATO officer in plain clothes lurking on the fringes of the vast traffic jam on the narrow, muddy road below took a glance at the crowd. The Albanians like Avni, Selimi commented to another ex-KLA man, went into northern Mitrovica because it seemed clear to them that the French were running an exclusively pro-Serb agenda, and because they saw the French as responsible for not having protected ethnic Albanians forced from their homes in the north over the preceding week. The breakdown between NATO, in the form of the French, and the Albanians, in the form of former KLA fighters, was now complete. Another KLA man opined to Western journalists that each side's actions would escalate the tension, and consequently the violence.

Nobody in Mitrovica was really sure whether Avni Haradinaj had a gun in his hand when he died or whether he had simply gone to northern Mitrovica to rescue an Albanian family, as one friend claimed at his funeral. What was certain, according to a K-FOR press release, was that all the evidence was buried with him. His death also clearly started a new chapter in Kosovo where two former allies – NATO and the KLA – began fighting each other.

In private, many of the French officers and NCOs knew that they were in an unwinnable situation, but after the events of February – twenty-two French soldiers were wounded on one particularly bloody day – they felt cornered by all parties. In their defence, they were trying to draw a demarcation line between two communities, the more hardcore and dominant members of which wanted simply to kill each other. There was, unsurprisingly, no love lost between Serbs and Albanians particularly those on either side of the River Ibar. The French response to their multinational military critics was to pooh-pooh their high-handed stance. It was the French, after all, that had to deal with Mitrovica, or Mitro-North and Mitro-South as it had become known, on a daily basis. How dare the operational gunslingers from the British Army lecture them about the importance of keeping Mitrovica multi-ethnic? What about the Brits in and around their Brigade Area near Pristina? How many Serbs were left there? How good had the British been at preventing their flight northwards in the face of Albanian revenge killings? And then there was the rather embarrassing reality that of the thirty-two national armies by now stationed in Kosovo (a variety of smaller countries like Portugal, Argentina, Romania, the United Arab Emirates and Poland were now contributing troops), the majority either refused to serve in Mitrovica or had only come to Kosovo on the strict understanding that they would not be deployed there.

The 2nd Battalion of the Green Jackets began rotating one company at a time in and out of Mitrovica in late February, preparing for a lightning deployment to the north of the town should it become necessary. A major and a company sergeant-major started planning for their sweep over both bridges across the Ibar and to estimate how far they could get into Mitrovica before they would be noticed by French patrols or observation posts. The French were quite well disposed towards the Green Jackets: during the day of large-scale violence when the French had taken some twenty-two wounded, a British sniper had come to their assistance. He had been positioned with his 7.62mm PM Accuracy International sniper rifle on top of a sandbagged position on the southern side of the River Ibar. Serb gunmen with Kalashnikovs were firing on French troops from apartment blocks in the northern part of the town. The Green Jacket sniper had opened fire on two Serb gunmen, killing at least one, much to the gratitude of the French.

However, the British troops discovered that they could not carry out sufficient reconnaissance of the northern part of Mitrovica, even after one sergeant-major and an officer had been for a nocturnal prowl around that part of the divided city. So the SAS were sent in. Pretending to be aid workers, a patrol of four SAS men went into the northern part of the town. Interestingly, although the SAS team was adapting to the situation on the ground by utilising such a pretence, this was one of the first times that, working in support of the international community, they would have masqueraded as aid workers. It was vital that they discover how far any prospective assault could get before it ran into the French – whom, it was feared, would immediately tip off the Serbs. So for a morning and half of an afternoon, the four men from Hereford drove around northern Mitrovica in a white Land Rover pretending to be aid workers, observing and noting down details of the French positions and the apartment blocks occupied by hardline Serbs, before walking back over the bridge to the British positions. However, before the British plan could be put into action, the Americans were sent in to deal with the truculent French and the hostile Serbs.

The Americans were sent into Mitrovica North in March 2000 ostensibly to carry out Operation Ibar, a vast weapons search encompassing the whole of the north of Kosovo designed to show the Serbs who was master. At dawn on a freezing morning of blizzard and wind, the men from the 82nd Airborne Division ran into trouble within an hour of arriving in the northern part of the town. As they attempted to erect a barbed-wire roadblock across one of the main streets, the 'Bridge-watchers' arrived with Oliver Ivanovic, local firebrand politician, karate club proprietor and nationalist. The Americans were told that they couldn't erect the barricade; instead of simply dominating the ground, the environment and the situation, they backed down and moved the wire. The Serbs had scored the first point. Apparently, the Americans had no weapons in their tactical armoury between use of massive armed force and withdrawing. It was to be a day that would bring into sharp focus US shortcomings in peacekeeping situations. The wire was taken down, the Serbs chortled and looked triumphant and the Americans withdrew to a nearby apartment block to begin searching for weapons.

The snowfall began to slow as the light turned from night into a cold, grey, murky morning. The entire American company lined up outside a block of flats, waiting for the order to go inside. Further up the street, two French infantrymen lounged against a wall, grinning as they watched the heavily armed Americans. From their right, a small, old Serb woman dressed in black came out of the entrance to her block carrying a small tray on which was balanced two tiny cups of espresso coffee. She walked up to the two Frenchmen and held out the tray. They smiled, thanked her formally in Serb and bolted down the coffees.

The Americans, meanwhile, viewed their surroundings with complete suspicion. The operation, their Special Forces Commander Colonel Eberle had told them, would last five days. So they trooped into the block of flats, weapons swinging, and queued up on the stairs, M-60 machine-gun bullet belts clinking with oily menace against the scarred, greasy wood of the banisters. All of them were pointing their M-16 assault rifles upwards as the operation to search the block of flats got underway.

Downstairs, outside in the thinning snow, the 'Bridgewatchers' were waiting.

When the Americans emerged some forty minutes later, they formed up again against the wall near the main entrance to the apartment block. Behind the building in a large expanse of waste ground that doubled as car park were the Humvee jeeps and trucks that had bought them from their base at Camp Bondsteel in eastern Kosovo. The 'Bridgewatchers' milled around in the snow, tossing snowballs from hand to hand, judging the mood of the Americans. Suddenly one of the 'Bridgewatchers', a huge skinhead called 'Pagi', hurled a snowball with a rock inside it into the face of an American soldier. It caught him on the cheekbone, just below the rim of his helmet. The man screamed. The line of American soldiers braced, crouched, looked around them, clutched their weapons tighter and huddled together. Another snowball hit one of them on the front of his body armour, this one consisting of just snow. An American soldier pulled his M-60 heavy machine gun into his shoulder. Another cocked his M-16. The hail of snowballs increased. Suddenly the soldier who had been hit with the first strike pointed into the crowd and yelled, 'It's him, Sergeant, it was him who did it,' rather like an accusing school-child sneaking on another pupil, and pointed at the large, shaven-headed 'Bridgewatcher'. His sergeant stepped forward and, unclipping a can of pepper spray from his webbing, advanced through the ranks of the crowd and Maced the man in the face, shooting bright vermillion liquid straight into the man's eyes. He went down like a shot, clutching his hands to his face. What the onlooking Serbs saw was their leader lying in the snow screaming, bright red liquid pouring between his fingers as he held them over his face. They thought he'd been shot. There was a moment of near silence, a collective intake of breath, a grasping of weapons by the Americans. Then the snowballs turned into rocks, chunks of wood, planks, stones, loose cobbles, tin cans, branches, dustbins, anything the Serbs could pry loose from the ice and snow. The Americans had just crossed their public-order Rubicon.

An hour later, the hail of anything throwable battered, pinged, crashed, splattered, clanged and exploded against the green camou-flaged armoured sides of the US Humvee jeeps as they tore and slid around on the snow-covered streets of northern Mitrovica, racing as fast as they could for the bridge over the River Ibar and the safety of the southern side. There was even the occasional bullet fired by an invisible sniper from one of the towerlike apartment blocks that clustered in the centre of Mitrovica. A screaming mob of Serbs – women, children and adults – lined the streets yelling as the American trucks and vehicles passed by. One woman, in her desperation to find something to hurl, opened her handbag and took out a tissue, which she threw at them. The paratroopers of the 82nd Airborne clanged shut the top hatches of their Humvees as they swept past, the vast bulk of the .50-calibre Browning machine guns mounted on the roofs of the vehicles swinging limply in the icy wind as the hail of projectiles bombarded them out of northern Mitrovica. Colonel Eberle's much-vaunted five-day Operation Ibar had lasted less than three hours. After this debacle, the British never got their chance to take the north of the city. The French Ministry of Defence in Paris used the episode to their advantage and started muttering once again about decreasing the numbers of French troops in Kosovo if there was any further extra-national interference in their zone of control.

The SAS withdrew to their barracks in Pristina and began to use Kosovo almost as a training area of sorts. It had multiple benefits: it was reasonably close to the UK, they could drive around in four-wheel-drive vehicles wearing civilian clothes and carrying sub-machine-guns and simply look like every other international in Kosovo. In Pristina, the summer of 2000 became as scorching hot as the winter had been freezing cold. In the dust and bustle of the downtown capital, the British Army patrolled constantly; they were sometimes almost invisible, but they were always there. Turning a corner, one might observe a Fusilier crouching down, SA-80 in hand, and suddenly it would become apparent that there were another seven soldiers scattered around, across the street, in front of him, behind him, dominating the surrounding area with an effective patrolling 'zone' perfected during three decades of operations in Northern Ireland. If Kosovo did one thing, it provided undebatable, irrefutable proof that when it comes to tactics, operations and simple military know-how, the British Army really is the best in the world. Yes, they are badly paid; yes, when off-duty they make soccer hooligans look polite; and yes, the SA-80 with which they are armed is a personal weapon that has to be routinely held together with Sellotape. But everybody (even, grudgingly, the French) admitted that 'the Brits', as they were known, were the bees knees. In terms of implementing the emerging new international order, there were few more reassuring things to have on your side anywhere in the world than a battalion of

British infantry. You could drop them anywhere and they seemed to have an uncanny adaptability about them that enabled them, within days, to be up and about, improving things, mending things, making things, patrolling and, if necessary, fighting. Kosovo Albanians loved them. They were everything Albanians respected: tough, decisive, in charge and with a massive potential for violence, yet also calm, diplomatic and polite.

Kosovo's first introduction to the British Army had been 1 Para, the Irish Guards and the Gurkhas. Nothing could have endeared the British Army more to the Kosovo Albanians than the fact that they had driven the Serbs out of Pristina, and shot a few at the same time. Prime Minister Tony Blair and Lieutenant-General Jackson, felt the Albanians, were basically their saviours. Somebody had even named their little boutique in Pristina the 'Tony Bler [sic] Duty-Free'. On the menu in the Parliament Restaurant in Pristina, there is a Michael Jackson burger.

The menus of Kosovo were an experience in themselves. Albanian is a language that does not necessarily translate easily to English, and in the locals' attempts to accommodate the thousands of international soldiers, policemen, aid workers, politicians, spies and journalists suddenly thrust into their midst, there had been a few idiomatic slips. One favoured speciality in the Balkans is carp, a fish that seems to thrive in the muddy, litter-infested ponds and lakes dotted around Kosovo. The downtown Pristina restaurant serving only carp was called 'Krapi Restaurant'. Carp in filo pastry was translated on one menu as 'Krap in embers', while over at the Muriqi Restaurant, steak served without any sauce or garnish was 'domestic strip of meat'. At the Restaurant Bristol, 'Fruit Salad' became 'Sexy Salad', 'Sweetbreads' became 'Sex-Glands of Kosovo House' and 'Plums in Yogurt' became 'Kosovo's plums soured to you'. Rather more alarmingly – or accurately, depending on your point of view – on one particular press release from the UNMIK police, an Albanian had translated 'Rapid-Reaction Unit' as 'Quickly-Interference Gang'.

Like his French counterparts in Mitrovica, British Brigade Commander Brigadier Richard Shirreff of 7 Armoured Brigade, in his Pristina headquarters, was finding that a year into K-FOR's takeover of Kosovo, the Albanians that his colleagues from 22 SAS had trained in 1999 were now turning into their foes. The UN knew that ex-KLA men were responsible for the murders of Serbs and Roma gypsies, in addition to running extortion rackets, trafficking drugs and supplying weapons to ethnic Albanian rebels who were fighting in southern Serbia. A small Albanian rebel group calling itself the UCPMB, the *Ushtria Clirimtare e Presheve, Medveja dhe Bujanovec* or Liberation Army of Presevo, Medvedjav and Bujanovac, had sprung up in southern Serbia. The format was the same as in the old days of the KLA: the fighters were demanding greater political recognition and freedom from oppression for some 70,000 Albanian-speaking people in an area of southern Serbia abutting the boundary with Kosovo known as the Presevo Valley. The Serbs, whose territory it was, saw the UCPMB – quite rightly – as terrorists interested in spreading that thing of demonic anathema to all Slav people: Greater Albania. The Albanians saw them as freedom fighters. Up to the spring of 2000, their activities had been limited to blowing up a few Serb policemen with landmines, machine-gunning the odd stray MUP official and flitting backwards and forwards over the boundary with Kosovo. Their headquarters was in the tiny farming village of Dobrosin, a few hundred metres across the Kosovo–Serbia boundary to the far east of the American-controlled sector. Apart from the fact that logistical support for the UCPMB was clearly coming from Kosovo, they were of direct concern to K-FOR because they were operating bang inside the Ground Safety Zone (GSZ). There were all sorts of rules and regulations about the kinds of people, weapons and activities that were allowed inside the GSZ, but unfortunately for the UCPMB, they were not one of them.

The liberal warrior General Klaus Reinhardt, the outgoing NATO commander in Kosovo, had stated categorically in April 2000 that Kosovo would not be used as a transit point for illegal weapons to enter southern Serbia. But weapons and logistical support had continued to flow from the Kosovo Protection Corps (KPC), an organisation still funded by EU donors including the United Kingdom, to the tune of twenty million Deutschmarks (£7 million) up to the end of April.

Deutschmarks had, by now, become the official UN-sanctioned currency in Kosovo after the Serbs had fled; the hated *dinar* was no longer used. But there was a constant shortage of change in Kosovo, it seemed. Receiving sweets or a sachet of instant Nescafé in place of fifty pfennigs or a single Deutschmark of change was common. It was also common to receive 'atrocity gum' as change. This was pink or yellow bubble gum made in Turkey, each piece of gum wrapped in a small square of paper on which was printed a photograph. A selection of these were collectable and innocuous: one showed British Paras coming into Kosovo, another showed Major-General Jackson, another an American F-16 fighter plane. And then there were the atrocity shots. In one picture, an old Kosovan man lay on his sheepskin rug, blood sprayed on the wall behind him from where Serbs had shot him in the head.

British troops had, up to May 2000, been waging a desperate intelligence war to try to identify the perpetrators of recent killings of Serbs, the latest victims being two men blown to pieces after the minibus they were driving hit an antitank mine on a road south of Pristina that was used exclusively by Serbs. Violence was expected to increase as October and the province's first elections drew closer. In their intelligence war against Albanian extremism, the British Army was drawing on many different forms of intelligence gathering. One was what is known as 'Humint' or human intelligence. This included the use of informers, tip-offs from the local Kosovo Albanian population and simple questioning. Earlier the same week as the latest Serb killings, British troops had used a drone-like light aircraft equipped with cameras, known as an unmanned aerial reconnaissance vehicle or UAV, to overfly an Albanian village. Men were observed unearthing a sack from a pile of cow dung and dropping it into a well. The Brits then sent in a second intelligence asset: Floyd the collie dog. Known as 'Dog-Int' and attached to a Royal Engineers specialist search team, Floyd sniffed out the smell of a weapon in the emptied dung pit. The Engineers pumped empty a nearby well;

Lance-Corporal Rotherham, an Engineer diver, put on his wet suit and down he went. Ten minutes later, a Russian-made RP-46 machine gun and 350 rounds of ammunition that had been found at the bottom wrapped in a blanket lay in the grass next to the well.

These weapons discovered in the Drenica Valley were destined for men some 110km away, languishing in the baking summer heat of southern Serbia. In the tiny Serbian farming village of Dobrosin, in the oak forests and wheatfields of southern Serbia just 500m across Kosovo's eastern boundary with that country, renewed organised, home-grown Albanian resistance was taking shape in the form of the UCPMB. This small group of armed Albanian rebels was lending its weight to the international opposition to the regime of President Slobodan Milosevic. Inconvenient though the UCPMB were for K-FOR, they were fighting against the regime of Milosevic, and in the way that enemies of one's enemies become one's temporary friends, the UCPMB were not an unequivocally bad thing. There was also the very real possibility that the CIA was somehow involved in their operations. Milosevic had announced that week in June 2000 that Yugoslavian general elections would take place on 24 September 2000 and was finding himself in an increasingly beleaguered political position despite the approval granted by the Yugoslav parliament allowing him to run for two more four-year terms. American President Bill Clinton and German Chancellor Gerhard Schroeder promised to lend support to help the Serb opposition movement unite against 'Europe's last aggressive dictator', as they described him. In the midst of this struggle against Milosevic, the UCPMB were tactically very small pawns, but their energies were directed in the right direction as far as opposing Milosevic was concerned. The problem for the myriad military, domestic and foreign intelligence agencies from the thirty-five countries that were by now operating in Kosovo was that while the UCPMB wanted to fight Milosevic's policemen and soldiers across the baking heat of the fields and oak scrub of southern Serbia, they also wanted to kill Serbs inside Kosovo. In public, K-FOR could obviously not condone the latter, but it very much supported the former.

Theories and reports about the UCPMB abounded. They were not based inside Kosovo, and consequently nobody apart from the media ever got to go and see them. NATO troops were out of bounds in the Presevo Valley and Serbia, unless inside the GSZ and accompanied by Serb officials. The lair of UCPMB leader Shefket Musliu in Dobrosin was completely out of bounds to Serbs. For ten days in mid-July 2000, the Albanian fighters and the Serbs had been clashing with each other. Standing on the sandbagged fortifications of Outpost Sapper, a NATO boundary position straddling the demarcation line between Kosovo and Serbia, Captain Tom Hairgrove from Task Force 136 of the US Army's 16th Engineer Battalion could hear and occasionally see these engagements. Squinting into the 38°C afternoon heat haze as he overlooked the rolling fields of the Presevo Valley, he said that almost every day there was automatic gunfire and explosions going off, as well as machine guns, rockets and mortars going in and out. A US Army M1-Abrams tank was positioned just beside Hairgrove, and along the length of the barrel were painted the words 'Commie Killer'.

The Albanian rebels, meanwhile, were living in a rural community of dung-splattered streets, red-brick houses and fields of watermelons baking in the heat. Walking down the hill of Dobrosin's main street, the first thing visible was a picture of a Kalashnikov and the initials 'UCPMB' spray-painted on the Tarmac. Then the rebels would appear. They were a collection of former KLA fighters and local ethnic Albanians who had formed together in January 2000 in an effort to provide some safeguards against Serb oppression of the local 70,000-strong Albanian community. Black uniforms, cast-off camouflage, a logo with an Albanian double-headed eagle and every variant of Mr Kalashnikov's favourite invention were much in evidence. They had been training for several months, and in recent days clashes with Serb forces had intensified. It was very difficult to get any information from the Serbs or the rebels regarding casualties, but what was certain was that the UCPMB was attacking Serb police positions up and down the valley and that the Serbs were responding by trying to pinpoint the Albanian positions.

NATO was in a quandary. Should it intervene if the Serbs started attacking in strength, given that Serb troops with heavy weapons were not allowed in the Ground Safety Zone? In an attempt to try to find out what was going on in the valley, K-FOR had deployed as many intelligence assets as possible to the area. There had been repeated and verifiable reports that in the north of the British Brigade area, towards the town of Podujevo in northern Kosovo, the UCPMB had been training throughout that spring. Trench systems had been found in the Mojanee Valley, and gunfire echoed around the hills at night. The American military claimed privately that the British SAS had sent reconnaissance teams into the Ground Safety Zone in the Presevo Valley to see what the UCPMB were up to. The British, in return, claimed that the American intelligence apparatus was either training the UCPMB or at the very least was complicit with it by turning a blind eye to their activities and allowing them to cross backwards and forwards over the boundary in and out of Kosovo. Bulgarian and Ukrainian mercenaries were operating with the UCPMB, the Americans countered, training the Albanians. However, the Americans failed to explain why former KLA fighters, among them some of the most experienced guerrilla warfare combat soldiers in the Balkans, would need training by mercenaries of two nationalities whose loyalties would almost certainly lie with the Slavic Serbs.

The Presevo Valley was one of those places where the international community's first experiment in nation-state building and the construction of the world's first illiberal democracy could go badly wrong. The valley and the town of Bujanovac lay on the main highway that led from Athens to Belgrade. Bujanovac was a key fulcrum in the international drug trade, so much so that a French criminologist had named it 'the Medellin of the Balkans'. What if the Serbs and Albanians were actually battling over the control of the drug trade, and American assistance to the Albanians was in fact a way for the Americans to keep an eye on the flow of the international narcotics trade? The Americans knew that it was likely that Milosevic would be unseated by force or by popular vote in that September's elections, and that when that moment came, there would be no further use for the UCPMB, who would simply turn into armed mischief-makers. Nobody, apart from a few wise seers in NATO, had predicted the coming storm that would sweep through Macedonia the following year. A British Army lieutenant-colonel, Mark van der Lande from the Life Guards, had wisely predicted in private to those who would listen that the political economics of Macedonia could well prompt it to fall apart, but nobody seemed to be listening. All eyes were focused on Serbia, or internally on Kosovo. This was, after all, the Balkans, and everybody was forever predicting war.

CHAPTER FOUR

At Play in the Fields of the Greater Albanian Anti-State

Macedonia and Serbia, 2001

Seen from the cramped cockpit of a British Army Gazelle helicopter flying at 600m, the oak-covered hills of south-eastern Kosovo looked calm and beautiful in the clear, late-winter sun of early November 2000. Eastwards, the slopes rolled into Serbia, while to the south-west, along Kosovo's border with Albania, reared the snow-covered peaks of *Bjeshket e Namuna*, the so-called 'Accursed Mountains'.

'In another time, this would be pretty,' said Lieutenant-Colonel Tim Chicken through the Gazelle's radio-intercom system. Huddled in his camouflage windproof smock, the Royal Marine commander braced himself as the helicopter turned and swooped down through the forested valleys to its landing site on a hilltop. Any semblance of calm and serenity disappeared as the downdraught from the helicopter rotor-blades thrashed the rough grass of the wooded clearing and Lieutenant-Colonel Chicken ducked out to greet one of his Marine company commanders. Laden down with SA-80 assault rifle, spare magazines of ammunition, radio and chest-webbing, Major David Wilson's camouflage was mud-splattered as he ran forward from the cover of the oak trees. His pace was urgent yet celebratory. Wilson's unit, X-Ray Company of the Royal Marines' 45 Commando, had just scored another hit against the ethnic Albanian rebels they were tracking along the windblown, deserted stretch of Kosovo's eastern boundary with Serbia. An hour earlier, one of his corporals had been patrolling 100m short of the boundary line when he had spotted a piece of white sacking hidden under the cover of sticks and leaves. Several hundred metres deeper into the forest, the contents of the find were being laid out in the muddy grass.

'This is the kit that would be used by a small fighting group, probably left behind as they moved across the boundary,' said Sergeant Andy Goodhall, holding up a long belt of machine gun ammunition that stretched between his hands like a bronze anaconda. In front of him were laid out a variety of captured automatic weapons. 'RPG-7 rocket launcher, two Kalashnikovs, RPK light machine gun. Warsaw Pact, some Chinese stuff. Grenades, first-aid kits, ammunition,' continued Goodhall, down on his knees in the grass, nodding authoritatively.

'And this,' said one of his corporals, sighting down the barrel of a 7.62mm Dragunov sniper rifle, 'would look good on the wall of X-Ray Company's mess.'

The men were bivouacked among the trees in small camouflaged tents, living on ration packs livened up by the odds and ends – Tabasco sauce, curry powder – they had brought from their barracks in Pristina, where for the majority of their six-month tour of Kosovo they had been patrolling the streets and keeping the peace. But here on the boundary with Serbia they were doing what they had been trained to do: long-range, flexible patrolling, establishing checkpoints and carrying out observation duties. As Kosovo was still technically part of Yugoslavia, the dividing line with Serbia was officially called a 'boundary' and not a border. The Royal Marines were essentially state-of-the-art combat soldiers: while they all understood the validity of peacekeeping, as soldiers they had long been keen to get involved operationally.

Lieutenant-Colonel Chicken commented a few minutes later that it couldn't really get any better than this. His men had been on the streets of Pristina for five months and now, finally, they were out on the ground doing what Royal Marines were meant to be doing. He turned into the wind to look east, across the boundary line into Serbia, to where the Albanian rebels that his men were tracking were involved in a low-key guerrilla war with Serb police and the Yugoslav Army. The lads, said Chicken, were fully 'spammed-up'. The Marines had watched over the preceding two years as their rivals from the Parachute Regiment had landed one plum posting after another. 1 Para had been on point duty during the entry of K-FOR into Kosovo in 1999; in 2000, the Paras had led the Operation Palliser intervention in Sierra Leone while the Marines waited offshore; and then 1 Para again, accompanied by the SAS, had gone in on the short, sharp, medal-heavy Operation Barras at Rokel Creek to rescue the Royal Irish hostages just two months previously, in September 2000.

An hour later and 3km away, 45 Commando's lieutenant-colonel was sitting inside the turret of a Warrior armoured personnel carrier, looking across the valley into Serbia at a small cluster of farmhouses 1.6km away, magnified ten times by the vehicle's optic sight. 'Fort Benning', as the Marines had christened the farmstead, was an Albanian rebel training camp. Hidden on the forested slopes were covert observation posts manned by British troops and American paratroopers, keeping a twenty-four-hour watch on the rebels' activities. The task for the British and the Americans was to prevent the rebels from getting their men and equipment backwards and forwards across the boundary into Serbia. The Marines were under no illusion that the Albanians were very well motivated to live out in the inhospitable countryside for any length of time. Around their observation post were muddy roads, patches of snowy slush lay in the hollows and the wind swept icily through the oak trees. Here and there were the burned-out, destroyed houses, the collapsed roofs, the torched barns left behind by the fighting that had taken place in 1998 and 1999 between the Albanian rebels of the KLA and the soldiers and paramilitaries of Slobodan Milosevic's former regime in Serbia.

Nearly two years later, in the dying days of 2000, things had moved on faster than anybody had ever expected. The KLA had been disbanded and demilitarised, 44,000 soldiers under NATO command occupied every inch of Kosovo and the UN was making a chaotic but well-intentioned stab at government in the tiny breakaway province. Serbia no longer shuddered under the corruption, paranoia and isolation of Milosevic's regime – opposition leader Vojislav Kostunica had come to power the previous September in a welter of tear gas and strident revolution as Belgrade's parliament was stormed. For the Albanians in Kosovo, there had come the sudden realisation that in the interests of regional geopolitical wellbeing, Balkan stability and a safer Europe, the West was prepared to do serious business with Belgrade, their former enemy. For the spammed-up, muddy Marines of 45 Commando and their American paratrooper allies a few kilometres up the road, the new foe was now Albanian, not Serb. The rebel fighters and illegal weapons that NATO was trying to seize belonged to the *Ushtria Clirimtare e Presheve, Medveja dhe Bujanovec* – the Liberation Army of Presevo, Medvedjav and Bujanovac or UCPMB. The UCPMB rebels, who now numbered anywhere between 1,000 and 2,500 depending on whether one talked to them, the Serb police or NATO military intelligence, now had a straightforward list of demands: independence for that strip of southern Serbia, home to 70,000-plus Albanians, an end to a campaign of alleged Serb 'oppression' and possibly even the integration of the Presevo Valley region into an eventually autonomous Kosovo.

The problems for NATO and the Belgrade authorities were compounded by the fact that the rebels' activities were taking place inside the Ground Safety Zone (GSZ), the 5km-wide security buffer strip that ran inside Serbia parallel to Kosovo's boundary. Under the Military Technical Agreement (MTA) signed between NATO and Belgrade in June 1999, only lightly armed Serb local police could enter the buffer strip, and NATO could only intervene in the case of dire armed violations of the MTA. Consequently, Serbs and rebels clashed there frequently.

The reality of the problem lay in places like the small village of Lucane, bang on the eastern extremity of the GSZ, where a narrow river divided the Serb Army outside the buffer zone from the Albanian rebels within it. By late January 2001, the Serb Army and the Albanian rebels had traded heavy mortar and machine-gun fire across the river. Both sides blamed the other for starting it. Showing journalists around the *de facto* front line in Lucane, Albanian rebel commander Shefket Musliu held up the twisted remnants of an 82mm mortar bomb. It was Yugoslav, from across the river, said the camouflage-uniformed commander, standing with a dozen rebel fighters looking at the white bullet-splattered wall of an Albanian house. 200m away across the front line, behind their sandbags, the shapes of Serb Interior Ministry Police flitted past the blown-out windows of nearby houses.

Back across the boundary in Kosovo, the Multinational Brigade Area next to that part of Kosovo's boundary next to the GSZ was controlled by the Americans. An additional British unit had by now, in January 2001, moved into the area near the American position inside Kosovo. Reinforcing the Royal Marines was a unit from the Princess of Wales's Royal Regiment that had been detached down to the border to track Albanian rebels trying to cross it. Twenty bumpy minutes up the mud-drenched road from the British positions was the village of Zegra, where the American 82nd Airborne Division had set up their tents, watch towers and barbed wire in a complex of olive-green canvas tents and all-terrain Humvee vehicles. The British troops were there to provide reinforcements for the American operations on the boundary, and it came as no surprise to anybody that the British Marines and soldiers were rising to the task rather well. The situation on the ground played to the tactical strengths of the British troops, as Britain's then-senior commander in Kosovo, Royal Marine Brigadier Rob Fry, had commented to journalists in a characteristic display of understatement. Essentially, he had explained, the British were providing the military expertise for those kinds of guerrilla operations, while the Americans were providing massive amounts of hardware, support, helicopters and signalling capabilities. The Royal Marines and their British Army colleagues from the Princess of Wales's Royal Regiment had, in fact, proved so adept at seizing rebel weapons and capturing fighters crossing between Kosovo and Serbia that, in the interests of providing a united NATO front – which meant not antagonising the Americans – British officers were bending over backwards to stress that these successes were simply part of a larger multinational effort.

Since World War II, the British Army, Special Forces and otherwise, had been honing their skills on this sort of operation everywhere from Borneo to Bosnia. In a response that in hindsight seems ghostly and prescient, the Americans would defend their lack of experience with the riposte that they were not the ones who had had a terrorist war on their doorstep for nearly thirty years, a reference to the British military's tendency to cite experience gained in Northern Ireland as a reason for their operational successes in Kosovo. The Americans, however, did soldier differently. In Mitrovica, more violence had flared in January 2001, with French NATO troops as the target of Albanian rioters. The Princess of Wales's Royal Regiment, nicknamed 'The Tigers', were sent in as reinforcements, and after a swift dose of British Army rubber bullets, the Albanian rioters had largely elected to leave 'les Brits', as the French called them, alone.

'Serbs and Albanians understand violence,' said one Kosovo Albanian in Pristina in June 1999 after watching British paratroopers operating. 'The British Army understands fighting.'

During the week in January prior to these latest troubles, while British soldiers were patrolling southern Mitrovica with their French counter-parts, swinging purposefully through the streets and engaging with the local population, the Americans had sent a contingent into town. All but six of the US unit's vehicles swiftly settled themselves into a secure car park, while a handful of troops gingerly ventured out on to the streets of Mitrovica, which were already being guarded by hundreds of Danish, German, French, Greek and British soldiers. For the Americans, Mitrovica was dominated by memories of their failed weapons-search operation the previous spring, when they had been chased out in a volley of snowballs. Even when the Americans were questioning rebel prisoners inside their own base they kept their helmets and body armour on. Their rules of engagement went with them wherever they were deployed. Rightly or wrongly, hanging over many US operations abroad lurked the shadow of Osama bin Laden, of the bombings of the US embassies in Nairobi and Dar es Salaam in 1998, of the USS *Cole*, attacked in Aden harbour in 2000, of Islamic fundamentalist cells dedicated to the destruction of the 'Great Satan'. 'Force Protection' as it was called, was the order of the day.

Back on the muddy hillside near the boundary hamlet of Dragibac Mahala and the rebel training camp, Major David Wilson took a break from marching up a hillside to explain to journalists the risks posed to British soldiers arresting Albanian rebels. There had been a couple of 'Mexican standoffs', he explained, and recently one Albanian rebel had tried to open fire when the British attempted to arrest him, but his weapon had jammed. Between the UCPMB and the British Army there existed, however, a grudging respect. One of the would-be rebels' last tests at the training camp was to see if they could get through the British lines without being caught. The rebels said that if the British managed to catch their men, then they didn't want them anyway. How long was the conflict between Serbs and the UCPMB going to last? No one knew for sure, but for as long as it continued it was likely that NATO would keep British troops on Kosovo's boundary as the last-war-but-one in the death of Yugoslavia continued to flicker. This time, though, for the Albanians the war was not so much about fighting Serbs as about attracting international attention and political recognition for the UCPMB and Albanians in Albanian-speaking parts of southern Serbia and northern Macedonia.

Inside Serbia, 40km north-west of Major Wilson and his muddy Marines, UCPMB rebel commanders were driving up a road towards the rebel-held town of Veliki Trnovac, where initial discussions about peace negotiations between the rebels and Belgrade were due to be held. Spirits were high: a bandannaed rebel fighter loosed off his pump-action shotgun through the open window of his Toyota four-by-four. Kalashnikov rounds cracked. At the side of the muddy track lay a blasted Serb vehicle, a ragged Serb police uniform hanging in tatters in the bushes, a single boot placed next to it. A rebel vehicle approached from the opposite direction and a tall, black-uniformed fighter got out; the UCPMB leaders told him they were on their way to the peace discussions. His answer to the idea of the talks was short and direct:

'Fuck the dialogue.'

Back in Kosovo, it was ironic that a territory where the ratio of policemen and peacekeeping troops to members of the civil population was almost the highest on earth should be one of the world's most significant criminal crossroads. In tiny post-war Kosovo, there was at that point more than one NATO peacekeeper or international or local police officer for every twenty of the 1.8 million-strong population. That hadn't stopped the province from being a meeting point for Albanian, Serb, Macedonian, Montenegrin and other Eastern European criminals, all dealing in weapons, illegal immigrants, drugs, prostitutes, trafficked human beings, cigarettes, petrol and other questionable commodities. The UN was alarmed by the $7–$13 billion that international organisations estimated was generated annually by transnational crime groups. Consequently, that week in January 2001 the UN was holding a week-long convention on organised crime in Palermo, Sicily, presided over by Secretary-General Kofi Annan. The convention hoped to lay down new laws that would oblige each of forty signatory states to adopt new measures to deal with the problem of organised crime.

Also at this time, far away from freezing Kosovo and sunnier Sicily in Islamabad, the Russians and Americans wanted a UN arms embargo put in place against the Taliban to clamp down on the 4,000 tonnes of illicit opium produced the year before in Afghanistan, 90 per cent of which came from Taliban areas. Meanwhile, the Iranian Army said that it had killed sixty or more Afghans in December 2000 along its borders with Pakistan and Afghanistan, most of whom were thought to have been involved in the drug trade. Halfway between the hopeful exhortations of Sicily and the clampdown in central Asia lay the Balkans, and Kosovo. That muddy, litter-strewn experiment in multinational tutelage was of concern to international criminal intelligence organisations because of its geographical location: it lay between Bulgaria, Macedonia, Montenegro, Serbia and Albania, where border controls were flexible and groups like the UCPMB held sway. Illegal commodities, especially drugs, moved predominantly from east to west, and the Balkans lay in the middle of the route from Afghanistan, Pakistan and Turkey to the West. International agencies feared that 4–8 tonnes of heroin from Pakistan, Turkey and Afghanistan passed every month through Serbia, Macedonia and Albania *en route* to Western Europe. Most of this bypassed Kosovo, where NATO troops on the lookout for illegal weapons would be quick to spot lorries filled with drugs, and instead flowed through Serbia to the north or Albania to the south. Elements of the Serb Intelligence Service and the German and Austrian police forces operating in Kosovo were convinced that the UCPMB were simply in place to try to guarantee some sort of Albanian hold over all the drugs flowing along the Athens–Belgrade highway: an illegal taxing point on the motorway where it passed Bujanovac in Serbia would put the Albanians in an extremely strong position. The difficulty with the level of policing in Kosovo meant that as the drug supply now had to move through Serbia, Albanians were forced to deal and negotiate with the Serbs, and thus wanted control of the Presevo motorway region to strengthen their bargaining hand.

What did flood through Kosovo, however, were thousands of illegally trafficked teenage girls from Moldavia, Romania, Bulgaria and the Ukraine, lured by offers of non-existent jobs in Western Europe and then sold into sex-slavery. They ended up in countries such as Italy, the UK and Switzerland, but the Deutschmark- and dollar-rich communities of international police and contractors and Russian soldiers in Bosnia and Kosovo also provided lucrative markets. The Albanians in Italy had established a monopoly on prostitution in that country, filling a void left by successful anti-Mafia trials in the early 1990s. After ten years of war and assorted civil disturbances, the Balkans were also awash with all kinds of weapons. Kosovo acted as a kind of centralised clearing house for many of these, from handbag-sized pistols to heavy mortars. International criminals wanting weapons on the cheap went to Kosovo and Bosnia: the large expatriate communities in both places made it easy for them to blend in. The antitank rocket that had been fired at London's MI6 HQ by the Real IRA in the autumn of 2000 was thought to have come from Kosovo. In a traditionally armed feudal society with a ferocious appetite for both domestic and clan violence, where fifteenth-century traditions of the blood feud still commonly applied, armed crime was commonplace. So was kidnapping, and the smuggling of anything from cigarettes to petrol to building materials.

Bringing all this criminal activity to heel was a huge problem: the UN fielded 3,500-plus police officers of some thirty nationalities, as well as a variety of competing intelligence agencies. Some police, like those from Northern Ireland's Royal Ulster Constabulary, the Canadians, Austrians, Scandinavians and Egyptians were hugely proficient at tracking down and arresting Albanian and Serb gangsters. Others, from countries with different policing traditions such as Jordan and sub-Saharan Africa, simply were not. Faced with the massive problem of ethnic violence during the previous eighteen months, the UN had had little time or technology up until early 2001 to concentrate on purely criminal activities. Realising this, Albanians had quickly discovered that nothing absorbed international efforts and distracted attention from shipments of drugs or weapons more successfully than a timely ethnic murder. In the southern Kosovo town of Vitina, Albanian criminals had made it pretty plain to the UN police that if they clamped down on their criminal activities or hindered them in any way, then the Albanians would retaliate and occupy vast amounts of UN police time by carrying out a high-profile ethnic killing. The ensuing random drive-by machine-gun attack on an old Serb couple that claimed the lives of two Serb octogenarians too poor to flee Kosovo caused ripples all the way from Vitina to New York. Crime busts didn't. The Albanian clan-based gangs had also realised that they were next to impervious to informers, whom the UN couldn't afford to pay anyway.

Normally hostile groups such as Albanians, Serbs and Macedonians found common ground over crime, and Kosovo's criminal pie had been carefully sliced. Albanians from Albania controlled the south, along their national border, and moved heroin, immigrants and prostitutes south to Adriatic ports for shipment on to gangs in southern Italy operated by Albanian families entrenched there for three or four generations. Counterfeit cigarettes in their millions went north from Albania to the rest of the Balkans. In the east of Kosovo, Albanians with Italian links trafficked cigarettes, petrol and women to and from Montenegro, while in the north and centre, Albanian and Serb gangs happily co-operated. The two main Albanian political parties that had sprung out of the disbanded KLA were involved with petrol smuggling, the trafficking of women and extortion.

In February 2001, NATO's attempts to crack down on Albanian extremism took another huge blow. On 16 February, eleven Serbs were killed, ten more very seriously injured and another thirty-five either wounded or considered missing after a massive explosive device blew up a coach containing fifty-seven Kosovan Serbs returning to the province from a trip to Serbia. The attack was the worst incidence of violence in Kosovo since August 1999, and took place near the town of Podujevo in the north-east of the province as a convoy of five buses containing 200 Serbs, escorted by Swedish NATO peacekeepers, was driving back into Kosovo from Serbia. The explosive device, around 70kg, was left in a culvert by the side of the road and detonated by wire. Even 100m distant from the twisted wreckage of the bus, it was clear that the bomb had been designed to achieve mass casualties and was, said Brigadier Fry of the Marines, an indiscriminate and premeditated act of mass murder. American and British helicopters evacuated casualties, including women and children, from the scene to British- and American-supervised NATO hospitals.

The attack had happened mid-morning and by late afternoon teams

of British and Swedish soldiers and international UN police had evacuated all the wounded, leaving the blackened, mangled metal of the coach
on the Tarmac. The blast had occurred at around 11.15 a.m. when a
regular convoy of five coaches containing Kosovan Serbs was returning to the province from the Serb town of Nis. They were under the escort
of five Swedish armoured vehicles, in place to prevent attacks on the
convoy by Albanians. The first coach in the so-called 'Nis Express' was
totally destroyed by the blast. The following four coaches turned around
immediately and drove back into Serbia, but of the fifty-seven people on
the first bus, all were casualties. At the site, things were taped-off with
orange scene-of-crime tape as dozens of British Army doctors, explo
sives experts and international policemen moved backwards and forwards
from the wreckage. Blasted metal from the bus was thrown up to 100m
on to a nearby hillside, while dozens of pages from school exercise books
belonging to children blown up in the explosion fluttered in the wind
and lay caught in thorn bushes and trees at the side of the road. Almost
immediately, things in Kosovo started to go very badly wrong. That the
attack had taken place in the British Brigade Area was extremely unfortunate for the Royal Marines of 3 Commando Brigade, who were due to
rotate out of the province ten days later. Even so, they had had a very
operationally successful tour, and the presence of the five Swedish
armoured vehicles, operating under British command, in the Serb bus
convoy was proof that whatever precautions 40,000 NATO troops took,
Albanians could still kill Serbs at will.

Within an hour of the attack, Serbs living in heavily guarded enclaves
inside Kosovo formed crowds and started attacking any Albanians they
came across. In the Serb enclave town of Caglavica, south of Pristina,
outraged Serbs blocked the main road south to Macedonia, dragging
Albanians from their cars and beating them. There were reports from
eyewitnesses that an Albanian woman was beaten nearly to death in
one incident. Angry Serb crowds gathered in the north of Mitrovica and
NATO officials feared that armed attacks by outraged Serbs on the
Albanian minority there could erupt. NATO armoured vehicles and foot

patrols sealed off all roads leading into the Serb enclave towns of Gracanica and Caglavica in an attempt to prevent further violence after a fortnight of anti-Serb aggression in Kosovo preceding the bus attack, involving more than twenty-five assaults, shootings and grenade and arson attacks on houses and the destruction of a church.

Up at the site of the bus explosion, as Black Hawk and Puma heli-copters clattered overhead in the warm late-winter sun, Brigadier Fry pointed out a lightly wooded knoll nearly a kilometre from the road where the explosive device had been triggered by a firing mechanism connected via hundreds of metres of wire to the explosives placed in the culvert at the side of the road. The message to Serbs from this attack was very, very clear: don't come back to Kosovo, this is going to be a mono-ethnic Albanian province.

Curiously enough, the most violent incident to happen in Kosovo for two years led to one of the least violent SAS operations in years. On 19 March 2001, 3,000 British and Norwegian troops, spearheaded by thirty men from 'G' Squadron of 22 SAS, led by Major Ivo Streeter, netted twenty-two Albanian men suspected of involvement in the bus-blast. 'G' was the Special Projects Squadron at the time and had been deployed from Hereford at the request of the senior British officer in Kosovo, Royal Engineer Brigadier Hamish Rollo. Four Albanians were 'detained' after questioning. It came as no surprise to anybody that all four men were members of the Kosovo Protection Corps. The arrest operation, which lasted twenty-seven hours, was spearheaded by British SAS teams because the Albanian suspects were all believed to be armed. Soldiers from the 1st Battalion, the Duke of Wellington's Regiment, as well as the 2nd Royal Tank Regiment and Norwegian line-infantry units, were also involved. The Duke of Wellington's – or Duke of Boots' – Regiment was the quintessential British line infantry regiment. They had replaced 45 Commando of the Royal Marines, who had rotated out of Kosovo at the end of February, and in the pantheon of British infantry battalions who had passed through Kosovo between 1999 and 2001, they were among the best. The battalion had served in Bosnia in 1994; their CO had been a company commander in Bosnia, where Major Ivo Streeter, who had led 'G' Squadron on the operation to arrest the Albanians suspected of blowing up the Serb bus, had himself been an SAS troop commander.

The operation in Kosovo was a success. The SAS men burst into the suspects' houses early on the morning of 19 March without resistance, subdued them – most were asleep – and plasticuffed them. One of the suspects later recounted the interrogation process that followed. Kneeling on a wooden pallet, with only his knees balancing on its sharp wooden edges, he was made to hold the increasingly agonising position for nearly twelve hours while masked British soldiers pointed handguns at him and threatened to shoot him if he didn't talk. The interrogation was carried out by a combination of British Intelligence Corps officers and Army and Military Police. Of the four suspects arrested, three were released for lack of evidence and in one of the most dramatically bungled K-FOR operations, the lead suspect, an Albanian called Florim Ejupi, escaped. He was being detained in the American detention centre at their base at Camp Bondsteel, a prison guarded by armed US soldiers and surrounded by barbed wire, searchlights and dogs, itself set bang in the middle of the vast American camp. The Americans made a characteristically feeble excuse and said that an inexperienced unit was on guard that night. Everybody else, from British to French, Norwegian and German military intelligence and diplomats, said that the Americans had let him escape simply because, as one of their former intelligence assets, they did not want him testifying in an open UN court. However, by late March 2001, the world's attention had turned away from Kosovo to the opening blasts of another fantastically violent Balkan conflict, the last war in the Balkans before the world changed for ever: Macedonia.

In the opening months of 2001, the NATO and UN mission in Kosovo changed from being one the main aim of which was the protection of Albanians from Serbs while the former – under international supervision – built a fledgling nation-state and the latter accepted their new role as a minority part of it. The change of regime in Belgrade had instant knock-on effects in Pristina: the activities of Albanian rebels in southern Serbia and, increasingly, in Macedonia, had effectively slotted them into the role of 'foe'. There was now greater dialogue between the international community in Pristina and the Serbs in Belgrade than there was with many of the hardline ex-KLA rebels. So in winter 2000 and early spring 2001, when a bunch of Albanian rebels started firing RPG-7 rockets into Macedonian police stations, and taking pot-shots at border outposts, and laying mines on isolated country roads in the mountainous north of the country, the stage was set for Macedonia to start fragmenting. The first main attack on a Macedonian state institution by Albanian rebels happened on 22 January 2001, when a Macedonian police station in the village of Tearce above Tetovo was attacked by Albanians from the NLA, killing one Macedonian policeman and wounding two others. Having worked so hard and so expensively to keep Kosovo's Albanian population intact and having finally seen the back of Slobodan Milosevic, the very last thing the international community wanted in the Balkans was another war. And that is exactly what the Albanian rebels from the self-styled National Liberation Army (NLA) were proclaiming by spring 2001.

By May of that year, spring had come to the cornfields and oak forests of northern Macedonia. Macedonian artillery gunners were slamming 122mm shells into a string of besieged villages held by Albanian rebels as the country's political leaders struggled to find a settlement that would prevent full-scale war. During the first week of May, in an exhibition hall housing the Skopje Arms Fair, dark-suited Slavic arms buyers and their thick-set bodyguards prowled in front of display cabinets showcasing Yugoslav 30mm grenade launchers, locally made Zastava M-85 copies of the ubiquitous Kalashnikov assault rifle, as well as Heckler & Koch sub-machine pistols.

On one of the stands, Iki Malinkovsky, vice-president of Micei International and the leading supplier of weapons to the Macedonian government, was courteous and welcoming. Dressed in dove-grey woollen suit and black shirt, with gold chains at neck and wrist that were discreet by the standards of a Balkan arms dealer, he poured brandy and Coca-Cola into plastic cups. Micei was the arms-dealing company that held the licence in Macedonia to represent such well-known weapons manufacturers as Browning, Remington, Walther and Heckler & Koch.

'In these months there is a bit higher demand for some products.' Iki smiled. 'We sell ammunition, high-calibre artillery shells, bulletproof vests, armouring – there is a lot of demand from the Macedonian Army. Business is doing well,' he said, proffering brochures and sighing contentedly.

'It's been great business for the arms industry over the last forty years in the former Yugoslavia,' said a colleague of his, Aleksandar Ljukovic from the marketing division of Yugoimport, based in Belgrade. 'We're talking some twenty billion dollars in turnover.'

32km away, around the village of Vaksince where Macedonian government forces and ethnic Albanian rebels had clashed for the preceding weeks, some of Iki Malinkovsky's ammunition was being put into use. Across clear green fields of spring corn, the Macedonian Army hurled 105mm artillery shells and heavy mortar rounds into the villages of Slupcane and Vaksince, which were defended by Albanian rebels. The old adage 'when the snows thaw, the Balkans go to war' could not have been more apposite.

Two months prior to this, in early March, as the first blossoms erupted on the cherry trees near Vaksince and the snow on the Sar Planina mountains some 48km further west, above the town of Tetovo in western Macedonia, began to melt, the newly mobilised Macedonian Army prepared for an offensive. Tetovo is Macedonia's second-largest city, dominated by Albanians and home to the small Balkan state's Albanian university. The Macedonian Army had trundled its heavy reinforcements into the town, where fighting continued between them and Albanian rebels in the hills for the sixth straight day running. Eight T-55 main battle tanks from the Macedonian Army, accompanied by armoured personnel carriers, dozens of troops and lorries towing 105mm howitzers rumbled into Tetovo in two separate convoys in the second week of

March as ethnic Albanian rebels dug in on wooded hills overlooking the town came under heavy mortar and automatic weapons fire from security forces.

Rounds from 122mm mortars, 30mm anti-aircraft guns and light machine guns thumped and crackled from Macedonian police positions in Tetovo's football stadium as, two days later, the Macedonian Army and police prepared for a fresh attack. Their targets were the ethnic Albanian rebels of the NLA who were trying to besiege Tetovo as part of their newly launched struggle for equal rights and increased political recognition in the region. The Macedonians were down in the centre of the town, the Albanians high up in the villages on the mountain slopes above them. Mortar rounds exploded in clouds of grey smoke, the reports echoing off the snowy mountains behind them and reverberating down to Macedonian and Albanian civilians in the town square of Tetovo 700m below.

NATO was, of course, facing another dilemma about whether or not to intervene and, desperate not to do so and find itself embroiled in another multi-ethnic Balkan war, decided that it would deploy further troops inside Kosovo to clamp down on the province's border with Macedonia in an attempt to stop the flow of Albanian rebels and weapons into Macedonia. NATO Secretary-General Lord George Robertson was chivvying NATO's member states to commit more soldiers to Kosovo. There was heavy, flurried international concern across Europe. At a fifteen-nation EU Foreign Ministers' Meeting in Brussels in mid-March, German Foreign Minister Joschka Fischer rejected a call from Austria that UN Security Council Resolution 1244 should be extended to allow NATO's K-FOR mission to operate in Macedonia. Russian President Vladimir Putin commented that 'the situation in Macedonia is getting increasingly out of control', while in Brussels Swedish Foreign Minister Anna Lindh sent a clear message of support to the Macedonian government following talks with their foreign minister, Srgan Kerim.

The NLA, whose initials in Albanian – UCK – were the same as the Albanian acronym for the former KLA, had three principal demands: a release of political prisoners, an internationally mediated census and a change of the country's constitution to state that Macedonia was a 'state of two constituent peoples'.

Also in March, Germany had dispatched four Leopard 2 tanks, along with an additional 100–150 soldiers from K-FOR's German sector in southern Kosovo, to protect a German NATO barracks in Tetovo where one German soldier had been wounded during fighting with Albanian rebels. Macedonia, which had largely escaped the violent wars and ethnic tensions of the preceding decade in the Balkans, was crucial to NATO because it controlled the supply routes to the Aegean for its 44,000-strong Kosovo-based peacekeeping force. In an address to the nation, Macedonian Prime Minister Ljubco Georgievski had said that Macedonia would 'win this war without losing a single foot of our territory'. He then added the proviso that following the failure of K-FOR's efforts in neighbouring Kosovo to clamp down on Albanian extremism, the West was responsible for permitting the creation of 'a new Taliban in Europe'. Very quickly, the situation in Macedonia was becoming a new type of emergency mission for the international community: one of preventive diplomacy backed up by a credible threat of force.

As March went on, two ethnic Albanians were killed and one Macedonian policeman wounded in continuing fighting when a ceasefire put forward by Albanian rebels collapsed, and further violence looked inevitable. Top EU officials met with Macedonian and Albanian political parties in Skopje, putting pressure on both sides to try to find ways to avert further conflict. European Commissioners Javier Solana and Chris Patten met with leading politicians in Skopje while 30km away mortar rounds exploded and automatic gunfire cracked as the Macedonian Army and police hit suspected rebel positions above Tetovo. Meanwhile, fighting between Macedonian security forces and rebels broke out in at least three different areas of northern Macedonia, including a cross-border clash on the frontier with Kosovo.

On one morning in the late-spring heat of the third week of March, two Albanian men were machine-gunned to death by Macedonian

Interior Ministry Police when they tried to throw a hand grenade at a sandbagged Macedonian police position near Tetovo's football stadium. The two Albanian men had jumped out of a silver saloon car, one of them attempting to throw a hand grenade, as two Macedonian policemen shouted warnings to colleagues nearby. A large group of journalists filming the police position watched as the two Albanian men were machine-gunned to death in a hail of at least 100 bullets from Kalashnikovs and belt-fed machine guns. The television cameras rolled as a Macedonian policeman stepped out from behind the sandbagged position to drag one of the dying Albanians out of the road. The Albanian man groaned and then shuddered violently, his head and torso vibrating up and off the ground in a welter of dust, flying grit and sand as the Macedonian policeman emptied his Kalashnikov ammunition clip into the man's head. It was a moment of supreme violence. The entire incident took place in less than a minute.

The two Macedonian policemen had been routinely stopping cars in front of their sandbagged position, where, with two belt-fed 7.62mm machine guns, they were pouring bullets in a steady stream up into the hills above them at suspected Albanian positions. The sandbags in their little emplacement were white and behind the chest-high position, eleven paramilitary policemen lay crouched down on the Tarmac of the road, empty bullet cases, apple cores, rolls of lavatory paper, Kalashnikov magazines and Macedonian tabloid newspapers lying in discarded piles. Most of the machine-gun fire coming from the position was ineffectual because the Albanians up the mountain were well dug in, the Macedonians were useless shots and they were firing at long range. But the Macedonians continued to blast off ammunition at the hated *Shqiptars* in the hills regardless of accuracy or efficacy, the media got their pictures and security was seen to be being protected.

During the last week of March, the near-war and fighting sped up and took on an energy of its own. Macedonian government spokesmen said that Albanian rebels had attempted to take over the village of Gracani, 15km north-west of Tetovo near the border with Kosovo, and that one Macedonian policeman had been injured in an attack involving an RPG-7 antitank rocket launcher. They also said that eight police officers had been pinned down under fire in a separate incident, while there were further unconfirmed reports that Albanian rebels had fired on Macedonian positions from across the border with Kosovo. Italian Foreign Minister Lamberto Dini said that the grouping of six nations (Britain, the US, France, Germany, Italy and Russia) that had dealt with crises in the Balkans for the last ten years would show 'zero tolerance' towards any ethnic violence, while the UN Security Council denounced ethnic Albanian attacks in Macedonia and urged NATO to do more to clamp down on the export of armed extremism and weapons from Kosovo.

As a British Ministry of Defence assessment team returned to the UK towards the end of March after consultative meetings in Kosovo to decide how to react to the situation in Macedonia – the conclusion being either to send in 45 Commando of the Royal Marines or do nothing at all – the Macedonian Army decided to storm the hills above Tetovo. If there was one army in Europe, the former Soviet bloc or the Adriatic crescent that was not equipped with the training, equipment or morale to take on experienced Albanian guerrilla fighters, it was the Macedonians. Their country was one of the poorest in the Balkans, had been a badly funded part of Yugoslavia until 1991, had seen nothing of the decade of violence that had racked the rest of the Balkans and its people had no fighting experience whatsoever.

Consequently, they decided to attack directly up a steep series of mountain slopes 450m high against a well-trained, well-armed and well-dug-in guerrilla enemy defending its native Albanian turf. Early one morning during the third week in March, in a blizzard of supporting machine-gun fire, booming T-55 tank shells and the arcing curves of mortar fire, the pride of the Macedonian Army advanced very gingerly up the hills behind Tetovo. This was close-range stuff: it was possible to drive into the suburbs of Tetovo, walk through some back gardens and suddenly be within 500m of the Albanian positions above. Cigarettes in mouths, old-fashioned steel helmets swinging on their heads with the straps undone, Kalashnikovs spraying rounds at everything that moved and huddled in tight, tactics-free groups of ten or more, the Macedonians went to look for the NLA.

To their massive relief, the NLA had largely disappeared. It would emerge later that the local NLA commanders had simply done a deal with the Macedonian government and the Macedonian Army and Interior Ministry chiefs on the ground, taken a couple of hundred thousand Deutschmarks in payment and vanished off to another sector of fighting. But in the centre of Tetovo and on the slopes of the hills above it, the ammunition still flew, the brass cartridge cases tinkled and rolled on the roads and pavements where the Tarmac had softened in the boiling early-summer heat and the fighting spread overnight like chickenpox across most of the north and west of the country.

After the debacle above Tetovo, the Macedonians called in their air support. After a period of calm in April, when each side waited for the other to play its hand, violence flared again on 25 April when eight Macedonian policemen were killed and six wounded in an Albanian rebel attack in the Sar Mountains above Tetovo. By now the NLA had mushroomed out of a dozen villages stretching across the north of Macedonia, lying in the shadows of the *Crna Gora*, the Black Mountains that run along the country's northern border with Kosovo. Since all these villages lay in the Albanian-speaking part of the country, the NLA were quick to realise that the local Albanian civilian population were potentially very useful as hostages. Knowing that many of the older Albanian residents of the villages that stretched between Skopje and the north-western town of Kumanovo had never lived anywhere else and were scared, poor and ill-educated, the NLA started rumours: any Albanians leaving their villages to escape the fighting and the Macedonian bombing would be considered traitors; in any event, those who got across the front line to safety would be attacked and possibly even eaten by the Macedonians. So, in the tiny villages of Slupcane, Lipkovo, Otlja, Vaksince, Matejce and Nikustak, stretching along the bottom of the mountains, the Albanian civilians stayed put. The NLA's human shield was in place.

The attacks on these villages by the Macedonians very rarely included assaults by ground troops. That was not, essentially, what Macedonian military tactics consisted of. They preferred instead to line up their 105mm howitzers, their 120mm mortars and their tanks in the soft, green swathes of the summer cornfields that rolled across that part of the country. Warm summer rain would fall gently through a hedge of hazel and blackthorn in some field 1.5km distant from an Albanian-occupied village while the air rang with the sound of spades and crunching earth as the Macedonians dug in. Behind their new positions in the corn were piles of soil from the digging. Bright red poppies uprooted by army shovels lay tossed on the piles of brown earth, beside which lay heavy blue suits of body armour, bandoleers of machine-gun ammunition and assault rifles put aside while their owners sweated and dug in the warm, early-summer air.

Once the heavy weapons were in place, the Macedonians would open fire. Tearing salvoes of shells and mortar rounds accompanied by thousands and thousands of rounds of machine-gun fire would be launched into the target area of each Albanian village. For the Macedonian soldiers and international journalists standing in the vivid green of the cornfields under the warm summer rain watching these onslaughts, it became difficult to believe that anybody could survive such an assault. The village of Slupcane was bombarded by 105mm and 122mm howitzers, T-55 tank guns, mortars and machine guns every day for a month at the height of the fighting, from mid-May to mid-June. The Albanian civilian population would be in the basements of their houses, the Albanian fighters well dug into positions to the front of villages, ready to fend off any infantry assault. The red-brick houses took shell after shell, the streets were stitched with bullets and the hamlets and villages were blown senseless. Casualties just had to be enormous, particularly as the Macedonians had started making liberal thrice-daily use of helicopter gunship assaults from the half-dozen Mi-24 Hind-D choppers that they had hire-purchased from the Ukrainians.

Flown by the Russians, these flying tanks had pummelled the

mujahideen in Afghanistan, firing salvoes of 37mm rockets from their underwing pods and then *whirring* out thousands of rounds from the Gatling guns set in their noses. Flown by drunk Ukrainian mercenary pilots in Macedonia, it was a somewhat different story. They would *thwack* and *thunk* their way from their base at Petrovec Airport outside Skopje, flying at very low level, and then take some ten minutes to line up for an assault against one of the villages. Rockets would be *whooshed* off and then the pilots would open up with their Gatling guns as the Albanians responded with RPG-7 rocket launchers and heavy machine guns.

A round of intense, behind-the-scenes political negotiation between Albanian and Macedonian leaders to adjust the country's constitution in favour of the Albanians, who felt themselves discriminated against – especially in the fields of employment and education – had, by late May and early June 2001, been underway for a month. But despite this and a round of preventive shuttle diplomacy by EU Commissioners Javier Solana and Chris Patten, as well as condemnations of rebel actions by everybody from the US State Department to the EU and NATO, the violence continued.

American military advisers, Ukrainian helicopter gunships, Bulgarian tanks, Croat and Serb mercenaries and Yugoslav weapons were just some of the resources that former Cold War foes from the United States and ex-Warsaw Pact countries were delivering to Macedonia as it struggled to contain the violent armed insurrection by the Albanians. Yet in spite of the abundance of hardware, it was obvious that the Macedonian Army and Interior Ministry Police were in a no-win situation. Heavy artillery, mortar and machine-gun duels between Macedonian government troops and the NLA continued throughout the month of May as the Macedonian Army bombarded three rebel-held villages outside the key town of Kumanovo, 24km from Skopje. The Macedonian Army had three choices: firstly, they could withdraw, cease firing and allow the rebels to continue occupying over 160sq. km of Macedonian territory; secondly, they could go in, confront the rebels on the ground in hand-to-hand combat and win back the lost territory; or thirdly, they could carry on as they were and simply allow the rebels to continue to attack as they pleased.

Based back up in Pristina were a handful of former members of 22 SAS, soldiers who had left the Regiment and put themselves out on the international 'Circuit', the informal security network that employed many former members of Britain's Special Forces. In Kosovo they provided 'close protection' or 'CP' to UN and EU officials and Western diplomats, advised the liberal humanitarian echelons of the aid world on security and assessed security, risk and various other commodities on behalf of a variety of international clients. They moved around Pristina with a calm air of self-assurance, mostly discreetly armed, carrying small rucksacks wearing functional clothing and with only the occasional Heckler & Koch MP5 in evidence. In the varying climatic extremes of Kosovo, it was safe to say that they were always dressed for the weather. Clustered around a table in the UN HQ café, half-drunk macchiato coffees at their elbows, hand-held radios, clipboards and files in front of them, they waited for their 'principals', the people they guarded, to emerge from meetings, keeping an eye on the international ebb and flow around them.

Two of the Hereford men who guarded the head of the EU Mission in Kosovo had an office in the UN headquarters. It was an oasis of military calm and protocol amidst the fluttering chaos, telephone chatter and endless meetings of international UN bureaucrats who dashed around the corridors outside the Hereford men's office. Inside, all was calm. The air was that of the Sergeants' Mess. On the wall were photos of the lads in uniform in the First Gulf War. Also attached to the wall was a metal locker in which the former SAS men kept all the security equipment they needed – or liked to think they would need – in order to protect a senior EU bureaucrat in a post-conflict Balkan environment. There was Mace spray, handcuffs, body armour, spare pistol magazines for 9mm Glock and Sig-Sauer handguns, torches, laser-sights, extendable truncheons, a couple of daggers, sets of marker-pens, maps, torch batteries and a copy of *Fighting Knives Monthly*. The men from Hereford were firmly decided about Macedonia. What the Macedonian Army needed to do was master the timeless business of the infantry assault. Few things in life, they thought, could not be achieved by a company of well-trained infantry moving tactically and operationally on to a position. If it was left to them, well, a couple of hundred blokes could sort out 'Mac-Land' in a week. Bit of a kick in the bum, that's what the Macedonians needed.

Their assessment was quite apposite. The Macedonian MOD had, a couple of years before, hired a private American security company made up of former specialist military personnel, mostly ex-SF and Marines, known as Military Professional Resources International (MPRI), from Alexandria, Virginia. MPRI had taken on a contract in 1998 to train the Macedonian Army up to the standards required of a national army for NATO accession. Both sides expected different things of the contract. In the case of the Macedonian Army, the opinions of MPRI and the Defence Ministry in Skopje differed. The Macedonians, like all self-respecting Balkan men, wanted big, expensive, powerful, flashy, noisy toys that would destroy people of any ethnicity apart from their own. They wanted helicopters, armoured vehicles, black Humvee jeeps with chrome bumpers – the lot. These the Macedonian MOD and Interior Ministry bought privately off their own bat with funds diverted from other cash-strapped government ministries. What they did not want to hear from the Americans was that they had to learn about things like patrolling, about how to walk across a cornfield in formation, at night, without routinely bursting into tears. Unfortunately, the Americans had also told them in 1999 that it would be unlikely that they would ever face a military threat from one of the countries on their borders. Consequently, two years later, battling Albanians from across their northern border, they were more than slightly irked by the Americans' advice.

MPRI were a curious bunch. On the one hand they were a firm that did things quite legitimately – and well – in many places, such as Columbia and Macedonia. Their policy was American foreign policy and they were sometimes the executors of it, particularly as their company was run by William Cohen, a former US secretary of state for defence. They were frequently used as the unofficial extension of any deniable Pentagon policy that was too questionable or simply too illegal to be assigned to the regular US military. However, like parts of the US Special Forces and various parts of the military, MPRI was not, politely and diplomatically put, an organisation that epitomised irony, flexibility or self-deprecation as much as it might have. What it did do, whatever the calibre of the men it employed, was epitomise the best and worst extremes of US foreign policy. The men from MPRI were often the ones deployed on the ground to ally themselves with or to train whichever rebel army, gang of self-styled freedom fighters or lunatic village headman it was that the US State Department had decided was the democratic flavour of the month.

The Americans in Pristina, both diplomatically and covertly, had kept closer ties with the ex-KLA fighters than many realised. The British foreign intelligence community was trying to retain a modicum of sensible influence over the bad boys of the Kosovo Protection Corps, the ex-KLA hardmen who had disappeared off to fight in Macedonia, in a variety of ways. Simply put, the British Foreign and Commonwealth Office diplomats and those staffers cross-posted from the Secret Intelligence Service wanted Kosovo to be at peace. Peace in Kosovo, for the British, meant an atmosphere in which democracy could flourish and where multiethnicity meant exactly that, rather than a province where a massive Albanian majority lorded it over a fistful of terrified and impoverished Serbs and gypsies who lived squalid lives of security-free poverty under the barbed wire and tank barrels of NATO troops.

The difficulty was that the British, Americans and other NATO armies had trained, armed, financed and supported the KLA. Now that the KLA was formally disbanded, the diplomatic Western powers-that-be were trying to shoehorn the ex-rebel leaders into new incarnations as democrats. The problem was that the Kosovo Albanian hardmen had by now swallowed so much international democratic medicine that they risked gagging on the spoon. Responsible control of political office meant one thing for a fast-track Foreign Office political secretary from Whitehall and something completely different for a former leader of the KLA. The Albanians, simply put, had other ways of doing things, and democracy was not much evident in their history. Leadership of a political party for them meant having access to the reins of criminal, political and social power. They also resented being told what to do by a bunch of internationals who, they thought, changed their minds and their allegiances like the wind and talked a lot while seemingly incapable of solving the simplest of problems. It was now midsummer 2001. The international community had been running the province for two years and there was still no remote sign of reliable supplies of water or electricity, despite the hundreds of millions of Deutschmarks that the EU and UN had poured into the energy sector. Why should they, the Albanians, be told what to do by some well-intentioned political science graduate from Brussels, some scion of European political economics big on education but short on experience, sitting in a white UN Toyota four-by-four braying on a mobile telephone about nation-state building? Wasn't it them, the Albanians, who had suffered? And here they were, two years later, being told in hectoring terms by the international community that they shouldn't take any form of revenge on Serbs. That all communities should live together in harmony. It was a bit much. And the Albanians could see that now that the hated regime of Slobodan Milosevic had gone up the spout in Belgrade, it would not be long before the Western bureaucrats in Pristina were giving their share of sympathy, time and money to the Serbs, while the Albanians got left behind. Again. The EU, UN and NATO? Nothing but a bunch of fickle colonial whities, thought many of the Kosovo Albanians.

The fickle colonial whities were, unfortunately for the Albanians, the ones controlling the purse strings and the political and social roadblocks that littered the route to modernisation and membership of the EU. Kosovo, they said, was doomed to remain a failed experiment in international tutelage consigned to a socio-economic time warp unless it got with the EU, NATO and UN programme and cleaned up its act. Many within the international sector, NATO in particular, were firmly of the opinion that if the Kosovo Albanians could not abide by Western rules, then they should not be surprised if they got a taste of Western stick.

The international diplomatic community in Pristina was run by the five-nation grouping known as 'the Quint' – the Italians, British, French, Germans and Americans. Firmly in the middle, mostly exercising reason, restraint and a modicum of common sense and *realpolitik* pragmatism, were the British. It fell to them to calm the latest flurry of international ruffled feathers, such as when the Italians began to discover in late 2000 and early 2001, for instance, that the Americans were – predictably – playing all sorts of complicated and self-defeating intelligence dirty tricks behind their backs. Or it would fall to the men from London to pour oil on the waters of troubled Gallic pride over the latest showdown in Mitrovica. The British Office – there was no formal 'embassy' in Kosovo as it was not a sovereign state – had been run from 1999 to 2001, successively, by a brace of astute senior diplomats backed up by some idiosyncratic, low-key yet effective political secretaries. While many of Prime Minister Tony Blair's policies and implementers thereof fell flat on their faces in Britain in a puddle of awful middle-ground political mediocrity, somehow when transported abroad both policies and staff seemed to thrive. Thus it was in Kosovo.

For the British, multi-ethnic democracy in Kosovo would mean that Britain could withdraw her hard-stretched infantry battalions, stop spending so much money on the little aspirant state and notch the intervention and subsequent experiment in international tutelage up as a success. Sometimes, though, the British diplomatic schemes seemed a little odd, as when some hardline ex-KLA men were sent off on a diplomatic white-elephant trip to Prague to learn English on a course organised by the British Council. In reality, though, what the shadowy political and intelligence analysts from MI6 were really doing, behind their bluff, welcoming diplomatic exteriors, was desperately trying to line up all the bad-boy Kosovo politicians against each other using a series of fake assurances that effectively played all sides against the middle. They hoped that the *really* bad boys in the Albanian ex-KLA community, the Serb-killers, the drug-running, wife-beating organisers of prostitution rackets, the ones who had no chance of ever being dragged into the democratic fold, would be informed on and sidelined by their marginally more intelligent colleagues. It was hoped that these more reasonable men would see that, when pragmatic push came to realistic shove, shopping their former comrades-in-arms to The Hague tribunal or the UN police in Pristina was a sure-fire way to keep in with the internationals, British and American, who really pulled the strings in Kosovo. So when Messrs Thaci, Haradinai and Ceku came to clink glasses with their international sponsors at the British or American cocktail parties, the smell in the air was not that of singed hors-d'oeuvres but of a frayed trust. And by midsummer 2001, the Kosovo Albanian ex-rebel community turned political animal smelt this change in the air whenever a British diplomat or American intelligence officer got out of their four-wheel-drive vehicles.

Consequently, when some MPRI officials turned up, in borrowed US uniforms, in the snow and slush on the mountainous Kosovo–Macedonian border in March 2001 when the first wave of the NLA insurgency was just beginning to peak, it wasn't clear whether they had come to look at how their former KLA-turned-NLA protégés were doing in their incipient border struggle with the Macedonians, or whether they had come for a look from the Kosovo side of things at how their training operations with the Macedonians had turned out. Not for the first time, the Americans were actively involved in training and assisting both sides at the same time. Knowing this, and knowing that that day in the snowy village of Debelde, high up in the *Crna Gora* mountains along the Kosovo–Macedonian border, would be a good day to observe all the different comings and goings on the frontier, was the reason why the man sitting in a covert observation post 150m above them had dug his artfully concealed hole where he had. He had sited the observation post well, and the countryside was like home. The mountains and oak forests here at this time of year were, after all, little different from those that covered the Black Mountains in mid-Wales, or the fields and hills that ran above the river near Pontrilas, the training ground south of Hereford where this officer from 22 SAS and his colleagues from the Regiment had honed their skills. The mission for the SAS officer had been to dig himself into a 'hide' on the muddy, snowy hillside, small enough for him to be completely camouflaged and invisible. From this hole he could monitor the comings and goings of the Americans, the Albanians, MPRI personnel and the Macedonians. His mission was to observe, and for twenty-seven days he and a rotating group of three other SAS men did just that, watching the physical proof unfold on the ground of the way in which the Americans seemed to be backing all sides against the middle.

Nearly four months after the SAS officer had sat in his 'hide', it was late June and scorching midsummer in Macedonia. The days of war seemed to blend into one, and the conflict that blazed across the entire north and west of Macedonia seemed to have consumed the country with that curious entropic energy that war brings with it. Seen from the air, villages burned in straight lines from west to east, north to south, defining the limits of Albanian-occupied territory.

Standing in a hotel in Skopje at breakfast time, journalists and international observers could watch and hear the creaking, whacking *thud* of pairs of Mi-24 Hind helicopter gunships as they flew off to attack Albanian villages. Every day there were artillery barrages across the cornfields on to a string of villages that stretched in a curving 56 km-long line from Kumanovo in the west to the villages above Tetovo in the east. Tens of thousands of Albanian refugees poured across the mountains into Kosovo; under the burning midsummer sun, the simmering hum of ethnic violence sounded across the whole of Macedonia. Every day seemed to bring the breathless concern of Western diplomats trying to kick-start a seemingly hopeless peace process, or a senior Western official standing on the front steps of a hotel saying that Macedonia was only hours away from complete, all-out war.

By the end of June, the Macedonian parliament was meeting to endorse the new multi-ethnic government formed in the hope that greater political recognition for the country's 600,000-strong Albanian minority would halt the wave of rebel violence. Outside the chalet-style house back in Lipkovo where the rebels had set up an impromptu headquarters in the rural mountain village, Mi-24 Hind helicopter gunships from the Macedonian Air Force swooped over the nearby rebel-held village of Vaksince, which was already heavily damaged after two months of almost constant shelling. The Macedonian government of President Boris Trajkovski had long refused to negotiate with the rebels, labelling them 'terrorists', yet months of continuous shelling of several villages they occupied between the town of Kumanovo and the Kosovo border had had little impact on rebel movements.

In Lipkovo, black-uniformed rebel fighters armed with Kalashnikov assault rifles, the Albanian double-headed-eagle insignia of the NLA sewn on their sleeves, showed journalists two basements and cellars where fifty-five women and children crouched underground, taking refuge from the shelling and mortar fire. The dusty streets of Lipkovo, poppies and wallflowers growing everywhere, were busy with dozens of rebel fighters but largely untouched by shelling, unlike the next-door hamlets of Vaksince and Slupcane which had been heavily blitzed by army shelling.

Back in the blasted streets on the other side of the rebel front line, the kind of rebel fighters the Macedonians were going to be up against were readying for yet another battle. A Macedonian policeman had just been killed and another wounded in a village near Tetovo on 21 June and the ceasefire seemed to be fragmenting. The promised all-out assault on the Albanian rebel villages seemed closer. On a ruined street in Slupcane, where every house, telegraph pole, wall, car, door and roof seemed to have been attacked with a furious, giant tin-opener that had torn everything apart in the form of a hail of artillery and cannon fire over the last month, stood eighteen-year-old Shodra Zenuni. She was one of the few women fighting with the Albanian rebels in northern Macedonia. Kalashnikov assault rifle slung over her shoulder, long brown hair swept back in a ponytail, the Albanian double-headed-eagle insignia of the NLA on the shoulder of her Italian-manufactured camouflage uniform, Shodra stood in the centre of this destroyed village in northern Macedonia, hit by weeks of Macedonian government shellfire, and said simply: 'I am a soldier.'

Until she was fifteen, the Albanian teenager from the Macedonian town of Kumanovo had studied in Lausanne in Switzerland. Then the war against the Serbs in Kosovo had taken her to join the KLA, after which she moved with the struggle to Macedonia along with her father, a former Albanian political prisoner in Macedonia. When NATO Secretary-General George Robertson said at an EU foreign ministers' meeting in Tirana that NATO had to assist Macedonia in her struggle against ethnic Albanian rebels by helping Macedonia to 'aggressively cleanse' its borders with neighbouring Kosovo, he was talking about finding a solution to the problems posed by fighters like Shodra. Standing in the summer heat of the wrecked village street, the young rebel looked around at the red-brick houses of rebel-held Slupcane, blown up, burned down, smashed and pockmarked by successive days of Macedonian government artillery fire, T-55 tanks shells, mortar rounds and machine-gun bullets. The roof of the village mosque had taken a direct hit and broken glass, burned timber and fallen telephone wires lay everywhere. Ukrainian Mi-24 helicopter gunships had blasted vast chunks out of some of the houses, and out of some of the local livestock. In a litter-strewn stream a brown chicken pecked hopefully at the bloated carcass of half a horse. The other half lay upside-down in a blasted tree, impaled on the sharp white stumps of broken branches. Macedonian artillery units had broken the ceasefire that day by shelling Slupcane and the neighbouring villages of Vaksince and Orizare, shattering a day of calm after the expiration of the government deadline for the Albanian rebels to lay down their arms or face 'elimination' by the Macedonian Army.

The first NLA rebels arrived within 8km of the capital, Skopje, on 8 June. On that boiling summer evening, rebel Commander Hoxha and his men had arrived in the small town of Aracinovo, on the fringes of the Skopje suburbs. The Slav villagers had fled. The Macedonian forces, terrified, had set up a roadblock at the far end of the town, where it turned on to the main road leading to the motorway and the capital itself. Hoxha, an Albanian who had either spent several years in the Haute-Savoie region of France working as a waiter in Annecy or had served in the French Foreign Legion, depending on whose claims one listened to, stood in the evening sun, licking a chocolate ice cream and staring at the tower blocks of the capital. Behind him, some of the Wahhabi-ist Islamic fundamentalist fighters who served with the NLA stood watching him, green and white headbands with Koranic texts written on them wrapped around their sweating foreheads. One of them was staining down the telescopic sight of his Dragunov sniper rifle at the sun as it set over Skopje. Hoxha had his heavy mortars arriving behind him, he told two British journalists from *The Economist* and Agence France-Presse, and it would be a day at most before he would strike at the heart of the Macedonian government.

On 21 June, after a fortnight of shaky ceasefire, the government called his cards. Macedonian Mi-24 Hind helicopter gunships flown by ex-Soviet mercenary pilots spearheaded the massive all-out dawn assault by Macedonia's government forces on the rebel positions on the edges of the capital, aimed at pushing back them back from the outskirts of the city. Just before dawn at 4 a.m., gunships blasted rebel positions with air-to-ground rockets, following up with an artillery and tank barrage into Aracinovo, 8km from Skopje's outskirts. By late afternoon, after twelve hours of heavy fighting, army and police units were clashing with rebel forces in Aracinovo and a string of villages north-west of Skopje. From a sandbagged police roadblock set up in the village of Singjelic, just 500m outside Aracinovo, mortar and artillery shells could be seen landing in the town as heavy bursts of automatic weapons fire crackled between both sides. On 22 June, NATO Secretary-General George Robertson would warn Macedonians and Albanians alike that this tinderbox southern Balkan state was 'close to civil war', and this latest offensive effectively buried a fragile truce between the army and the guerrillas as peace talks in the capital stalled.

During the four-day fight for Aracinovo, Commander Hoxha told journalists by mobile telephone from inside the red-roofed suburb that three civilians had been killed in the fighting and eighteen injured. As massive plumes of smoke billowed from burning houses and T-55 tanks blasted rebel positions in and around the town, Macedonian TV said that five soldiers had been wounded in the fighting. Commander Hoxha threatened to retaliate with a mortar attack on the capital and on nearby Petrovec Airport, a vital regional hub as well as a logistically key base for the massive NATO mission in neighbouring Kosovo. He had already responded with mortar fire towards villages outside the capital. As Ukrainian-made Mi-24 Hind helicopter gunships clattered at tree-top level over the summer cornfields blasting rebel positions with rockets, tanks and BTR armoured vehicles fired down into Aracinovo from the dusty hillsides surrounding it, toppling the minarets of two mosques and setting several houses on fire. Further west, Macedonian forces came under fire from rebel mortars and Russian-made Kolya rockets as they attacked rebel positions around the villages of Slupcane and Orizare, between the northwestern city of Kumanovo and the Kosovan border. Two Mi-24 gunships blasted rockets into NLA ammunition storage bunkers in Mojanci and Oralnci, two villages outside Aracinovo, as rebels tried to regroup under tank and artillery fire.

By the end of the second week in June, the fifth Balkans war that so many international diplomats, generals and politicians had struggled to avoid was screaming over the horizon so fast you could hear it coming. The Macedonians had tried ineffectually to take Aracinovo for four days. Despite pouring a huge volume of tank, artillery, rocket and small-arms fire into the town, the NLA were very well dug into a network of trenches and dug-outs. Assaults by the Tigers, the Interior Ministry's Special Forces, had failed. The NLA had a commander in Aracinovo who knew the art of defensive warfare well. One Western intelligence official commented that a well-known ex-KLA fighter and leader of a minor Kosovan political party was taking his summer off to fight in Macedonia.

Desperate to avert further disaster, and to remove the NLA rebels from the fringes of Skopje, the Americans took drastic action. After four days of fighting, a rather tremulous ceasefire held over the dusty cornfields and in the shrapnel-strewn streets of Aracinovo. The American 82nd Airborne Division arrived with some civilian contractors from neighbouring Kosovo, some large air-conditioned coaches and a convoy of armed Humvees to escort them. To the utter fury of the entire Macedonian military, civilian and political establishment, the Americans simply gave the 300–400 NLA fighters in the town a lift to safety.

The NLA fighters were dropped off by coach several kilometres away, on the outskirts of the village of Umin Dol, from where they made their way back to their positions on the other side of the front line while Macedonian soldiers watched in horror as the heavily armed fighters disembarked from the coaches like so many guerrilla day-trippers. It was yet another example of ham-fisted US intelligence at work: in one fell move the Americans had demonstrated to the Macedonians that they were unequivocally biased towards the NLA. The following night, outside the parliament building in Skopje, the reaction of the Macedonian electorate was to the point.

On 25 June, a Macedonian soldier from one of the army's Special Forces units known as the 'Scorpions' stood on top of the remains of a black limousine belonging to the Macedonian presidential motorcade, waving his Kalashnikov and kissing the Macedonian flag. The limousine had been destroyed by demonstrators venting their fury on President Boris Trajkovski and his government. In his other hand, the soldier grasped a large Serbian Orthodox cross, which he waved wildly at the thousands of Macedonian Slav demonstrators pushing determinedly towards the main doors of the parliament building, trying to storm it. Jumping up and down on the roof of the scarred Mercedes, he screamed at the crowd about how he had cried at the funeral of his friend, who had been killed by Albanian terrorists. Police and army reservists emptied magazine after magazine of automatic gunfire into the air, making no attempt to restrain any of the 10,000-odd demonstrators pushing towards the parliament building, which some twenty managed to enter, tearing the national flag off its halyard over the entrance and opening fire into the air right outside the building.

TV journalists, including a crew from the BBC, were attacked, and anybody remotely suspected by the crowd of being a foreigner was turned on and attacked or abused. The images shown on TV screens could have been the storming of the parliament building in Belgrade the previous year, prior to the fall of President Slobodan Milosevic. Demonstrators screamed for the resignation of President Trajkovski, shouted that NATO were traitors and demanded that Albanians should be put in gas-chambers.

But for the majority of Macedonian Slav citizens, it was a completely non-violent affair. Children walked around with their parents, licking ice creams; Skopje's citizenry came out for an evening stroll and went to watch their parliament building being stormed. As automatic gunfire crackled into the air, police reservists sat on the kerb, quietly munching hamburgers and paying no attention. Outside the Fresh fast-food outlet, somebody spray-painted 'NATO = Nazis' on to the wall while a couple kissed quietly on a bench. This was not the fall of the Berlin Wall. This Macedonian Slavic *laissez-faire* had been the saving grace of the country so far, the one thing that had stopped Macedonia from sliding into civil war along with the rest of the Balkan states.

Luckily for the ethnic Albanian rebels of the NLA, they were not up against the Serb paramilitaries or soldiers who had run rings around them in Kosovo. They were up against the mainly lethargic, sleepy Macedonian security forces, described by one British military expert as 'badly trained, badly equipped and badly led'.

'Macedonian Slavs are like the Serbs,' ran the popular saying among the more cynically minded of the international community, 'except they lack the killing skills.'

The country had been largely at peace since 1991, when it had gained independence from the Yugoslav Federation, and a decade of peace and prosperity showed. This was not a country that particularly wanted a fight, nor indeed was it ready for one, which is one reason why the Albanian rebels had managed to make such an impression so far.

Over in Kosovo, NATO was still desperately trying to clamp down on the flow of weapons and equipment across the border. One day in July, an American patrol noticed three Kosovo Albanian men outside a house in the village of Grno Zlocucane, on the Kosovo–Macedonian border, only because all of them had serious gunshot wounds. On a reconnaissance patrol trying to prevent ethnic Albanian rebels from infiltrating into Macedonia across Kosovo's wooded, mountainous border, the US peacekeepers from 'B' Company of the Second Battalion, 502nd Infantry Regiment, approached with extreme caution. They discovered that one man had serious gunshot wounds in his abdomen and another had been hit in the shoulder, while the third man had wounds in his left leg and his right leg – and all the toes on his right foot – were broken. Carrying out a rapid search of the house, the soldiers discovered another twenty-four men inside, along with a variety of pistols, hand grenades and knives. Taken to the detention centre at the massive US military base at Camp Bondsteel, the Albanians were just some of the forty-four men picked up in Kosovo within one forty-eight-hour period, suspected of belonging to Albanian rebel units that had been fighting the Macedonian Army. It was midsummer in the oak forests and on the mountain slopes of Kosovo's southern border with Macedonia, and NATO peacekeepers were struggling to maintain a hold on the flow of rebel fighters and military equipment moving across the Sar Planina mountain range into Macedonia. Above the town of Tetovo, the Macedonian Army had used Sukhoi Su-25 ground-attack jets against rebel positions for the first time.

Even higher above Tetovo, in the freezing winds at heights of up to 2,440 meters just inside Kosovo, British soldiers from the 1st Battalion, the Duke of Wellington's Regiment, set up a series of positions in July designed to interdict rebels trying to cross the border. British troops had discovered that many of the male civilians they arrested had small mirrors on them, which they used to signal back down the mountains to their rebel colleagues, indicating that a particular route was safe. It was an operation that the men from the Duke of Wellington's Regiment excelled at, and consequently the Albanians took to trying to cross into Macedonia in border areas controlled by the Germans or Americans, where the boundary was much more porous. Further to the east, in the forests outside the Kosovan town of Strpce, German and Ukrainian NATO troops manned observation positions, trying to spot rebels using tractors and horses to transport guns, food and ammunition along mountain tracks into Macedonia and wounded fighters back out into Kosovo.

In addition to the efforts of the hundreds of British, German, American, Ukrainian, Italian and Polish troops, other measures were being taken. In a special order, US President George Bush had banned five organisations, including the NLA and several individuals in Kosovo believed to be linked to it, from receiving financial assistance from abroad and had frozen their assets in the United States. Hans Haekkerrup, the charmless and ineffectual Danish diplomat who, though terrified of the Albanian hardliners, had replaced Bernard Kouchner at the head of UNMIK, took what he saw as a drastic step: he removed several key NLA leaders who were also members of the Kosovo Protection Corps from that internationally sponsored organisation.

War in Macedonia continued into July and August 2001. During the particularly bloody week of 8–14 August, there were many deaths. Eight government soldiers were killed in an antitank-mine blast outside the capital on 12 August, a day on which a ceasefire had supposedly been agreed. On 13 August, the 'Ohrid Peace Agreement' was ratified at Lake Ohrid in southern Macedonia. In spite of this, during 13–15 August, Macedonian troops and paramilitaries, assisted by local villagers, killed twelve Albanians in the village of Ljuboten outside Skopje in revenge for the mine attack. As the week went on, five Macedonian police reservists were wounded after police units, backed up by Mi-24 Hind helicopter gunships flown by Ukrainian pilots, fought with Albanian rebel units near the village of Radusa, north-west of the capital on the mountainous border with Kosovo. Twenty soldiers and policemen, at least five rebels and two civilians had been killed and more than thirty people wounded in the worst violence since late January. Large parts of Macedonia's second-largest city, Tetovo, were controlled by one brigade of the NLA, who had clashed daily with the army and police in the northern and eastern quarters of the city. For four nights running, there had been violent demonstrations in Skopje as groups of hardcore nation-alist youths had gathered in front of the parliament building in the capital and then gone on the rampage, destroying Albanian-owned businesses, stoning Western embassies and attempting to cross the River Vardar to attack the Albanian-dominated quarters of the city. Chanting slogans such as 'NATO are Nazis' and 'Albanians to the gas-chambers', these were the supporters of hardline Prime Minister Ljubco Georgievski's VMRO party, the same nationalist youths who made such easy recruit-ing fodder for Slav paramilitary organisations increasingly involved in anti-Albanian violence.

Under the supervision of the EU's senior negotiator, François Leotard, and American Envoy James Pardew, Macedonia's leading political parties were still determined to put their signatures to a peace deal hammered out during months of frustrating talks between all sides, behind the scenes, which had frequently collapsed as Albanians or Slavs walked out in disgust, or as increasing violence intervened. Everybody involved – Mace-donian, Albanian and international negotiators – were in accord about one thing: the deal, which attempted to guarantee greater political and constitutional rights for the country's 600,000-strong Albanian minority, was the very final, utterly last chance Macedonia had before the country spiralled completely out of control.

Were the peace deal to be signed, NATO would arrive. Led by Britain's flamboyant Brigadier Barney White-Spunner – a Household Cavalry officer who combined his military duties with occasional journalism, writing for *The Field* magazine – and spearheaded by elements of the Colchester-based 16 Air Assault Brigade, including a reinforced battal-ion of the Parachute Regiment, a 3,500-strong multinational NATO mission was ready to deploy to Macedonia to collect the rebels' weapons under a voluntary disarmament scheme. One of the reasons that Mace-donia was falling off the edge of a cliff was that the gaps between the country's two main ethnic groups were widening with each day, and with each violent incident. Ask the five Macedonian road-menders who had been kidnapped during the week of 8–15 August by Albanian rebels as they erected road signs on the hard shoulder of the main Skopje–Tetovo dual carriageway. Beaten with spades and sticks for several hours, NLA fighters had then carved the men's initials on their backs with knives before forcing them to perform oral sex on each other in a trench and trying to anally rape them with a stick. Every such incident fed into the churning hatred each side had for each other, making each successive act of violence more mindless, less relevant.

It had been scorchingly hot in Macedonia that week in August and the leaves on the chestnut trees in the central cobbled square in Skopje were wilting in the heat. In the warm night-time air, affluent Slav families paraded under the awning of Dal Met Fu, a brightly lit terraced café, ice-cream parlour and restaurant that sat under the chestnut trees by the newspaper kiosks in one corner of the square. Roma gypsy children barely old enough to walk begged ceaselessly at tables, only scared away by the micro-skirted Slav waitresses *fizzing* them with the occasional jolt from an electric cattle-prod. By day, the veranda tables were the preserve of the jostling ranks of the international community – NATO soldiers and journalists, as well as International Red Cross delegates with their burning agendas and urgent expressions. The whole international crowd were scowled on by the thick-necked Slav paramilitary leaders in their black shirts and grey suits, guzzling lunchtime tureens of liver stew in the 32°C heat and washing it down with brandy, red wine and coffee. Their afternoon would bring a heavy, sweating siesta on the fake leather of the Interior Ministry sofas, slumbering off a couple of hours with a daydream of light orange flames dancing on the ochre tiles of ethnically cleansed Albanian villages. Or perhaps it would involve a drive down the motorway to that special motel outside Veles for an hour of misogynistic Balkan sex with one of the trafficked, heroin-addicted Moldovan teenagers with the bruised lips and sloppy smiles, girls press-ganged into prostitution five countries away and shipped to Macedonia to face the music as sex-slaves for the entertainment of Macedonian hardmen and German NATO peacekeepers.

What hopes did the peace talks have? On 10 August, in the Albanian quarter of a small village outside the central Macedonian town of Veles, eleven-year-old Tafil Vejseli's parents let their children sleep outside on the terrace as it was so hot. Enraged by the deaths earlier in the day of ten Macedonian Army reservists in a rebel ambush outside Skopje, local Slav paramilitaries armed with automatic rifles were out looking for Albanian blood. Driving past the Vejseli house, they opened fire. Tafil stood up to see what the noise was and a 7.62mm high-velocity round blew half his chest out. The following day, Macedonian police had to protect the mourners at his funeral from further attacks by Macedonians.

But the Balkans is a land of surprises. From 14 August onwards, advance NATO troops arrived in Macedonia on a mission that would assess whether a fragile ceasefire between warring rebels and government forces was stable enough to allow a further 3,000 troops to deploy to collect weapons from Albanian rebels. More than 500 troops, including over 100 British soldiers from the Colchester-based 16 Air Assault Brigade, arrived at Petrovec Airport. The Albanian rebels had reiterated their intention of laying down their arms. Rebel leader Ali Ahmeti, who had masterminded the six-month insurgency campaign that had seen NLA fighters advance to the gates of the capital, said that his men, estimated at 2,500-strong, would be handing in all their weapons to NATO forces. But the British commander of NATO's Operation Essential Harvest, Brigadier Barney White-Spunner, warned that a ceasefire in place between the two sides would have to hold before he and other NATO officials recommended to the alliance's Brussels headquarters that the time was right to deploy the larger force from thirteen nations to carry out the weapons collection.

Such was the background situation for some thirty British paratroopers from 16 Air Assault Brigade's elite Pathfinder Platoon, specialising in reconnaissance and long-range patrolling, who were about to strike out into the northern Macedonian countryside to scout out access routes into rebel-held areas. The Paras were to be accompanied by three or four four-man teams of soldiers from 22 SAS, who were to occupy observation positions high up on the mountains overlooking Macedonia. Lightly armed with only their personal SA-80 assault rifles and driving Land Rovers mounting 7.62mm GPMGs, the British troops were just part of a dual-track process that was to see intensive negotiation meetings held between NATO officials, the Macedonian government and rebel commanders.

On 21 August, high up in the mountains of war-torn western Macedonia, two British Army Lynx helicopters had landed one after the other on the tiny football pitch of the small village of Sipkovice in a boiling cloud of brown dust whipped up by their rotor-blades, Army Air Corps door gunners cradling 7.62mm GPMGs as the helicopters settled. A small typhoon of dust, grit and stones hailed through the air into the faces of the four-man Parachute Regiment reconnaissance team already on the ground, who minutes earlier had laid out a turquoise and fluorescent pink marker-strip in the middle of the pitch and then guided the helicopters in by radio. Out jumped three British NATO officers, a civilian negotiator from the British Foreign Office and an Albanian translator. Waiting for them on the steps of the village school next to the football pitch were a group of black-and-green-uniformed Albanian rebel fighters, clutching Bulgarian Kalashnikov assault rifles and waiting to escort the NATO team in to meet their leader.

'Typical Brits,' laughed one rebel fighter, a brand-new chrome-plated 7.65mm automatic pistol stuck in his belt. 'They're not on time.'

Minutes later, a black Audi saloon with blacked-out windows roared to a halt at the top of the mountain track and out stepped the rebels' political leader, Ali Ahmeti, and the military chief-of-staff of the NLA, Gezim Ostreni, a red beret on his head. The group of Albanians and British officials was ushered into classroom number six, the door was closed behind them and the meeting started. In the corridor were three rebel fighters and a British Army sergeant with a thick South African accent who acted as a bodyguard, laden down with communications equipment, an SA-80 assault rifle and a Fairbairn-Sykes commando knife stuck down the front of his chest-webbing.

For over an hour, the only person who entered the room was the school janitor, taking in plates of Jaffa Cakes. The rebel leaders of the NLA had been meeting with NATO officials in this school-room for at least four days, trying to hammer out the modalities of a deal whereby NATO soldiers would collect the rebels' weapons once the NLA agreed to disarm. At the same time, NATO ambassadors from the nineteen-member alliance were meeting in Brussels and considering whether to deploy a larger force to Macedonia to collect the rebels' guns.

On the football pitch in Sipkovico, the Pathfinder Platoon's sergeant-major, who asked to be called 'Jock', was crouching behind a half-destroyed house, radioing in co-ordinates as around him village children, some dressed in miniature rebel uniforms, some clutching bows and arrows, looked at him excitedly. 'Hot here,' quipped a Pathfinder sergeant, maroon Parachute Regiment beret on his head. Inside the school, the meeting continued. The South African sergeant refused a Jaffa Cake.

Sipkovice, which lay nearly 600m above the western Macedonian town of Tetovo, had been a rebel stronghold since the early days of the NLA's insurgency nearly six months before. Many of the red-roofed buildings in the village had been hit by machine-gun fire, mortar rounds, artillery shells and helicopter gunship rockets as the Macedonian Army and police had repeatedly tried to dislodge the rebels. Down below on the sweltering northern Macedonian plain lay the Albanian-controlled town of Tetovo, where a crowd of angry Macedonian Slavs gathered, threatening to burn down an ancient mosque after a thirteenth-century Orthodox church was blown up. The government blamed the rebel insurgents for what it called an act of 'barbarism'. Religious sites had become foci for frequent attacks in Macedonia and especially in Kosovo as extremists of both ethnicities vented their fury on their ethnic opponents. Such incidents did not bode well for the ceasefire that had to be in place and holding stable before further NATO troops would be deployed.

Heavy rain had drifted off the peaks of the Sar Planina mountains,

ABOVE In the wake of the night-time dash for Pristina Airport made by the Pathfinders of 5 Airborne Brigade early on Saturday 12 June 1999, men from 1st Battalion, the Parachute Regiment, are deployed by Puma helicopter on the road to Kosovo's capital. © *Crown Copyright/MOD*

BELOW Men from 1 Para crouch down against the dust of a Puma helicopter landing as their platoon advances up the road to Pristina, Saturday 12 June 1999. © *Crown Copyright/MOD*

ABOVE British Chinook helicopters fly over central Kosovo, June 1999. © *Crown Copyright/MOD*

BELOW A British paratrooper observes the graves and burial site of more than sixty Kosovo Albanians, Monday 14 June 1999. © *Crown Copyright/MOD*

OPPOSITE BELOW Four days after taking control of the streets of Pristina, a mixed patrol of British paratroopers wearing both the maroon and dark green 'DZ flashes' of 1 and 3 Para on their airborne smocks are briefed by a sergeant before going out on patrol, Wednesday 16 June 1999. © *Crown Copyright/MOD*

ABOVE A British paratrooper escorts three Kosovan civilians arrested after the discovery of an illegal handgun, Sunday 20 June 1999, Pristina. © *Crown Copyright/MOD*

ABOVE In a textbook demonstration of crowd-control, some 150 British soldiers from 2nd Battalion, the Royal Green Jackets, manage to hold back up to 7,000 Kosovo Albanian demonstrators on the bitterly contested bridge in Mitrovica, Kosovo, February 2001. *Associated Press*

BELOW Macedonian Interior Ministry Special Forces from the 'Tigers' unit return fire with a belt-fed machine gun against ethnic Albanian rebel positions dug in on the hills above the town of Tetovo, western Macedonia, Thursday 15 March 2001. *Associated Press*

ABOVE A Macedonian Army MI-24 Hind helicopter gunship fires rockets at Albanian rebel positions in the town of Aracinovo, outside the capital, Skopje, during heavy fighting in June 2001. *Associated Press*

BELOW A British Special Forces soldier with Northern Alliance troops during fighting at the fortress prison at Qala-i-Janghi, northern Afghanistan, 2001. The team at the fortress found itself operating alongside numerous photographers and camera crews from the international media, resulting in this rare instance of a British Special Forces soldier caught on camera. *Associated Press*

ABOVE British Royal Marines patrol in Afghanistan, February 2002. © *Crown Copyright/MOD*

BELOW British paratroopers on patrol in Iraq during Operation Telic, 2003. © *Crown Copyright/MOD*

ABOVE Australian SAS soldiers on an armed Land Rover, Iraq, 2003. *Australian DOD*

BELOW Seen through a night-vision device, this shot shows Australian SAS men on a heavily armed vehicle in Iraq, 2003. *Australian DOD*

Two men of an Australian SAS patrol in Iraq, 2003. The soldiers' weaponry is a perfect example of customised Special Forces equipment: a 40mm M-203 grenade launcher has been attached under the barrel of a 5.56mm assault rifle, to which is also attached an infra-red laser sight device and a torch.
Australian DOD

keeping the dust down on the football pitch as the Lynx helicopters swooped in again to pick up the negotiation team. Ali Ahmeti stared out of the classroom window. He was confident, keen to reiterate the message of the NATO mission. 'Perhaps,' he said rather overoptimistically, 'discrimination against Albanians has come to an end.'

Somewhere up in the mountains above him, where the mist scudded past rock outcrops and the ground was soaked by rain, small outposts of British SAS soldiers were dug into the ground, two or three men in each observation post, binoculars trained on to the small passes and valley tracks where Albanian rebels could still move back and forth from Kosovo. Small children and a gang of teenagers from Sipkovice had been watching the men on and off for two or three days, they said, and for five Deutschmarks they were prepared to point out the Special Forces men's observation posts.

Things moved quickly after that. On 22 August NATO in Brussels approved Operation Essential Harvest. On 23 August, the Macedonian peace deal – called, rather grandly, the 'Framework Agreement for Peace' – was passed in the Macedonian parliament by ninety-one votes to nineteen. On 26 August, 3,000 NATO troops including British paratroopers and French Legionnaires began deploy to Macedonia for Operation Essential Harvest, which was formally scheduled to last for thirty days from 27 August to 27 September. In all, some 3,000 weapons were eventually collected, including a few ground-to-air missile systems, but mostly old Kalashnikovs and machine guns. By January 2002, using proceeds from heroin dealing in Austria, Switzerland and Germany, the Albanians in Macedonia had swiftly re-armed themselves. But Macedonia remained at peace. Preventive diplomacy had paid off, for once.

A few days later, an Albanian taxi driver stopped at the sandbagged police road-block that barricaded the main road leading from Skopje up to the Kosovo–Albanian border. For months now, as an Albanian, he had got used to harass-ment, occasionally a fist in the face, as the price he had to pay for passing by the Macedonian police post. He had learned that if each time he was stopped at the checkpoint he had a few tangerines, a few cans of Coke or bottles of beer as small presents for the policemen, they waved him on.

But that day when he stopped by the pile of sandbags, where the barrels of the machine guns pointed through the observation slits, nobody came out to stop him. Nobody seemed interested in his offerings of a can of Coca Cola and four tangerines. The five policemen were sitting behind the dug-out on sandbags, as usual, but their attention was focused intently on a small transistor radio.

Later that evening, outside the US Embassy in Skopje, local Macedonian teenagers jumped up and down whooping with joy, waving and laughing at the US Embassy security guards as they held up copies of the evening paper, its front page consisting of nothing but one huge photograph of burning tower blocks.

It was 11 September 2001.

CHAPTER FIVE

First Strikes in the War on Terror

Afghanistan, 2001

The unmanned aerial vehicles (UAVs), known by their codenames Predator and Global Hawk, swung through the dark skies above the mountain peaks and ravines that lie along Afghanistan's southern border with Pakistan. The cameras installed in the undersides of their fuselages *whirred* constantly, tracking backwards and forwards over the terrain 600m below, guided by the unseen hands of their CIA and US Air Force controllers on the ground. They were circling over two particular valleys and three ridge-lines, looking for the telltale heat signatures emitted by convoys of vehicles or large groups of people huddled around cooking fires. If the pilotless drones had carried on flying north, they would quickly have spotted the heavy glow of lights from the city of Jalalabad, 56km to the north, itself about to be liberated from Taliban control. But they didn't. They circled back. Feeding video images in real-time through night-vision lenses, the UAVs presented their American controllers with a never-ending aerial map of the valleys and ridge-lines that surrounded the village of Tora Bora. For now the sky and the ground beneath were relatively quiet. It was 5 November 2001.

The drones were not deployed the following night above that section of the White Mountains, where the Tora Bora and Milawa valleys intersect with the ridge-lines of Agam and Wazir. They had been deployed on another mission, and so when a convoy of dozens of four-wheel-drive vehicles drove into the Afghan village of Garikhil on the night of 6 November, it went unobserved from the sky. Garikhil lies at the foot of the Tora Bora complex of mountainous ridges and valleys, where the peaks flare up to heights of 3,650m. Tora Bora, which means 'Black Dust', is another small hamlet that gives its name to the complex of mountainous slopes, ravines, ridges and valleys, all crisscrossed by stony, unmetalled roads, donkey paths, tracks and sweeping masses of moraine and vast rockfalls. The sides of the valleys and the mountains are layered and pocked with caves; some are vast, some tiny. Some are systems of vaulted chambers and yards of passageway; others are simply large holes scraped by man or eroded by nature into the face of the mountains. It was in the White Mountains on the Pakistan–Afghanistan border, south-south-west of the Khyber Pass, that the Afghan *mujahideen* resistance to the Soviet invaders during the 1980s had been at its most successful. The passes, valleys and mountains are lined with abandoned positions, Soviet and Afghan. Rusted shells of vehicles and tanks lie in the arid dust of the valley. It was here that the Afghan fighters earned their nickname of '*dukhi*' or ghosts from the Russians.

The convoy that arrived in Garikhil on the night of 6 November carried several senior al-Qaeda and Taliban figures, including a Saudi financier of Osama bin Laden – a theologian called Abu Jaffar who had travelled to Afghanistan from Pakistan and Saudi Arabia to give Osama bin Laden $3,000,000 in cash. Allegedly now in captivity according to some newspaper reports, Jaffar has since stuck to his story that bin Laden was in the convoy that night, and that on arrival amidst the dust and mud houses of Garikhil, bin Laden convened an immediate meeting with the Ghilzi tribal elders. These elders and their parents, grandparents and great-grandparents had been smuggling anything of value across the Afghan–Pakistani border for generations, doing deals of money, diamonds, heroin, opium, guns and hostages, happily double-crossing other clans and switching allegiances like the wind changes directions. In short, behaving like solid, reliable, predictable and dependable Afghan tribal elders.

From the convoy of more than 100 four-wheel-drive vehicles, packing cases were unloaded and tarpaulins stripped off. A film of powdery road dust as fine as talcum powder covered every surface. Yet when the 400 Kalashnikov assault rifles were unpacked they were spotlessly clean. They were a present from Osama bin Laden to the Ghilzi elders. The deal was simple: with the fall of Kabul imminent, Mazar-i-Sharif about to be taken by the Northern Alliance and Jalalabad and Kandahar about to be surrounded by US and coalition forces, bin Laden was running out of places to hide.

Next to the border with Pakistan, the White Mountains were a perfect hiding place for bin Laden and his legions of foreign fighters – Arabs from Egypt, Yemen, Chechnya, Saudi Arabia and Pakistan. In return for the AK assault rifles – the weapon of choice of every Afghan – bin Laden arranged his escape route into Pakistan, knowing that when the moment came he could rely on the Ghilzi to whisk him to safety on donkey or horseback across the border into Pakistan. Moving around Afghanistan for bin Laden was about to switch from the ludicrously easy – driving in a convoy of over 100 four-by-four vehicles – to the almost impossible, where surveillance by coalition Special Forces, US aircraft, Predator drones and every combination of thermal-imaging equipment would make movement almost out of the question. Simply put, prior to this point, if Afghan informers had tipped off one of the myriad Western intelligence agencies working inside Afghanistan that bin Laden was in a particular area at a particular time, even if the full manpower and electronic assets of the US-led coalition could have been deployed to find him, the al-Qaeda leader could still have continued to move around almost as he pleased so long as he kept on the move. However, by mid-November, with the capital Kabul fallen, the Taliban regime deposed, the main cities of Mazar-i-Sharif and Jalalabad either fallen or toppling and Kandahar set to fall on 6 December, Tora Bora became bin Laden's last stand. Hundreds of Arab fighters had gathered with him, knowing that their only escape route was across into Pakistan. The last chance in Afghanistan that the coalition troops of US Special Forces General Tommy Franks would have of seizing – or killing – bin Laden would be around Tora Bora.

The first ground combat strike made by the Americans in Afghanistan after the attacks on the twin towers of the World Trade Centre in New York on 11 September 2001 had taken place on the night of Friday 19 October and the morning of Saturday 20 October, 96km south-west of Kandahar. More than 200 US Army Rangers from the 75th Airborne Rangers, commanded by Colonel Joe Votel, jumped on to a desert airstrip codenamed 'Objective Rhino'. Prior to parachuting in, the Army Rangers had been filmed by a military media operations cameraman with a night-vision lens, the greeny-black images showing them laden down with parachutes and equipment, among which were photographs of New York Fire Department men raising the 'Old Glory' American flag over 'Ground Zero', the site of the now-collapsed World Trade Centre. These photo-cards, they boasted, would be left on the dead bodies of the Taliban that they killed. The attack on the airfield was intended to show the Taliban regime, al-Qaeda and the world at large that the Americans were able and willing to launch retaliatory strikes in the opening assault of their war on terrorism.

Four C-130 Hercules Combat Talon aircraft dropped two companies of men over the airfield: in typical American style, the entire assault was filmed by a US Department of Defence team and subsequently broadcast on television. As the Rangers swept through buildings on the edge of the airport runway, coming under hostile fire, they responded in kind: official estimates put the number of Taliban or al-Qaeda fighters – known by the US as 'AQT' – at around forty. This number is not backed up by anything other than Ranger estimates.

Simultaneously, US troops from Special Forces Operational Detachment Delta (SFOD-D) – or Delta Force, as it is often known – were carrying out a raid on a compound just outside Kandahar allegedly occasionally occupied by Mullah Mohammed Omar, a senior Taliban official who was related to Osama bin Laden by marriage. The Delta Force operators – Americans tend to call their SF troops 'operators' rather than just 'soldiers' or 'men' as the term lends an additional edge of operational urgency, a tang of assurance, a heady whiff of no-nonsense machismo – landed on Black Hawk and Pave Low helicopters. They surrounded the compound where Omar was meant to be, unaware that he was absent. Dozens of men from Delta Force went in on the raid and the compound did yield up, admittedly, Taliban intelligence material. However, on the way out of the unoccupied compound they were ambushed by a larger group of Taliban fighters who had been awoken by the sound of the helicopters landing. There was a heavy fire fight and up to twenty or more Delta Force commandos were injured. The US Department of Defence put the figure at twelve. It was on exiting the compound, into the subsequent fire fight, that not only did things start to go wrong for the troops on the ground, but also for relations between the Delta Force establishment and General Tommy Franks' US Central Command (CENTCOM) back at MacDill Air Force Base in Florida, and for the US military's strike strategy in Afghanistan.

Subsequent to the attack, it turned out that the 'compound system' that the Delta Force troops had hit in fact consisted of a potholed road, three mud huts and a small walled compound. It was here, on these hills overlooking Kandahar, that Mullah Omar had his summer house, and there had been a slight chance that he would have been present in the house during the period of the assault. The first detailed account of the raid emerged when American writer Seymour Hersh published an article in the *New Yorker* magazine. A wealth of investigative material, controversy, claim and counter-claim followed into what consisted, essentially, of the first American attacks on the Taliban in what was already becoming known as 'the Global War on Terrorism' or 'War Against Terror'. General Richard B. Myers, the US Chief of the Joint Chiefs of Staff, insisted that both raids had been launched to demonstrate the ability of 'Special Operations Forces to deploy, operate and manoeuvre in Afghanistan without significant interference from Taliban forces'. A week prior to the assaults, President George Bush had said in a news conference that 'slowly but surely we're smoking al-Qaeda out of their caves so we can bring them to justice'. For the American soldiers on the ground in Afghanistan, however, the 'War Against Terror' was getting off to a shaky start. It transpires, from British and American military and intelligence sources, that the operations took place something along the following lines.

Prior to the US Army Airborne Rangers' assault on Objective Rhino, the airstrip 96km south-west of Kandahar, a small team of Airborne Reconnaissance Pathfinders had been dropped in to scout out the airfield to make sure that there was no opposition present. Only then were the Rangers given the order to jump. It remains entirely unclear whether or not they encountered any resistance, despite official claims that up to forty Taliban were killed during the operation.

The situation was very different for Delta Force in the middle of the night at Omar's compound just outside Kandahar, where the US troops appear to have met with some very 'significant interference'. On the night of 18 October, approximately 100 soldiers from US Delta Force SF teams had gathered on the flight deck of the USS *Kitty Hawk* aircraft carrier and then flown to Dalbandi Air Base in Pakistan, some 32km from the Afghan border. Their descent on Mullah Omar's compound had been preceded by a blizzard of support fire launched from the air by an AC-130 Hercules Spectre airborne gunship. These prized components of the US armoury are impressive machines: deploying multi-barrelled Gatling and miniguns as well as a 105mm howitzer, they can circle a target in the air, lock on to it by flying in a preplanned arc and keep their fire trained on the target throughout the aircraft's manoeuvres. This was not the first attempt on the life of Omar: his headquarters in Kandahar and a vehicle in which he was believed to have been travelling had been hit by missile and air strikes during the days immediately prior to the Ranger assault on his summer home; US air strikes had been hitting Taliban positions inside Afghanistan for two weeks by this stage. Common thinking suggested that if his compound was left untouched he might seek refuge there, believing that the Americans knew nothing of its existence. By the time the Hercules gunship had blown vast chunks out of its infrastructure, it was clear that they did.

After the attack on the compound by gunship fire, the Delta Force teams went in. A company of Army Rangers had also been deployed by helicopter a few hours before the Rangers arrived on the ground as a stop-and-cut-off group some distance from the target, intended to prevent any Taliban fighters from fleeing the area. However, the Taliban, once they emerged, were in full contact with the Rangers. In his *New Yorker* article, Hersh quotes a senior Special Forces source who said that once the Delta teams came out of the compound 'the shit hit the fan'. Significant interference from the enemy had become a reality.

Trapped in a series of volleys of fire from Kalashnikov assault rifles and RPG-7 rocket launchers, the Delta Force men started to take casualties. The American Department of Defence later put the total at twelve; unofficial estimates put the figure much higher at twenty-two. There were hints that the casualty figures had been deliberately mismanaged by the US DoD and that a man was only considered a casualty if he had sustained a wound that required stitching and prevented him from walking. US helicopter gunships were called in to enable the Delta Force commandos to pull out. They had intended to leave behind a small four-man team to provide further surveillance of the area; this group of men was also forced to pull out after withdrawing to a pre-arranged rendezvous point. In the face of intense, orchestrated and accurate fire from the Taliban, who had bracketed the American soldiers with barrages of rocket fire, the commandos withdrew to their helicopters and exfiltrated. One man is reported to have lost a foot and at least three were seriously wounded. General Myers subsequently described this resistance as 'light'. Except, clearly, to those on the ground. He then went on to say, curiously, that 'there were some other wounds from some of the activity that was ongoing but none of it was inflicted by the enemy'. Inflicted by whom, then? Friendly fire? Was Myers admitting that on this first combat outing for US ground forces in Afghanistan, so well publicised that part of the operation was staged for camera, that American soldiers had shot each other in action? A Chinook left behind part of its landing gear – the Taliban claimed that they had hit it with an RPG – and the American Special Forces left behind large, tattered pieces of their strategic reputation.

Much was made of the botched assault: Delta officers had, it was claimed, subsequently approached journalist Seymour Hersh because they wanted to publicise how an operation that they felt could have been successful had turned into an elaborate, badly planned publicity stunt. It was CENTCOMs handling of the affair, they said, that was at fault. The principal result of the raid in operational and strategic terms was that Franks and the Pentagon were obliged to rethink how they were going to handle the remainder of the ground war. If anything was going to impinge on the way in which the Americans fought the ground war in Afghanistan, and how Operation Enduring Freedom would subsequently be carried out, it was this operation.

Facing each other off across the arid Afghan terrain, Osama bin Laden and General Franks both held extremely strong hands – so strong, in fact, that their aces almost cancelled each other out. Bin Laden's main strength was the flexible and fluid nature of the ways in which he could hide. To be able to pinpoint his position and deploy air strikes or military personnel on the ground to intercept or kill him, the coalition had to know in which exact village, building or cave he was hiding at any given time, and had to be able to hit such a target without causing excessive civilian casualties. On more than one occasion, for instance, bin Laden travelled by public bus, knowing that coalition air strikes would not deliberately hit such a target. Consequently, the CIA, MI6, Delta Force, the British SAS and agents from the American FBI and National Security Agency (NSA), as well as the various foreign military and domestic intelligence agencies from France, Germany, Norway, Australia, New Zealand, Denmark and Canada present in Afghanistan, had to rely largely on one source of information: informants. If they could discover in which part of the whole of Afghanistan to target their Predators, their Global Hawks, their satellite sweeps, their Special Forces patrols, their helicopter snatches, then they had a chance against bin Laden.

On one occasion in December 2001, a Hellfire guided missile was fired from an American Predator UAV at a Range Rover in a convoy in which bin Laden was thought to be travelling. This was probably the closest the Americans got to killing him, except swabs of mashed tissue and bloody fragments of corpse taken from the wreckage and sent away for DNA testing proved not to be his. (FBI technicians had travelled to Saudi Arabia in November 2001 to take tissue samples to assist in this DNA testing process, scraping them with wooden swabs from the insides of the cheeks of fifty-three members of the extended bin Laden family.)

The information for this strike came from an informant who, like many Afghans, was prepared to change his allegiances without a moment's thought if it meant having a chance of winning all or part of the $25 million bounty that the US State Department had put on bin Laden's head. Prior to the start of the coalition bombing campaign, Osama bin Laden had been highly mobile, travelling across Afghanistan from one al-Qaeda training camp to another, not staying in one single location for more than twenty-four hours. The areas controlled by the Taliban were the areas where al-Qaeda could most effectively operate; consequently, as the Taliban-controlled areas fell into the hands of coalition troops, as well as Northern and Eastern 'shura' or Alliance fighters, so the areas of operational liberty available to al-Qaeda diminished correspondingly. Thus it became easier for the coalition to narrow down their areas of search. As the Taliban were defeated across the length and breadth of Afghanistan – like most Afghans, they were proficient in the guerrilla tactics of the small, mainly unopposed mountain ambush, but were utterly lost in anything remotely resembling conventional warfare – so the pool of potential informants grew. Eager to save their own lives, many Taliban fighters simply dumped their black turbans, switched sides and attempted to demonstrate their new fidelities by selling or giving away information regarding the whereabouts of the remaining Taliban or al-Qaeda cells.

Thus the only way in which General Franks could begin to hope to isolate al-Qaeda on the ground was to defeat and topple the Taliban regime. At his disposal he had the coalition Special Forces, access to military and foreign intelligence and the services of the CIA. Using this combination of assets, a variety of fighters and tribal leaders were co-opted to form the Northern and Eastern Alliance, who in turn toppled the Taliban for him, backed up by the massive assistance of US air support. He also had more conventional forces which he used to physically occupy the land space and air space of Afghanistan once the Taliban had been beaten. This in turn led to an ability completely to deny ground space to al-Qaeda, meaning that their fighters – and by extension bin Laden – were increasingly forced into less and less territory, making it easier and easier for Franks to track them down using electronic air assets and his Special Forces.

Therein lay the American general's military dichotomy. By playing his two strongest cards – an ability to defeat the Taliban and an ability to occupy and dominate Afghanistan – he was, in effect, calling bin Laden's hand. Osama bin Laden's ace of spades, as it were, was his ability to move within Afghanistan undetected. Once the coalition and the Northern and Eastern Alliance had occupied Afghanistan, he had nowhere to move. His ace had been trumped. He either had to face down the Americans, the British and the Australians in open, semi-conventional battle or flee. He knew he could not hope to win the first scenario, but he needed to tie down the prime military assets of the coalition for a minimum of two weeks in November and early December 2001 while he made good his escape. Franks had played both his top cards, but in doing so he indirectly forced bin Laden into fleeing.

One advantage Osama bin Laden had was that he understood not only how Afghan and Arab fighters waged their wars, but also how Western Special Forces, particularly the Americans, carried out their operations. Bin Laden reckoned that he could outthink, outfight and outmanoeuvre the soldiers of Delta Force, the Green Berets, the Army Rangers and the Navy SEALs. This reckoning was based upon the fact that he knew that some of the tactics in these forces' operational repertoires had changed little since the same American units had been training the *mujahideen* to fight against the Russians in the 1980s. The main difference, of course, was that this time around the Americans had at their disposal enormous air assets and the practical ability and budgetary wherewithal to deploy them at will. In their advance across northern Afghanistan, American Special Forces had deployed aerial munitions to devastating effect, often employing the simple tactic of bombing anything – houses, armoured vehicles, trench positions, gatherings of Taliban fighters, pick-up trucks – that stood in their way. The use of co-opted Northern and Eastern Alliance allies, with *de facto* US SF team leaders, combined with comprehensive use of aerial assets meant that the human cost of US casualties could be kept low. In terms of human resources, this was an inexpensive way to wage war, but in terms of costly state-of-the-art aerial munitions, it was pricey.

British Special Forces, bin Laden knew, were another matter entirely and presented the major obstacle to him effecting his escape into Pakistan, and thence to freedom. He knew the extent to which the Americans would rely upon their electronic assets and upon air power. He had watched closely the way in which the Americans had co-opted the Northern Alliance into winning the battles for Kabul and Mazar-i-Sharif. He knew that they would attempt the same strategy around Tora Bora and suspected that their tactics would be considerably less successful there.

The fighting on the plains around Kabul and against the fortress at Mazar-i-Sharif had been in open country where American air dominance had made short work of many of the Taliban positions. Around Tora Bora, the fighting would be in and around cave systems at heights of up to 3,960m above sea level, where the initiative would be with the defenders. Secondly, the Uzbek General Abdul Rashid Dostum knew that by accompanying the Americans on their 'liberation' of parts of northern Afghanistan, and by fighting alongside them, he would effectively stand to dominate and occupy these areas – and subsequently assume control of such lucrative commodities as the drugs trade and smuggling – once they had been wrested from Taliban control. There was, therefore, massive personal motive at stake when it came to the allegiances of the Northern Alliance. Bin Laden knew that there was a direct link between controlling territory in Afghanistan and the subsequent demands that somebody like General Dostum could make for a strong political position in any future interim administration in Kabul. This would not be the case in the border areas around Tora Bora where the Ghilzi and other Pathan tribes were more loyal to the Taliban, would look violently askance at any US attempts to bring in Uzbek 'northerners' and had, in many cases, already been bought off by bin Laden, as in the village of Garikhil. Thirdly, the troops who would be doing most of the fighting at Tora Bora would be a group of about 900 Yemenis, Algerians, Chechens and Egyptians, the most hardcore, radical and loyal of al-Qaeda's foreign fighters, very different from many of the Taliban who in some cases were little more than enthusiastic teenagers with guns.

There were unconfirmed reports that a British SAS unit had been involved in an incident at the same time as the US assault on the compound of Mullah Omar near Kandahar. Although no British Ministry of Defence or British military sources can confirm this, American author Robin Moore, in his paean to the US Special Forces operations in Afghanistan entitled *Task Force Dagger – The Hunt for bin Laden*, has the following to say:

An additional target, believed to contain several high-ranking members of the Taliban and al-Qaeda network, was hit by the Counter-Revolutionary Warfare Wing [sic] of the 22nd SAS. Operating in four-man 'bricks' or teams, more than forty SAS commandos hit their target simultaneously, killing or wounding more than twenty-five enemy and capturing several enemy

soldiers. One important aspect of using the SAS so early was that
they had Pashto speakers, which was the southern dialect in the
Kandahar region . . . the SAS also took casualties, with several of
their assaulters wounded.

Is this true? Robin Moore is probably the single author in the United
States with unfettered access to US Special Forces. Moore had gone to
Vietnam in 1964 after attending US Army Jump School at Fort Benning
in Georgia, allegedly with the special clearance of John F. Kennedy. He was
at that time the first and only civilian to go through the SF qualification
course at Fort Bragg. After this, he wrote a book, *The Green Berets*, which
later became a film starring John Wayne. He also co-authored 'The Ballad
of the Green Berets', a rousing, patriotic dirge that a generation of would-
be US Special Forces soldiers grew up on in the 1960s. Its lines are
unquestioningly gung-ho and patriotic:

Fighting soldiers from the sky,
Fearless men who jump and die.
Men who mean just what they say,
The brave men of the Green Beret.

Thus goes the first verse. Regardless of the imbued bias towards the
American military way and the one-sided and intensely patriotic prose
that Moore writes, it must be admitted that he has excellent contacts in
the US Special Forces community. In nearly 400 pages in *Task Force
Dagger*, he details the vast majority of US Special Forces Green Beret
operations carried out in Afghanistan, reported directly to him by soldiers
whose names are used to identify them, except in the case of Delta Force
– soldiers of all ranks from trooper and private to general. Is the story
of the 22 SAS operation in the first days of the ground war true? As we
shall see later, it is not impossible that it is, but that it was covered up
by the British MOD and SF establishment because they did not want to
publicise the fact that the SAS was also in action and had already

taken casualties during the attacks around 'Objective Rhino' that took place on 19–20 October.

However, according to some accounts, 'A' and 'G' Squadrons of 22 SAS – the units that would be deployed into the Afghan theatre of operations – were still in Hereford at this time, but it is possible that the attack was carried out by Special Forces troops from the SBS. Robin Moore may be mixing this operation up with a later one – Operation Trent, perhaps – or whoever in the US SF community gave him the information may have been misbriefed themselves. It is difficult to imagine a number of SAS men being wounded in an attack that left twenty-five enemy dead without some aspects of the British media becoming aware of the casualties. Or perhaps not. *Task Force Dagger* is, despite the hyperbole and the cloying jingoism, well sourced. Moore has spoken to dozens of US SF 'operators', some of whom would have known about UK Special Forces operations. As it stands, the operations on which British Special Forces teams were engaged in Afghanistan would appear to be as follows:

– 18–22 October: Possible SBS involvement in operations around Kandahar

– Early November: Operation Determine – search and reconnaissance missions in north-western Afghanistan

– Mid-November: SBS operations in and around Mazar-i-Sharif, particularly at Qala-i-Janghi fortress

– November onwards: SBS and Royal Marine deployment to Bagram Air Base, Afghanistan

– 18–20 November: 22 SAS involved in Operation Trent, south-west of Kandahar

– 22 November to early December: Operations around Tora Bora.

Some time during October 2001, two operational squadrons from 22 SAS, 'A' and 'G' Squadrons, numbering more than 100 men, along with SF-trained signallers from 264 (SAS) Signals Squadron, medics, mechanics and pilots, were deployed from the UK to forward operating bases at an air force base at Thumrait in Oman. More than fifty men from the Special Boat Service (SBS), the amphibious equivalent of the SAS and drawn mainly from the Royal Marines, were deployed to Afghanistan along with some 150 Australian troops from the Australian Special Air Service Regiment. Canada had, at the request of the United States, also dispatched men from its specialist Joint Task Force Two to the Middle East.

Look at photographs and listen to accounts told by Australian, American, Canadian and British Special Forces, as well as by Afghan fighters and international journalists, of the fighting in Afghanistan in November and December 2001, and one thing immediately strikes you. The British SAS, accompanied by small groups from the SBS and Royal Marines from the Mountain and Arctic Warfare Cadres, were not fighting classic Special Forces warfare. In Bosnia, in operations such as those around Gorazde, small groups of four to eight men had been operating together, acting as forward air controllers and Joint Commission Observers. In Iraq, during attacks on Saddam Hussein's air bases in western Iraq during the First Gulf War, the men from Hereford were deployed in mobile Land Rover patrols remarkably similarly to the way in which they had been operating in the Western Desert in World War II. In Kosovo, before and after the NATO bombing campaign, their role had been in keeping with typical SF diktats: small groups of men, training and assisting the local guerrilla force whose aims were most sympathetic to and symbiotic with the regional policy of the British government, guiding in air strikes, marking the sites of mass graves, snatching war criminals. But in Afghanistan, while it was all textbook Special Forces stuff for the Americans, it was much less so for the British.

'A' and 'G' Squadrons of 22 SAS were operating in mobile columns of Land Rovers and during Operation Trent in Helmand Province their reconnaissance teams were deployed by HALO parachute drop. Yet in their assault on the al-Qaeda positions in Helmand Province, prior to the limited actions at Tora Bora, they were essentially being used as a company of light infantry. Yes, their war-fighting prowess, organisational skills, some combat experience and basic capacity for fire-and-manoeuvre second to none were what enabled them to outfight the Taliban and al-Qaeda's foreign fighters. Yet the nature of their role meant that they were Special Forces soldiers being used as highly trained infantry. This had the benefit of keeping casualties to a minimum, yet there are increasingly loud voices within the British Army questioning the operational doctrine of further training, through combat experience, the already highly trained at the expense of the operational efficiency of regular line infantry units.

Before discussing the large 22 SAS operation in Helmand Province that took place in November 2001, it is important to consider briefly the deployments of British Special Forces up to and including Afghanistan, to list the ways in which they have been used operationally since World War II and then, more significantly, to compare the main ways in which they were deployed between 1980–2001 to reveal how much these deployments diverged from or complimented the changing and developing nature of international community interventions and missions. The deployments were as follows:

World War II
Special Forces operations in the Western Desert and in Europe involved reconnaissance missions and attacking enemy airfields, aircraft, ports, radar, shipping and communications facilities. Operated with the Special Operations Executive. The majority of operations were behind enemy lines

The break-up of the British Empire
1952–65: Malaya and Borneo. Deployed on offensive operations to track Chinese Communist terrorists and Indonesian insurgents

1960s and 70s: Oman, Aden, the Radfan and Dhofar. Assistance missions to friendly Middle Eastern regimes at risk from insurgency carried out by predominantly communist-orientated armed groups

1969 onwards: Northern Ireland. Counterinsurgency and anti-terrorism operations

1977–2002

1977: Mogadishu, Somalia. Hostage-rescue

1980: United Kingdom. Hostage-rescue at the Iranian Embassy

1981: The Gambia. Military assistance to friendly African regime during an attempted *coup d'état*

1982: The Falkland Islands, Chile and Argentina. Close-target reconnaissance, attacks on enemy airfields, acting as forward air controllers

1988: Columbia. Counterinsurgency and antinarcotics training to the government, hostage-rescue

1990–91: Iraq. Operation Desert Storm. Vehicle- and foot-based patrols used to locate and destroy enemy missile sites and communications systems

1993–5: Bosnia, Croatia, Serbia. Joint Commission Observers for UN peacekeeping troops, forward air controllers and reconnaissance teams in and around enclaves such as Gorazde, Maglaj, Srebrenica and Bihac

1997: Albania. Hostage-rescue

1988–99: Thailand, Cambodia, Algeria, Israel, Central Africa. Training, assistance, anti-terrorist and advisory missions

1999: Kosovo. Forward air control, training and assistance to the Kosovo Liberation Army, locating sites of war crimes, actions in support of NATO troops

2001: Macedonia. Reconnaissance missions and observation duties in support of NATO mission and British elements of K-FOR

1993–2002: Bosnia-Hercegovina, Republika Srbska, Croatia, Kosovo. Operations to arrest war crimes suspects.

This breakdown reveals that up until 2001, the operations of Britain's Special Forces had been textbook stuff: hostage-rescue, training foreign armies, anti-terrorism activities, guerrilla operations behind enemy lines. Some of these deployments were routine training, assistance and attachment missions with foreign governments, while others, particularly in Bosnia, Kosovo and Macedonia, were operations complementing international interventions, including peace-support and peacekeeping operations. It was only in Afghanistan in 2001 that they were, for the first time since 1971, essentially used as infantry. The target was a suspected al-Qaeda headquarters and hideout in Helmand Province, south of Kandahar. The units chosen for the assault were 'A' and 'G' Squadrons of 22 SAS. There were several reasons why the Regiment suddenly found itself being deployed effectively as a company of light infantry in Helmand Province, among which were a desire both to give the SAS an operational role independently of the Americans while at the same time trying to avoid British casualties. It was also to be a deployment that would make Britain's senior Special Forces commanders think twice before they allowed their precious, expensively trained assets to be used in this way again.

CHAPTER SIX

High Noon in Helmand

Afghanistan, 2001

'A' and 'G' Squadrons of 22 SAS, totalling some 140 men with their attendant attached and support personnel, had most likely been deployed to Afghanistan at the end of October and the beginning of November 2001. During the last week of October, the men had transited from Oman into Pakistan, and then to Northern Afghanistan on a deployment code-named 'Operation Determine'. Their mission, much to the frustration of the men who were dying to get into action, was to be one of surveillance and reconnaissance (S & R) against the Taliban and al-Qaeda forces. It was now some six weeks after the two hijacked aircraft had been flown into the World Trade Centre towers, and by this time American Green Beret teams such as Texas 12, whose 'target-lasing' activities were assisting the Northern Alliance in their advance across the north of the country, had been in action for the best part of a month.

The SAS men were extremely keen to join the Americans on operations, and the US Central Command (CENTCOM) headquarters in Florida was under pressure from the British military and political apparatus to allocate 22 SAS a target. The difficulty was that it was debatable whether or not there was anything for them to do. Operation Enduring Freedom was an American-run operation. If there was one thing that the Americans had learned from the Kosovo campaign, it was the difficulty of trying to forge an operational consensus of opinion and decision making between multiple states. In Afghanistan, post-11 September 2001, the Americans were in charge and intended to keep it that way.

In the run-up to NATO's entry into Kosovo, there had been a very clearly defined role for British Special Forces teams because a sizeable British contingent was involved in NATO's multinational Kosovo Force (K-FOR), and the SAS were operating in support of it both inside and outside Kosovo. British aircraft were bombing Kosovo and British soldiers were guiding in these British air strikes in a campaign where one of the three main Western political protagonists, Tony Blair, was the British prime minister. Moreover, the conflict in Kosovo was on the fringes of Europe, it affected EU states much more than it affected America, Britain was welcoming thousands of refugees from Kosovo and the British were set to take over the capital and centre of the war-torn province once it was liberated.

Afghanistan and its occupation, or invasion, or liberation, whichever way you looked at it, were of uniquely American derivation, a direct result of the attacks in New York, a direct strike at those whom President Bush's administration believed to be responsible for the world's largest terrorist incident. When an American Special Forces officer stood up to give a classified military briefing in October 2001 and delivered the following homily to his men, it was by no means completely misrepresentative of American public sentiment:

> This is not war as you have ever known it before. This is vengeance for the women and children they murdered on 9/11. Our responsibility is to implement that vengeance. Fight as though your families were killed in New York. You are America's avenging angels. Your goal is justice and you are authorized to use all means necessary towards that end.

American Special Forces teams took fragments of concrete from the destroyed World Trade Centre towers with them to Afghanistan to bury; US Rangers parachuted into action carrying photographs of New York firefighters raising the American flag over the ruins at Ground Zero. For a country, and particularly a city, that felt itself – justifiably – to be under attack, the mission was somehow personalised. In the days immediately after the attacks, much of the vocabulary used by the Bush administration as justification for the subsequent 'War on Terrorism' would have struck a chord with other nations who had felt their values, lifestyles and freedoms so directly threatened. As with Rwanda's Tutsis, Kosovo's Albanians and the Israelis, there was more than a touch of self righteous victimhood creeping into American rhetoric. Suffering was being copyrighted on the Hudson River. Of course, it wasn't long before one of the late-twentieth-century's more overused descriptive terms for mass death reared its head. On 17 October, addressing a gathering at Great Britain's Sussex University, a lecturer by the name of Martin Shaw bit the vocabulary bullet and described the attacks of 11 September as a 'genocidal massacre'.

The strikes against the Taliban and al-Qaeda in Afghanistan were co-ordinated, planned assaults against a terrorist regime that was believed to have been responsible for previous attacks against American interests, such as the USS *Cole* in Aden and the embassies in Kenya and Tanzania in 1998, in addition to being responsible for thousands of civilian deaths in New York. Much has been made of the overtly unilateral way in which the United States responded to the terrorist strikes of 11 September 2001, of the 'our might is right' approach of a president that many foreign critics saw as nothing more than a neoconservative simpleton cowboy. Others welcomed the forcible deposition of the Taliban regime – an armed, morally flawed, human-rights-abusing dictatorship whose denial of the most basic standards of civic, legal, ethical or religious legitimacy had made them an international pariah and rogue state whose removal, if necessary by force, had become a form of moral imperative under the terms of international moral, if not necessarily customary, law.

The United States and other NATO members had not felt it necessary to seek the justification and legitimacy of a UN Security Council Resolution when it had come to bombing Kosovo and Serbia. Thus, when it came to bombing Afghanistan and instigating a forcible regime change by removing the Taliban, the US and NATO were prepared to fly in the face of international legal principles and take on the Taliban and al-Qaeda without the 'permission' of the UN. In the event, of course, they didn't have to. UN Security Council Resolutions 1368, 1373 and 1377 supported the anti-terrorist actions undertaken by Operation Enduring Freedom, which began on 7 October 2001. NATO invoked an Article V [1] response to the attacks of 11 September, which categorised them as an attack against all NATO members. Even without the backing of the Security Council Resolutions and the support of such huge bodies as the Organisation of American States, America would have resorted to the cover of Article 51 of the UN Charter [2], which they have long interpreted to mean that a member state has a right to what is known as 'anticipatory self-defence'.

For the SAS, what this effectively translated into, on the ground, was a conundrum. Prime Minister Tony Blair had sworn that Britain would stand 'shoulder to shoulder' with the United States and the pride of Britain's armed forces had happily responded. It was now a question of finding them something to do that would justify the huge effort, expenditure and commitment involved in sending half of the operational capability of Britain's entire land-based Special Forces halfway around the world. The problem was that there were no hostages to rescue; no friendly armies to train; no air strikes to guide in; no mass graves to locate; no rogue leaders to be taken out by snipers. The Americans were doing it all. So a solution had to be found, and quickly, that would enable 22 SAS to justify its role in the face of massive American material supremacy.

'G' Squadron had returned from Oman in late summer 2001, and approximately a whole troop of the squadron had been serving in Macedonia in support of 16 Air Assault Brigade on Operation Essential Harvest. The whole squadron had recently carried out a desert training exercise in Oman. The squadron commander, Major Ivo Streeter and the troop from 'G' Squadron who had been in Macedonia had routed back to the United Kingdom on a C-130 Hercules flight from Skopje to Brize Norton in Oxfordshire. If it was clear to the government analysts and generals that the opening chapter of President George Bush's much-vaunted 'global war on terrorism' was to centre on the removal from power and destruction of the Taliban regime in Afghanistan, then everybody in Hereford knew that many of the Regiment would hopefully soon be taking part in the action on the ground. Many of the squadron had been able to train in the desert in Oman on Operation Swift Sword in 2001, so the shopping list of equipment that Streeter and his men decided to take with them had been reasonably well tried and tested in conditions resembling the hotter parts of Afghanistan.

One of the many operational difficulties 'G' Squadron had worked out that it would face in Afghanistan was that they would on occasion probably be fighting alongside the Afghan fighters of the Northern Alliance, who often operated in civilian clothing. The exigencies of the domestic terrorist threat brought on by their service in Northern Ireland has meant that the SAS are obsessively keen to keep their identities hidden, and if the wearing of civilian clothing on mission in Afghanistan helped them to maintain a lower profile, then that was a plus. American Special Forces tend to dress in civilian clothes that are almost a uniform, with baseball caps turned backwards, night-vision-goggle attachments clipped to the front of their caps, wrap-around sunglasses, ZZ-Top beards and highly customised weaponry. The men from 'G' Squadron may have looked more low-key than their American counterparts, yet be they in Kosovo or Macedonia, Bosnia or Iraq, Afghanistan or Columbia, they tended to stand out by dint of being armed, British and not in uniform.

Considerations of what clothing to wear came second to the equipment that the squadron would be taking with them on the deployment to Afghanistan. The Americans had by an early point in the war – late October 2001 – established an enormous forward operating base (FOB) at a huge airfield codenamed K2 in Uzbekistan. It was uncertain whether or not the men from 22 SAS would be transiting via this base. 'A' and 'G' Squadrons were becoming increasingly frustrated with their 'S & R' role in Afghanistan, while the American Green Beret teams that were operating with the Northern Alliance had been busy advancing across half of northern Afghanistan. So when the SAS squadrons learned that they were to be dispatched back to the UK, via Oman, at the beginning of November, the irritation and frustration of the SAS soldiers increased. Were they destined to miss out on the entire war in Afghanistan after all? Following the abortive US Delta Force and Ranger raids near Kandahar in October, the American desire to avoid further casualties had percolated down to the deployment of between 100–150 Special Forces personnel whose main task was liaising with the Northern Alliance, advising them in battle and co-operating with the CIA's Special Operations Group, whose tasks essentially consisted of everything to do with bringing the various Northern Alliance groups on side. The CIA Special Operations Groups included former members of US Delta Force and the anti-terrorist Development Group, or DEVGRU, formerly known as SEAL Team 6. These men, who had transferred to the CIA, were part of a sub-grouping known as Military Special Projects or Special Activities Staff.

By early November, the two SAS squadrons, under their commanding officers Major Streeter and Major Edward 'Ed' French, were back in Hereford. Their frustration was complete. A tan in a Hereford bar was of no use to the men if all they could do was then admit that no, they hadn't been singeing the trailing locks of Osama bin Laden's beard or getting dirty knees with the Northern Alliance, but stuck on patrol duties in the middle of a great big sandy, rocky nowhere, helping the Americans to 'take out' the Taliban.

Then, suddenly, it seemed that whoever was lobbying for the Regiment up on high had been successful. By the beginning of the third week in November the SAS squadrons transited through Oman again, back into Afghanistan and on to the mined, bullet-holed, pockmarked, war-blasted Tarmac at Bagram Air Base, 40km north of Kabul.

Bagram was an old Russian air base that would become a key position not just in the coming fall of Kabul, but in launching the air-assault operations that, after the fall of Kabul, would be concentrated in southern Afghanistan, around Kandahar. After the capital fell, the Taliban would have nowhere else to go. Bagram had last been used by the Soviets, and the entire base bore the signs of a decade of neglect. There was a bullet-riddled control tower, rusting aircraft fuselages, broken-down buildings, a hangar that was completely colandered with bullet holes, discarded and broken jet engines and a thick layer of dust lying everywhere. These were just some of the more noticeable aspects of the abandoned base. The less noticeable ones were the hundreds and hundreds of antitank and antipersonnel mines scattered, laid and planted everywhere. Along with men from 'M' or 'Maritime' Squadron of the Special Boat Service, a combined party of some 100 Royal Marines had secured the airfield during the second week of November. At least the two SAS squadrons now had a base from which they could operate, and from which aircraft could take off and land.

A complete breakdown of British Special Forces operations in Afghanistan is difficult to source definitively from this point onwards. It seems, from a variety of defence, intelligence and Special Forces sources that the operations in which they took part were as follows.

Elements of 'M' Squadron of the SBS were occupied at Bagram Air Base, and were shortly to see limited action at Mazar-i-Sharif. They were also employed on reconnaissance of Kabul, and in providing immediate interim protection for British intelligence officials from the SIS and British diplomats as they began operations to re-establish themselves in the capital. A British battalion, 2 Para, was to head up the first International Security and Assistance Mission in Kabul.

Two SAS squadrons, 'A' and 'G', now at Bagram Air Base near Kabul, were shortly to take part in an operation in Helmand Province in southern Afghanistan, followed by limited operations in conjunction with US Special Forces. SBS troops would carry out operations around Tora Bora and elsewhere in the country, as well as 'national interest operations' without the Americans.

In two areas in particular the SAS had learned their lessons well from the First Gulf War in 1991. The first was the necessity for completely accurate electronic warfare systems, particularly when it came to guiding in air strikes, and communications systems that were compatible with those of their American and Australian allies. They were keenly aware of the potential for being hit by 'friendly fire' strikes by the Americans. The second lesson they had learned was in the use of their mobile, heavily armed Land Rover patrols. The SAS had suffered the first time around in the Gulf when the operational capacity of some of its patrols – including the notorious and well-publicised failure of the Bravo Two Zero mission – had been severely hampered by the soldiers being deployed on foot as opposed to in vehicles, and by having signalling equipment that didn't work. This time around, British SF teams were determined not to make the same mistakes.

If utterly necessary, the SAS would be deployed into action by freefall parachute drop, but given the choice they would prefer to be lifted in for the most part by Sikorsky MH-60 Pave Hawk or MH-53M Pave Low helicopters from the dedicated Special Forces flights of the US Air Force or alternatively in RAF Chinooks, as well as C-130 Hercules aircraft. If they went into action in vehicles, the men would simply drive out of the back of the Hercules down their loading ramps, their vehicles equipped with sufficient ammunition, fuel, water, explosives, weaponry, communications equipment and food to allow them to operate for ten days at a time. Laden down with 7.62mm general-purpose machine guns (GPMGs), .50-calibre Browning heavy machine guns, .50-calibre Barratt sniper rifles, 40mm automatic grenade launchers and Milan antitank missile systems, the weaponry on the Land Rovers was complemented by the personal fire power carried by the men themselves.

Among the personal hardware reportedly sported by the men from 'A' and 'G' Squadrons, as well as by SBS men, operating in Afghanistan in late November 2001 were the following items: PM Accuracy International sniper rifles; Canadian Diemaco C7 and C8 (carbine version) assault rifles, some with M-203 40mm grenade launchers slung under the barrel;

Remington Wingmaster and Franchi SPAS-12 assault shotguns; Swiss Sig-Sauer and Belgian Browning handguns; plus flare guns, combat knives, small hatchets, machetes and chain saws for coping with small trees and scrub. The Diemaco assault rifles, which are essentially Canadian copies of the M-16A2 and the Colt M4 carbine, were the most popular weapons with the SAS soldiers. The SAS squadrons are also reported to have taken a variety of Heckler & Koch weapons to Afghanistan, including the perennially popular MP5 sub-machine-gun and the G3KA4 variant of the popular 7.62mm G3 assault rifle. This has a shorter barrel and a retractable stock, but retains the benefit of the heavier 7.62mm round. When fired on full automatic setting, it sports a muzzle flash up to 1.8m long. There were also examples of the new Heckler & Koch G36, by then standard issue to the German *Bundeswehr*. Along with the G36K, its more compact version, which sports a shorter 20cm barrel, the G36 is an admirable weapon. It has a transparent magazine, enabling the user to count the number of rounds he or she has expended, in addition to being accurate, robust and coming complete with an inbuilt optic sight. The butt is a folding skeleton, but of A-frame design and thus not a hindrance to accuracy and strong enough to replace a traditional solid one. Up to five clips of ammunition – 150 rounds – can be carried effectively on the weapon.

Given the choice of using 5.56mm or 7.62mm ammunition, there are two long-argued, long-disputed and varying schools of thought [3]. When all is said and done, a discerning group of men, given the choice, will carry a selection of both. Between eight men the ideal choice of weaponry would be: one 7.62mm GPMG, one belt-fed 5.56mm Minimi squad support weapon, one Heckler & Koch G3 assault rifle with telescopic sight, one 7.62mm PM Accuracy International sniper rifle, two Diemaco C8 carbines and two C7 assault rifles, all with 40mm M-203 grenade launchers attached, plus additional MP5s and shotguns.

The one weapon that would figure nowhere is the much-lamented, shoddy piece of equipment with which the world's best army, the British, is equipped as standard: the SA-80 A2 assault rifle. In terms of pathos, the sight of British soldiers in Kosovo having to operate, at the height of the NATO and UN deployments, in front of the armies of forty-one other nationalities – European, American, African, Asian, Russian, rich, poor, developed, Third World, all of whom were better armed than them – was shaming. Defending the weapon in 2000, General Sir Charles Guthrie, a former CO of 22 SAS, said, 'I wouldn't like to be hit by it.' An unlikely event, which assumes that its user would actually have been able to fire it, if it hadn't jammed in his hands or fallen apart in the first place. A Royal Marines sergeant's view of it was succinct and more to the point: 'It's a pile of shite.'

Alongside their weaponry, the SAS men carried electronic communications kits, with most soldiers possessing a global positioning satellite (GPS) system. There were also laptop computers for sending encoded satellite messages and for assistance in guiding in air strikes, the occasional Palm Pilot and one of the most vital pieces of equipment – the laser-guidance systems designed to put 'smart' bombs on to their targets. These come in two shapes and sizes; the more efficient is the Litton Laser Systems AN/PEQ-1 Special Operations Forces Laser Marker, or SOFLAM, which weighs 4kg and comes with a GPS set inside it. At 5km it can 'paint' a 3sq. m electronic laser 'spot' on a target, enabling it to be hit by an air strike. By the time Operation Enduring Freedom came around, many of the SOFLAMs were the 1-A designation that came with a night-vision sight, which enabled the operator to see the 'cast' electronic spot from 3km away. The SOFLAM consists of a large pair of binoculars set on a tripod, to which is attached a cable and a small electronic trigger attached to the laser marker itself. The operator looks through the binoculars, aims at the point he wants to electronically 'paint' and pulls the trigger, sending a beam of laser light down the aimed path. The missile or bomb dispatched on to this target simply locks on to the 'painted' area.

By the end of November 2001, the towns or cities of Mazar-i-Sharif, Jalalabad and Kabul had fallen to the Northern Alliance, backed up by American and British forces. Only the hardline Taliban stronghold at

Kandahar still held out, itself to be deserted by the Taliban on 5 December. The Americans of the 5th Special Forces Group were concentrating their efforts to find Osama bin Laden around Tora Bora. They had brought in Eastern Alliance Security Commissioner Hazarat Ali from Jalalabad to lead the Alliance operations around the White Mountains; Ali had brought 2,000 men with him from Jalalabad. They were spurred on by American encouragements that Osama bin Laden was hiding near Tora Bora, which meant that there was a distinct possibility that the Afghan group who found him, or informed on him, would be eligible for the $25 million bounty on his head. The Americans were giving every kind of incentive to the anti-Taliban fighters, from food, to weaponry mostly in the form of Kalashnikovs, to clothes.

Between the beginning of October and the middle of the last week of December, including the period when operations south-west of Kandahar and around Tora Bora were at their height, it is claimed that the US 3rd and 5th Special Forces Groups, along with intelligence teams from MI6 and the CIA – predominantly the latter – gave out just over $3 million dollars, mostly in cash, promissory notes or gold sovereigns, to buy the allegiance of Northern and Eastern Alliance Afghan fighters. This money was flown in by the CIA, accompanied by US Special Forces soldiers, to Uzbekistan and Pakistan, and then into Afghanistan, to Bagram Air Base and Camp Rhino, the base at Dolangi, either on Chinook or MH-53 Pave Low helicopters under heavy military guard.

By the last week in November, the SAS and SBS teams that were to carry out the fighting near Tora Bora and in Helmand were in place at Bagram and Dolangi; at the former, they had been joined by Mountain and Arctic Warfare Cadres, Royal Marines. 'G' Squadron had flown into Bagram Air Base, where they had been reunited with some of their SF colleagues who had been operating along with the US Special Forces in the north of the country, particularly around the fortress at Mazar-i-Sharif.

The SBS, MI6 and the Americans had been involved in the fighting around the fort at Mazar, where a riot by Taliban prisoners had escalated into massive violence.

On 24 November 2001, the towns of Taloqan and Kunduz in northern Afghanistan had fallen to the Northern Alliance under the command of General Abdul Rashid Dostum. Up to 800 Taliban prisoners, including a large number of Chechen, Pakistani and Egyptian fighters, were given assurances that they were going to be able to surrender to the Alliance fighters. They were taken to the prison fortress at Qala-i-Janghi – the name means 'Fortress of War' – outside Mazar i Sharif. The CIA operatives who accompanied them, however, had other instructions from the Pentagon and from US Secretary of State for Defence Donald Rumsfeld. The Afghan Taliban fighters could be allowed to go free, but any foreign fighters – the Islamic fundamentalist mercenaries who, for Rumsfeld and the White House, formed the bedrock of al-Qaeda support for the Taliban – were to be imprisoned, at best, or preferably killed in battle. When these foreign fighters, gathered in the courtyard of the Qala-i-Janghi prison, realised that they were not only going to be forced to surrender to 'infidels' from the CIA but also questioned by them, trouble exploded.

Part of the problem was that on being captured, the al-Qaeda and Taliban (AQT) fighters had not been as thoroughly searched by the Northern Alliance as they would have been by Western soldiers. The AQT had simply put down their visible weapons, surrendered and been transferred to the huge 350m across by 100m long courtyard of the fort, which itself resembled a Crusader castle, rising up out of the desert. Two CIA officers, one known as Johnny 'Mike' Spann and another identified only as 'Dave' but whose surname was Tyson, were inside the prison compound questioning the fighters. The uprising began when Taliban fighters managed to overpower their Northern Alliance guards. 'Dave' and Spann were able to open fire and kill four of the rioting prisoners with a Kalashnikov and a handgun before Spann was killed. 'Dave' fled on to the walls of the prison as the Taliban and foreign fighters, who had broken into a weapons store in a corner of the fort, began to open fire on Northern Alliance troops. On the ramparts of the fort, 'Dave' approached a German television crew from the ARD network, demanded to use their satellite telephone and called the US Embassy in neighbouring Uzbekistan for air support and backup. Within two hours, as the fighting and the standoff inside the prison continued, US Special Forces arrived, accompanied by two white Land Rovers containing eight men from the SBS. The Americans and the British set up positions on the walls of the fortress and began the process of calling in an air strike. The SBS soldiers took three 7.62mm GPMGs from their Land Rovers and, using these alongside their Diemaco carbine rifles, opened fire on the rioting prisoners below.

Three US Special Forces soldiers were injured when one of the first bombs to be dropped, a 900kg joint direct attack munition (JDAM) targeted by an American FA-18, fell 600m short of the Taliban positions inside the fort at which it had been aimed. Five Northern Alliance soldiers were also killed. The attack on the prison continued throughout the night and the next day. During the night of 25–26 November, fearing that a breakout of some 600 armed AQT prisoners was about to take place, the commanding officer of Taskforce Boxer, a US SF co-ordination team, ordered a C-130 Spectre gunship to circle and open fire on the former prisoners, now armed combatants, inside the fortress. Up to 450 Taliban and other Arab prisoners were reported killed, many of them allegedly executed by the Northern Alliance or burned alive in underground basements after diesel fuel and petrol were poured in on them and then ignited. The basements were later filled with water to extinguish the flames. When the fortress was finally pacified, hundreds of Taliban bodies, many half-burned, many with their hands tied behind their backs and clearly executed with single shots to the head, were discovered inside the vast, sprawling prison compound.

War crime? Massacre? Legitimate killing in time of war? It depends on whose account you listen to. Two officials from the International Committee of the Red Cross, beholden to uphold the seven basic principles of the Geneva Convention, who were inside the Qala-i-Janghi complex at the time of the incident say that from the moment of capture, the prisoners had not been granted their full rights, were not allowed to have contact with their families and had been tied up. Amnesty International, along with a variety of media organisations who investigated the incident afterwards, called it a war crime, alleging that the Americans had allowed the Northern Alliance to open fire on the Taliban and Arab prisoners and had then aided and abetted the killing by calling in air strikes upon them, thereby suggesting that it was a deliberate US – and by extension British – policy to execute prisoners. The egregious Robert Fisk from Britain's *Independent* newspaper described it, predictably, as 'a massacre'. The SAS, who were almost certainly not even there, were accused in other reports of having 'blood on their hands'. Former Foreign Secretary Robin Cook called for a war-crimes investigation into the incident. Other witnesses, however, among them American officials and Northern Alliance soldiers, say that the Taliban and Arabs had not even surrendered officially when they were brought to the fortress, and therefore were not real POWs. And, most importantly, even if they had been POWs, by choosing to take weapons from their captors and start firing on them, their status reverted to that of enemy combatants, and thus they had completely legitimised the use of whatsoever pieces of ordnance the British and Americans chose to use against them. The incident at the fortress was very heavily reported around the world in every broadcast medium. Three separate documentaries were made about the fortress riot. Yet around the same time as the incidents at Qala-i-Janghi were taking place, from 25–28 November, Major Ivo Streeter and 'G' Squadron of 22 SAS were engaged in some of the heaviest fighting the SAS had seen since World War II south of Kandahar. Not surprisingly, the SAS operations in remote Helmand Province passed off without any immediate media coverage, while the fighting in Qala-i-Janghi was comprehensively filmed, photographed and reported on simply because foreign correspondents were there.

Meanwhile, by 30 November the Americans had begun their assault on Tora Bora, 56km to the south of Jalalabad. American Special Forces had already begun fighting for control of the Milawa Valley, which controlled the only entrance to the village of Tora Bora and the slopes above it where Osama bin Laden was reported to be hiding. On the ridge-lines above the Agam and Wazir valleys, lines of bomb craters were mushrooming, evidence of American air strikes designed to dislodge al-Qaeda fighters who were allegedly dug into the cave systems on the forward slopes. The old bunkers and cave systems built by the *mujahideen* were once again being put to good use. Dozens of US intelligence reports flashed backwards and forwards from the Pentagon: one, typically optimistic, which like a firework thrown into a pond fizzled briefly before disappearing, reported on 28 November that bin Laden's defecting cook, a man known only as Ali Muhamed, had given his whereabouts as being in a cave somewhere on a ridge-line above the Tora Bora and Milawa valleys. Another report said that bin Laden, along with 250 Yemeni fighters, 180 Algerians and 350 Chechens, was going to fight to the last in the fastnesses of the Agam or Wazir valleys. The Pentagon reported in off-the-record briefings that a cave system 350m deep with vaulted caves 9m high left over from the Soviet occupation of Afghanistan and equipped with an electrical supply and a small air-conditioned hospital was being used as bin Laden's headquarters.

On the ridge-lines outside the caves, trees were cut off at ground level by 6,800kg 'daisy-cutter' bombs. The ground was strewn with empty plastic bottles of 'Poland' brand mineral water left behind by the Americans, who had taken to writing messages on the rocks indicating what they were going to do to any Taliban they found. The CIA was using Mi-17 and Mi-8 helicopters of Russian make to fly money and equipment in for the Eastern Alliance fighters. American Special Forces were fighting handfuls of Taliban and foreign al-Qaeda fighters: one here, six there, twenty somewhere else. A pattern was established and repeated *ad nauseam*: one of the Eastern Alliance commanders would report that bin Laden or one of his fighters was in a particular location. American Special Forces would occupy the immediate area, often allowing the Afghans to lead the attacks on the caves. In each cave system the Americans occupied, CIA operatives were picking up swabs of body tissue from al-Qaeda corpses, along with bits of body parts, fingers, organs and jellied muscle sprayed up cave walls by air strikes. Everything was going back to mobile laboratories at Bagram Air Base for DNA testing to see if the samples bore any relationship to the DNA of Osama bin Laden. At night, Predator and Global Hawk UAVs tracked silently across the Afghan heavens; by day the sky was crisscrossed with the vapour trails of B-52 bombers unloading their payloads upon suspected al-Qaeda hideouts.

In late November, a Pathan leader near Tora Bora, Haji Zaman Gamsharik, asked the UN to administer a surrender by al-Qaeda fighters. The Americans were having none of this and Eastern Alliance Security Commissioner Hazarat Ali was brought in from Jalalabad to stiffen the mettle of the assault. The fact that Ali was a Jalalabad leader immensely unpopular in the area of the White Mountains – where his criminal rivals operated – led to further rifts among the ranks of Afghan fighters assisting the Americans.

Each day would start the same, said American fighters from the 5th Special Forces Group. Acting on information received overnight from UAVs, local Afghan informers and their own intelligence system, the Americans would formulate a strategy of attack on a particular area. As the operation around Tora Bora continued, the Afghan demands for money increased. An operation would often begin with a CIA official negotiating the cost of carrying out a particular assault with the Afghans. The fighters, under whichever leader claimed to have the particular piece of tactical information concerning al-Qaeda whereabouts, would then lead the Americans, some in pick-up trucks, others on foot or by helicopter, to a location. More money was frequently demanded at various stages along the way. The Americans seethed with tactical frustration at what they saw as the ludicrously double-crossing and duplicitous nature of the Afghans, who ultimately proved themselves to be interested in very little except the bounty money on bin Laden's head. General Tommy Franks from US CENTCOM, under immense pressure from Donald Rumsfeld, the White House and the world's media to produce results, felt himself going round in circles.

In between that week at the end of November and the middle of December, the two Squadrons of 22 SAS now in Afghanistan were to see more action than had been witnessed by any parts of the unit collectively since the 1960s and 1970s, when the Regiment was operating in Oman, the Radfan and Dhofar. The forthcoming deployment was to be called Operation Trent.

In the last week of November 2001, Major Ivo Streeter and 'G' Squadron, along with Major 'Ed' French and 'A' Squadron and some thirty-plus vehicles, mostly armed Land Rovers, were flown by US Hercules from Bagram to a forming-up position near Kandahar. A small party of men from Air Troop of 'G' Squadron had already been inserted by night via a HALO parachute drop to establish a tactical landing zone. The following day, the remainder of the two squadrons joined them; then the vehicles formed up and drove some 150km to assault an AQT position. This operation consisted of a two-squadron attack on a ridge-line near a set of buildings held by AQT fighters. 'A' Squadron assaulted the position while 'G' Squadron provided fire support. During this action, the 22 SAS Regimental sergeant-major was wounded along with four other SAS soldiers. The only details that participants and observers involved in this operation and battle in Helmand Province will give are that it took place on and around a ridge-line on a hillside and open plain, and that the British soldiers were not operating on a tip-off exclusive to them. Loosely translated from intelligence reports, it appeared that Streeter, 'G' Squadron, the CO of 22 SAS and the British SF hierarchy in Afghanistan were keen to operate in a more integrated way with the Americans and were prepared to undertake this operational compromise – of operating under US command and accepting targets designated for them by the Americans rather than choosing their own – if it meant being allocated a larger share of the available deployments.

They were also extremely keen to avoid unnecessary operations at any level with the wildly lacklustre Afghans, who had demonstrated an ability second to none to change their minds, their allegiances, their loyalties and their sense of priorities at the drop of a hat. Contrary to many reports, Afghans are sometimes extremely mediocre fighters – guerrilla or otherwise – when confronted with properly trained and equipped enemies. They can be wildly, almost madly brave and devoted to the cause for which they are fighting. However, their reputation for this fighting ability is based upon a sense of their perceived resilience to pain and socio-economic hardship; their so-called 'bravery' can sometimes not be described as such, but rather as a total disregard for logic, tactical reason and self-preservation, and with only an occasional regard for the tactical benefits that come with the occupation of the high ground.

The shortcomings of the Afghans' daily lives when not fighting are so little different from when they are that conflict will always be a winning option. Historically, their record shows them using the same tactics from the mid-nineteenth century against the British and the Russians until the present day against the Russians – second time around – and then against the Taliban, which merely means against each other. Against red-coated British infantrymen sweltering in a thick layer of high-buttoned serge in the summer heat in the 1870s – men whose tactical training had been polished on Hounslow Heath and consisted of little more than an ability to operate in three distinct formations – the Afghans' guerrilla tactics had worked spectacularly well. These tactics were based upon three things: knowledge of the local terrain and an ability to move freely and swiftly across it, developed as a result of habituation with the physical demands that this required; knowledge of how to occupy the high ground and carry out simple ambushes; and an occasional ability to shoot straight.

When confronted with a combination of Western technology – helicopters, automatic weapons, armoured vehicles – and developed Western counterinsurgency tactics, the Afghans went to pieces. The Afghan fighters facing the Americans and British at Tora Bora and Kunduz, or indeed assisting them, had largely been the first- or second-hand recipients of British, Russian or American SF training in the 1980s. Unfortunately, they had neither learned from it nor adapted to new situations by modernising it. Their levels of tactical advancement and, simply and diplomatically put, their psychosocial and political economic development were so hidebound by idiotic tradition and sociocultural isolationism that the Afghan rank and file was often incapable of learning or adapting. 90 per cent of Afghans cannot read; many Afghan men are incapable of dealing in any way, shape or form with women other than through violence or a tactic of zero tolerance, often preferring to have sexual relationships with adolescent males, both teenage boys and younger. They are intensely superstitious: most Afghans still think that human beings are outnumbered by politically active *djinns* created from the smokeless fire spoken of in the Koran. Needless to say, when equipped with modern technology – tanks, armoured personnel carriers, missile launch systems – they proved so bad at maintaining the equipment that it frequently broke down.

Some time during the last ten days of November 2001, a Hercules aircraft specially fitted with the modified oxygen consoles required for a high-altitude low-opening (HALO) parachute jump and crewed by men from the RAF Special Forces flight had been specially flown into Bagram Air Base from Oman for the operation about to take place somewhere south-west of Kandahar in between the Margo Desert and the Pakistani border. The parachute jump instructors and the air loadmaster had worked and trained with the SAS before, but even so, the nocturnal parachute descent was still risky. HALO parachuting is a complicated and dangerous skill to master. The eight-man patrol from Air Troop of 'G' Squadron, wearing a main parachute on their backs with a reserve slung directly below it, exited from the tailgate of the Hercules at a height of 6,100m or more. Inside the Hercules fuselage, they had been breathing oxygen from a console mounted towards the back of the aircraft; shortly before they jumped, they had switched their oxygen supply from the consoles to the small bottles mounted on their chest harnesses. Helmeted and goggled, they jumped off the back of the tailgate into the sub-zero night air, breathing oxygen as they fell at speeds up to 120mph. The air temperature and speed of their descent would have caused their goggles to ice up quickly, forcing them to use their gloved hands to wipe off the layer of white frost – an action that required perfect timing and hand co-ordination to prevent themselves from spinning out of control as they rocketed through the air. Only when they were at or below 1,220m did an automatic opening device pull open their parachutes for them, allowing them to descend to the ground on the 110sq. m of their tactical assault parachutes. Their rucksacks and equipment would have been balanced on the backs of their legs as they fell; as they neared the ground, these items were released to dangle from the parachute harnesses, hitting the ground scant seconds before the men did. Despite these difficulties, all the men from Air Troop jumped safely, signalled back to Bagram that they were in one piece and in position, and then proceeded to scout out possible landing zones for the Hercules coming in the following night.

Major Ivo Streeter and his men of 'G' Squadron, plus a group of signallers and engineers, thundered to the ground at the remote landing zone Air Troop had selected right on schedule. Touching down in three American C-130 Hercules, they were accompanied in another three US Hercules by 'A' Squadron. The 'Pink Panther' Land Rovers that would transport the men from the tactical landing zone to the target some 160km to the south-west had been strapped tightly into the aircraft at Bagram Air Base shortly before the men took off. The men landed on the south-western corner of a vast sandy plain long before dawn. The landing zone was almost entirely silent as the men and their vehicles emerged from the tailgates of the Hercules, a massive change from the thundering of the Hercules' engines and the roar of the Land Rover motors inside the aircrafts' cramped hulls. Streeter and his squadron sergeant-major had divided the three and a half troops of 'G' Squadron into three-man vehicle crews. The target of Operation Trent was, according to the intelligence reports that the British and Americans had received, a combination of a Taliban and al-Qaeda base where Osama bin Laden may or may not have been hiding, an opium storage plant and a system of trenches dug into the side of a 1,830m-high mountain. The SAS soldiers roared off the back of the aircraft in their Land Rovers and the vehicles immediately took up a circular defensive position around the makeshift airstrip; arcs of fire were covered with .50-calibre Brownings, 7.62mm GPMGs and C8 and C7 rifles. Then the Hercules lifted off in a boiling cloud of brown dust, rock chippings, sticks, leaves and stifling overheated air that had sat on the floor of the plain all night.

The ground opened out along the side of a dried-up riverbed, and behind the position where the soldiers had landed stretched the plain, intercut by paths, watercourses and long slopes of shale and boulder-strewn moraine. Streeter's plan was for the main body of the men to form a harbour position and forward operating base at the mouth of the riverbed. The terrain chosen by the eight-man recce team from 'G' Squadron's Air Troop had been perfect for landing a Hercules on or driving Land Rovers around except for one salient factor: the dust. Invisible from the air, it formed a layer 30cm thick in places, making driving visibility a nightmare for the column of vehicles. Their objective was located over and beyond the reverse slope of the mountains that lay to their backs. All Streeter knew about it was that a self-contained compound and group of houses somewhere on or near a sloping ridge next to a large mountain some 1,800m high, was being used by AQT groups as a staging point for fighters transiting into Pakistan. The infiltration distance to the target was an estimated 160km as the crow flew, which meant about 190km on the ground. The strength of the enemy presence, based upon a combination of Afghan intelligence, information gathered by the US from around Kandahar and depending on the movements of the AQT forces and how they were being staged onwards towards Kandahar and back into Pakistan, could be up to seventy men inside the houses, compounds, trenches or caves at any one time. Interpreted into real information, the two SAS majors commanding 'A' and 'G' Squadrons knew that they could be up against anything from two boys with a sling-shot between them, houses full of fresh air and nothing else, five men from al-Qaeda or the Taliban, or 200. There was only one way to find out: attack the target.

Mountain Troop of 'G' Squadron, under the command of young Captain Huw Wake, was given the first operational task. Their vehicles would provide the lead elements of the convoy as it approached the target. Summoning his four troop officers and their respective troop sergeants, Major Streeter brought the men together behind a large rock overhang. The distance from the centre of the circle where he sat explaining his plan to the outside perimeter occupied by his squadron's vehicles was several hundred metres. The air, now that the Hercules had departed, was very still. A long, dusty drive to the target lay ahead of them, and the time available to the SAS soldiers to make the drive, form up for the attack and still coincide with the availability of US-supplied combat air support (CAS) was very tight indeed. The American CAS was only reportedly available between 11.00 a.m. and 12.00 noon, so the men were obliged to attack in daylight. The first task for the thirty-odd vehicles, laden down with equipment and mounted with 7.62mm GPMGs and .50-calibre Brownings, was to reach the target. There the two squadrons would split up: 'A' Squadron would form up and assault the target on foot, while 'G' Squadron would provide covering fire from their Land Rovers and from a mortar line before sending in additional men if the assault became bogged down.

Once in front of the trench-lines on the side of the mountain, the CO of the Regiment, who was present on the ground with the Regimental sergeant-major, would command the battle from a centralised location where they could observe the movements of both units and also, crucially, be in a position to co-ordinate the air strikes that the Americans were going to make on the target. The CO reportedly wanted two troops of 'A' Squadron to cut over and behind a rock feature that stood between them and the cave systems and trenches. Somewhere in the target area there was a trio of buildings, one of which was being used as a command position by the AQT fighters. According to intelligence footage collected from UAV passes and the video equipment aboard Orion P-3 reconnaissance planes, the entrances to the trench systems and caves were at different levels. Once the two SAS troops had worked out the easiest way to make surprise approaches from above, beside and below the dug-out positions – which would almost certainly require killing the enemy fighters who would be on guard – then the rest of 'A' Squadron would follow into the attack.

After ten hours of driving, it was very dark again when Captain Huw Wake from 'A' Squadron led his fifteen SAS men into position in their Land Rovers at the side of what looked like a dried-up river. Ahead of and above them, the 1,800m-high mountain flared up in the darkness; behind and to the right were the men of two other troops; to their left were the formed-up Land Rovers of 'G' Squadron. Ahead were the Taliban and al Qaeda. For the SAS men who, between all 140 of them, had fought against Argentinians, Serbs, Iranians, Iraqis, IRA terrorists and sundry other nationalities from Africa and Central Asia, the Taliban and al-Qaeda were a new foe. Many of the SAS men in the two squadrons deployed on Operation Trent had never been in action before and the next few hours would see them in battle for the first time. As soon as 'A' Squadron departed towards the start-line of their attack, the CO of 22 SAS passed down a briefing to the remainder of his men – the HQ party and 'G' Squadron: they were to prepare for an immediate tactical move in their Land Rovers to support the assault. As the sun started to come up, the .50-calibre Brownings and 7.62mm GPMGs were readied, the 81mm mortars prepared on the firing line and the .50-calibre Barratt sniper rifles taken out of their protective packing on the Land Rovers. If 'A' Squadron discovered that the caves or trenches could be taken quickly, they would try to do it at dawn that morning, during the period when the rising sun would be in the eyes of any enemy on the mountain slopes in front of them. The men spent the first hour of the early morning lying in wait. Their Land Rovers were beside them, and when the attack was launched, the men of 'A' Squadron would charge forward and open fire from them and then continue the attack on foot when they came within effective firing range.

Weapons were given a final check. In the extremely dusty conditions of Afghanistan, where a fine, white-grey talcum-like dust permeated everything that moved, the men were not going to put any excessive oil on their weapons. If they could keep the magazine apertures and working parts of their weapons dry and clean of dust and the ammunition in their belts of 7.62mm and 5.56mm ammunition very lightly oiled and concealed from windblown dust as much as possible, then they would have been successful. In these conditions, it was an endless battle to prevent weapons from jamming at the crucial moment. Most of the men would be going into action carrying as much ammunition as possible, along with their medical and signalling kits, water, spare socks, main personal weapon, a sidearm, a knife, compass, distress flares and webbing. The officers and NCOs tended to leave it to their men to decide what they would wear on an operation like this where they were far away from the public eye. Consequently, the soldiers were wearing a combination of British desert camouflage trousers, baggy, side-pocketed combat trousers from army-surplus stores, tropical jungle trousers, even lightweight and waterproof cover-trousers worn over generously cut denims. There were a lot of *keffiyeh* scarves, in red, brown or black check, in evidence. Most of the men had customised their webbing vests, spraying them in every combination of grey, green, black and brown. The men carrying the C8s and C7s would go into action with up to 600 rounds of ammunition on them, as well as smoke, white phosphorus and fragmentation grenades, a Sig-Sauer pistol, a knife, machete or hatchet and all-important Maglite torches taped or inserted into plastic holders attached to the ends of their weapons. Those providing covering fire with the heavier-calibre GPMGs were carrying 600 rounds each, with extra belts of ammunition split up among their colleagues, while some of the men who were armed with C7 Diemacos, the cut-down, highly effective and very popular Canadian version of the M-16, were packing up to sixteen magazines each, totalling some 540 rounds. Almost every second or third man had an M-203 40mm grenade launcher attached to his C7 or C8. One of the men with a GPMG was also carrying an MP5 9mm sub-machine-gun and a dozen magazines in a day-pack slung over his shoulders. Everybody had more ammunition in their Bergen rucksacks, which would be carried in the Land Rovers until several hundred metres short of the attack area.

It was just after 7.00 a.m. when a signaller waved Ivo Streeter over to his Land Rover. 'A' Squadron had observed enemy moving in and out of the trenches, although they were largely staying inside them as the sun came up. The SAS men had been monitoring all approaches to the AQT positions and caves, but had not moved against any sentries yet, having concealed themselves to wait. 'G' Squadron was ready to open fire, and the Land Rovers of 'A' were ready to move off.

The mountain that lay in front of the SAS position was neither particularly steep, nor the route to it particularly harsh, nor the distance to the entrance to the trench systems particularly far. It was the hot, dusty temperatures and the rocky terrain that would make the fighting on the ground such hard going. The men would be moving forward at speed, stopping and starting, advancing, going to ground, moving and firing in that combination of fire and manoeuvre that the British Army calls 'pepper-potting'. Once the trenches were captured, the men would pull back to their vehicles, helicopters would be called in to pick up any wounded soldiers and the entire party would exfiltrate back to the landing zone for extraction.

In the end, the fire fight to capture the trenches, caves and dusty buildings lasted for four hours. It began just after 'A' Squadron in their Land Rovers appeared below and to the sides of the trench-line. Captain Wake's men had waited another forty minutes, after which he gave the order for them to begin their assault and open fire. The main body of the squadron formed a semicircle in front of and below the first trenches, from where Taliban fighters could be seen popping up into the open, spraying rounds from their Kalashnikovs around the trenches and loosing off RPG-7 rockets, while other enemy fighters were visible above the trenches with support weapons ready to join in the attack against the infidels from Hereford. The main assault took the form of a pair of encircling bull's horns, with fire support from 'G' Squadron, and at least twelve SAS managed to penetrate the primary entrances of the trenches and caves, killing at least six enemy fighters, all of whom were carrying Kalashnikovs. In some cases, the ground inside the entrances to the trenches dropped via a series of ledges and the one thing that the CO was keen to avoid was his men getting stuck inside any caves. All sorts of American ideas – to the SAS CO's mind mostly completely barmy – had been mooted for the best way to clear caves. Some had involved pumping large amounts of cyanide gas into them, as though a cave was an entirely non-porous entity where the risk of any gas escaping and killing Streeter's men was somehow considered an impossibility.

During the first assault, at least one SAS man was wounded. Fire support from US aircraft had been brought in to hit the trenches and the side of the mountain, some coming dangerously close to where the SAS men were pushing forward, shouting, shooting and scrambling their way as the machine-gun rounds of 'G' Squadron sprayed into the positions ahead of them. By the time two SAS men had made a courageous dash forward and managed to extricate themselves and the wounded man, seven Arab fighters had been hit. The provision of covering fire was difficult because of the narrowness of the intersection of arcs of fire and the danger of 'G' putting down fire on 'A'. Gradually, as fighting continued in the trenches, the al-Qaeda and Taliban fighters came out into the open. Some of the SAS men were in very good cover in front of the trench entrances. There was the equivalent of most of a squadron of the best soldiers in the British Army facing off an unknown number of men. The amount of ammunition flying around was extraordinary: one SAS officer was reportedly hit by two rounds on the ceramic plates of his body armour, and by a third bullet that hit the water bottle on his belt-kit. A very near miss. Over to the left of the right-hand elements of 'G' Squadron, Wake's men from Mountain Troop were opening fire with the ripping, thudding tear of a 5.56mm automatic weapon leading the way, backed up by the heavier barking chug of a GPMG fired on three-shot bursts. Also to the left of 'G' Squadron, the 'A' Squadron sergeant-major was moving from cover to cover, guiding his men and pointing out the positions of hiding Arab and Taliban fighters. When Streeter first looked at his watch it was over an hour since 'G' Squadron had gone into action. The noise was deafening, the sound of shouting drowned out by the ceaseless gunfire.

The trenches were not very deep and the caves, such as they were, did not extend very far back into the mountainside – in some cases it was as though bunkers had been dug into the slopes of the mountain. The SAS men entering the caves and openings in the rocks switched on the torches attached to the front of their automatic carbines as they advanced further into the darkness. Those men who had attached a secondary finger-grip to their C7 Diemaco rifles could hold on to their rifles with one hand and operate the switches on the bases of their Maglite torches, attached horizontally under the barrels of the weapons. A quick stab of a thumb against the base of the torch activated the light. For the first two men through the entrance of the first cave, the first thing they saw were three sleeping AQT fighters. Within two or three seconds of the enemy soldiers waking and fumbling for their weapons, they were dead. Several reports have mentioned that some of the SAS soldiers were using ceramic rounds instead of the normal lead-tipped, copper-surrounded 'FMJ' or full-metal-jacket standard 5.56mm ball ammunition. While the cave-assault teams were fighting inside the openings in the rock face, al-Qaeda and Taliban fighters were closing in from positions around the mountain slopes. SAS snipers in position above and to the side of the assault area opened fire on to the AQT fighters who were shouting and shooting and rushing over the rocks in their haste to get to the position where their colleagues were being attacked. About two hours into the battle, within thirty minutes of the first sniper rounds going into the AQT reinforcements, the sun was shining down hard on the enemy struggling on the hillside in the deafening, clattering, cracking rush of dust, cordite and shouts accompanying the battle.

It was sometimes impossible for the SAS soldiers to use combat air support as the proximity between them and the enemy was far too close; the angle of the slope on which they were fighting meant that if a bomb or missile dropped a few metres short – i.e. not vertically on to the Taliban or al-Qaeda positions but further down the slope towards the British positions – it would kill just as many SAS as enemy.

In battle most men, on radios and off them, shout constantly: partly as a natural reaction to relieve fear, and partly because of the sheer volume of noise around them from explosions, weapons fire, incoming fire support and orders being yelled out from one man to another. The Afghan dust rolled in the air, covering the men's uniforms, equipment and weapons, sticking to the blood pumping from one dying al-Qaeda fighter lying doubled up behind a rock, half of his stomach and intestines mangled with 5.56mm ammunition, bleeding noisily to death as dust and flies mixed in with the darkening pool of blood spreading out on the mountainside.

This was a battle with no quarter: the Taliban and al-Qaeda, according to SAS soldiers, US Special Forces, Australians and the Northern Alliance, were not in the business of prisoners and mercy. They carried on fighting and shooting and attacking until they were shot or stabbed to death or blown to pieces. Surrender was not in their lexicon. So they died for their cause. The trenches had been cleared by the time two hours of the battle had elapsed, and the action was then concentrated on fighting off the AQT who were advancing in a semicircle towards the SAS men from a group of buildings situated at the foot of the slopes and on the slopes themselves. The SAS positions in some cases now faced outwards rather than inwards, the only enemy threat inside the trenches, caves and rocky openings now lying dead in a tangle of twisted limbs, bloodstained blankets and lifeless eyes. After four hours, the battle was almost over. After four hours of dust, grit, blood, shouting, yelling, the coughing hoarseness of throats scoured raw by sand and dust, ricocheting bullets fired on full automatic, magazines changed in an instant, grenades booming, wounded men screaming as they died and the thousands and thousands of ejected brass cartridge cases sprayed high and right from assault rifles before their tinkling, clinking fall on the rocky ground was lost in the blasting noise of battle.

It was still completely dark in London at the headquarters of the Director Special Forces two hours later. The signal had come through from Tora Bora, via Bagram, and thence to Hereford. The operation was completed, the assault over. The final body count was yet to come, and the full effects of this operation on future deployments of UK Special Forces were about to play themselves out.

(1) Text of NATO Article V:

'The Parties agree that an armed attack against one or more of them in Europe or North America shall be considered an attack against them all and consequently they agree that, if such an armed attack occurs, each of them, in exercise of the right of individual or collective self-defence recognised by *Article 51 of the Charter of the United Nations*, will assist the Party or Parties so attacked by taking forthwith, individually and in concert with the other Parties, such action as it deems necessary, including the use of armed force, to restore and maintain the security of the North Atlantic area.

Any such armed attack and all measures taken as a result thereof shall immediately be reported to the Security Council. Such measures shall be terminated when the Security Council has taken the measures necessary to restore and maintain international peace and security.'

(2) Text of UN Article 51:

'Nothing in the present Charter shall impair the inherent right of individual or collective self-defence if an armed attack occurs against a Member of the United Nations, until the Security Council has taken measures necessary to maintain international peace and security. Measures taken by Members in the exercise of this right of self-defence shall be immediately reported to the Security Council and shall not in any way affect the authority and responsibility of the Security Council under the present Charter to take at any time such action as it deems necessary in order to maintain or restore international peace and security.'

(3) The 5.56mm round is more accurate, lighter, meaning that each soldier can carry more ammunition, and it is also NATO standardised, meaning that different nationalities, including US soldiers, can switch ammunition with each other. The round tends to 'tumble' upon hitting solid matter such as hard tissue or bone, meaning that it spins off its direct path of flight, turning end-over-end on itself to inflict tearing wounds as it ricochets off bones inside the body cavity. Combined with the 'vortex' that travels behind each bullet, it has the capacity to cause substantial internal injury and to wound rather than kill, meaning that other soldiers have to care for their injured comrade, thus removing them from effective battlefield duties. A South African policeman describing the experience of shooting a criminal with a 5.56mm R4 assault rifle – a locally manufactured variant of the Israeli Galil – claimed that it was very accurate but that the bullets went straight through the target, making the job of 'taking down' people a bit tricky.

The much heavier 7.62mm round is notorious for its 'one-hit' capability. A former SAS troop commander who saw action in Bosnia said that the G3 was the weapon of choice that should be issued to every infantryman: it has the 'elephant-gun' ability to either kill with the first round or to so severely dismember that the victim is rendered useless. It has all the accuracy and long-range capabilities of the Belgian Fabrique Nationale 7.62mm *Fusil*

Automatique Leger, known in the semi-automatic version adopted by the British Army in the late 1950s as the self-loading rifle. The G3 is simple to operate, clean and fire and can score a killing hit at ranges of up to 900m. An SAS corporal who served in Northern Ireland with 'D' Squadron in the 1980s described being in a car that was chasing a van from inside which two PIRA terrorists were firing from behind a steel plate. British 5.56mm bullets simply would not penetrate the metal; a G3 using armour-piercing rounds would have done, the corporal said. Supporters of the 5.56mm round will say that the added range offered by the 7.62mm round is unnecessary, as most infantry fire fights take place at ranges up to but not generally beyond 300–400m. However, in his epic memoir of serving with the British Army in Burma in 1944, *Quartered Safe Out Here*, George MacDonald Fraser swears that in World War II nothing came close to a .303 Lee Enfield for long-range accuracy; he bemoaned the sub-standard qualities of his issue Thompson .45 sub-machine-gun at the time, which, he says, he later threw in a river.

Human targets hit with a 7.62mm round are damaged in a different way than those hit with a 5.56mm round. The latter flies around inside the body, often ricocheting up the inside of the thorax and sometimes not exiting; a 7.62mm round hits the body, passes through and continues to travel on to a secondary target, taking whichever part of the body is hit along with it in its wake. A 7.62mm round will penetrate concrete, a wall, trees and brick and still go on to kill a secondary target. A Kenyan teenager shot in the shoulder at a range of some 30m by a Kenyan policeman armed with a G3 during anti-government riots in Nairobi in the summer of 1997 lost not just his upper bicep but also a sizeable chunk of fragmented collar bone and shoulder blade, blown out through the top of his back. In October 1995, on a street leading out of Moroni, the capital of Grande Comore, a Comorian soldier shot in the chest by a French Commando Marine using a 5.56mm Swiss SIG SG551 assault rifle at 100m range through the car window of a Renault 4 approaching a French road-block was killed outright. At least seven shots penetrated his torso but only two or three appear to have exited. Gravel and road dust stuck to the bloodied back of his camouflaged uniform just after he died in that curious, warm tropical half-light between dusk and dawn; the front of his chest was shredded, but the back showed very limited damage. However, the South African R4 – 5.56mm, again – had mixed results: the lighter rounds did not penetrate through the triple-breeze-block thickness of the corner of a wall behind which a target, a Somali gunman, was concealed.

The middle ground is occupied by the 7.62mm 'short' round as used in the Kalashnikov range of weapons. With the weight and length of a 5.56mm round, this has the 7.62mm calibre and penetrative power at ranges up to 300m, but not much further on account of its lighter charge. The benefit of the Kalashnikov is its simplicity and reliability, relative accuracy, durability and interchangeability of ammunition and magazines with other Kalashnikov variants. At long range this round can achieve an accurate killing hit at about 400m. Like all firearms, at very short range it is irrespectively lethal. Hutu war criminals found guilty of genocidal war crimes committed during the Rwandan genocide in 1994 were executed in public in Kigali in 1998: tied to railway sleepers in football stadiums and on sports pitches, they were machine-gunned at ranges of less than 10m by Rwandan gendarmes who expended an entire thirty-round magazine on each person, changed clips and fired on the next person. The victims were cut almost in half.

CHAPTER SEVEN

The War That Never Ended

Iraq, 2003–2004

In late 2003, an SAS NCO who had recently left the Regiment commented that the one incident in the preceding decade that had made the most difference to the unit was the 11 September 2001 attacks in New York. Prior to this, he said, operational deployments for the unit had been few and far between, limited to those in Sierra Leone, Bosnia and Kosovo, plus a few less attributable missions in places such as Chechnya, Columbia and Albania. The level of training required to keep the unit at an operational level still occupied much of its time and energy, however. Post-11 September 2001, Operation Trent in southern Afghanistan was almost the only time the SAS undertook a combat operation in the first six months of President Bush's 'War on Terror'. Compared to the vast machine of US Special Forces, which had enough men and equipment to be operational in several theatres at once, for 22 SAS, which needed to have one squadron on standby in the UK at all times, having two squadrons abroad simultaneously on operations, as in Afghanistan, left the Regiment little room for manoeuvre if other operational deployments were to be requested of them. Elements of three squadrons, reportedly 'B', 'D' and elements of 'G', were finally to deploy in and out of Iraq, and the Director Special Forces was eventually to call on the Territorial Army SAS to fulfil part of its Afghanistan commitments in 2004.

Was the Regiment operationally busier pre- or post-11 September? Had its roles or the nature of its deployments changed? One factor to be considered in answering these questions is that the SAS, outside of hostage-rescue and one-off missions abroad, tends to see more active operational service when it is deployed, in part or as a whole, in support of the British Army. Such was the nature of its deployments in Sierra Leone and Kosovo, and in the forthcoming conflict in Iraq.

It could be argued that a major contributing factor in the increased number and frequency of foreign deployments of the British Army, and subsequently its Special Forces, was the election of Tony Blair to prime minister in 1997. During Mr Blair's time in that office, the British Army has found itself being deployed abroad with almost the same frequency as it was in the 1960s as a direct result of several factors: Mr Blair's conviction about and commitment to foreign interventions abroad; frustration over the failures to intervene effectively in Rwanda, Somalia and Bosnia during the ten years before he took power; Mr Blair's close relationships with successive American presidents; and the events of 11 September 2001. It is this four-fold rationale, coupled with Britain's increasing desire to be a key player in the new international order, that have resulted in an increase in Special Forces deployments. There are a finite series of tasks, operations and results that the SAS can effect, but it is fair to say that since 1997 they have been deployed more often to more different places to do more different things than at almost any other point in their existence. And as we shall see, so many tasks are being asked of so few people, whose numbers risk shrinking for a variety of reasons we shall examine, that it is no surprise that the directors of Britain's Special Forces should start to question the necessity of deploying troops on operations like 'Trent'.

Subsequent to Operation Trent, British SBS teams were tasked with operations around Tora Bora, while the SAS squadrons returned home to Hereford. Their next operational deployment was to be in late 2002, when they began to be deployed to Iraq in even greater numbers than had been sent to Afghanistan, on a series of missions as diverse as anything the unit had experienced during their sixty-three-year history. The main difference, in the first instance, between their deployments to Afghanistan and their deployments to Iraq was that the latter were bound to be much larger and more extensive simply because the main strength of the regular British Army was being dispatched to the Gulf as well, thus increasing the subsequent role for British Special Forces. The Middle East was to occupy such a large amount of UAE Regimental manpower that with the main body of the British armed forces set to be deployed in 2003, it was natural that the SAS should have started deploying to the Middle East in 2002. Additionally, the first request the Americans had of the British was for their SF capability, and when the US started basing SF teams in Jordan in 2002, the SAS went too.

As early as October 2002, Special Forces were one of the major component parts of the vast combat effort deployed into Iraq by the US-led coalition to pave the way for the full-scale attack on the regime of Saddam Hussein that would begin on 20 March 2003. Commander General Tommy Franks – the artillery officer, four-star general and thrice-wounded Vietnam veteran – was the commander of US Central Command (CENTCOM). Normally based at MacDill Air Force Base outside Tampa, Florida, CENTCOM controlled the area of US military operational responsibility that stretched from the Horn of Africa to central Asia. If ever there was one theatre of operations in which every part of the Special Forces 'band of brothers' from Britain, the United States, Australia and Poland operated together it was Iraq in late 2002 and 2003. The country was one vast, violent, hyper-complex matrix of multinational SF activity even before the major land-war part of the conflict began.

Iraq drew upon every operational aspect of SF activity, from the British and Australian SAS attacking air bases, roads and communication sites in their mobile Land Rover patrols, to covert forward observation teams inside Iraq, Basrah and elsewhere guiding in air strikes. 'Psy-ops' (psychological operations) were conducted to 'turn' and 'shape' dissidents in the Iraqi regime. The CIA, Green Berets and US Delta Force were training the Kurdish *'peshmerga'* guerrillas in northern Iraq. By 2003, everybody who mattered in the coalition Special Forces community was there in Iraq.

Under the ultimate command of General Franks, the multinational Special Forces component of CENTCOM was the responsibility of Brigadier-General Gary L. Harrell. Harrell, nicknamed 'Shooter' by Franks, was a former Delta Force operator who had been one of the US Special Forces commanders during the misguided and disastrous operation to capture some of Mohamed Farah Aidid's senior lieutenants in Mogadishu in 1993. Prior to that he had commanded both the 7th and 3rd Special Forces Groups and had operated in Columbia during the hunt for Pablo Escobar in the early 1990s. Reporting to him in the SF operational grouping were four component nationalities.

The Australians' SF Task Force was made up of one reinforced squadron of some 100 SAS soldiers from their 1st SAS Regiment, based at Campbell Barracks in Perth, Western Australia. Accompanying them were 4 Battalion of the Royal Australian Regiment, a commando unit that had been brought along as a quick-reaction force essentially designed to infiltrate Iraq and extract the SAS soldiers if they got stuck. These troops were all under the command of Australian Defence Force Brigadier Maurie McNarn, who was in overall charge of the 2,000 Australian troops involved in Operation Iraqi Freedom.

Next came the US Joint Special Operations Command (US JSOC), consisting of the 75th Rangers, the 1st US Special Forces Operational Detachment Delta – or Delta Force – and, to support these soldiers in battle, the 160th Special Operations Aviation Regiment, with their MC-130 Hercules, eighteen Sikorsky MH-60 Pave Hawks, seven MH-6 Hughes 'Little Bird' assault helicopters and fourteen Chinooks. The 160th also had air tankers and helicopters for use in combat search and rescue (CSAR) missions. Attached to the US JSOC was the British Special Forces component consisting of some 215 British soldiers from 'B', 'D' and 'G' Squadrons of 22 SAS in their mobile, heavily armed Land Rover patrols, under the command of a former colonel from the Irish Guards. In addition to the SAS, there was 'M' Squadron of the SBS based on HMS *Ark Royal*, travelling with 3 Commando Brigade of the Royal Marines.

Next came the mighty US 5th Special Forces Group from Fort Campbell, Kentucky, which, with three entire Special Forces battalions of some 2,000 soldiers in total, completely dwarfed the tiny British and Australian contingents in terms of numbers. Then came the US Navy's Special Warfare Wing, with their Navy SEALs and 'DEVGRU', the former SEAL Team 6, and then to carry these men around, whisk them off into battle and extricate them from it were the aircraft and helicopters of the 16th US Aviation Wing. These included its MC-130 Hercules, some of them in the Spectre gunship role, and MH-53 Pave Low helicopters. The British had their Joint Special Forces Aviation Wing, consisting of 657 Army Air Corps Squadron with six AH-7 Lynx helicopters, plus eight CH-47 Chinooks from 7 Squadron RAF, based in Odiham, Hampshire. SAS men tended to be carried to drop-off points or parachuted into them from the Hercules aircraft of the RAF Special Forces Flight of 47 Squadron. To persuade the enemy by leaflet or broadcast from the air that it was time to surrender, or to attempt to win over the hearts and minds of the Iraqi people, were the 8th US Psychological Operations or 'Psy-Ops' Battalion and the 96th Civil Affairs Battalion (Airborne). Finally there were the Polish Special Forces commandos from the Polish Operational Reserve Group – the *Grupa Reagowania Operacyjno Mobilnego* or GROM.

As discussed in an earlier chapter, the SAS had learned its lessons well from the First Gulf War of 1991 and this time around, British SF teams were either lifted in via helicopters or Hercules from the respective specialist Special Forces flights of the RAF and US Air Force, or drove into Iraq in their Land Rover Defenders, known as 'Pink Panthers', or 'Pinkes'. Prior to and after the beginning of formal hostilities, infiltrating their vehicles as close as possible to Iraqi positions without allowing themselves to be seen, they established lying-up positions from which they could observe the movements of the Iraqi Republican Guard units and key Iraqi positions, and from which they could then guide in air strikes using every combination of 'smart' guidance equipment. The SAS and SBS would also be used in support of British infantry assaults around Basrah in the opening days of the ground attack on Iraq.

Long before the first British and American bombs were being guided in against Saddam Hussein's palaces and headquarters in Baghdad in March 2003, Special Forces units had been active inside the country. There were several operational priorities, each of which highlighted the combination of politico-military expertise now a mainstay of SF operations. One main priority was, obviously, to discover whether Saddam Hussein was concealing weapons of mass destruction (WMDs) and if so, exactly where. In autumn 2002, intelligence reports gathered from satellite imagery, from Iraqi military defectors and from opponents of Saddam Hussein's regime inside Iraq indicated to US and British military intelligence that there were sites of missile launchers in western Iraq which could potentially be used in attacks against Israel. The US Special Forces and intelligence apparatus had been denying since August 2002 that Israeli SF teams, or '*Sayerets*', were active in western Iraq. The truth was actually somewhere in the middle: the Americans had agreed with the Israeli Ministry of Defence that if a substantial British and US SF operation was launched to hunt down Saddam Hussein's Scuds and other missiles capable of firing on Israel, Jerusalem would rein-in its existing activities inside Iraq.

The Special Forces teams clearly had a vital role to play in preventing Iraq from bringing Israel into the war. Secondly, it was imperative for the coalition to know on which of his western Iraq airstrips – the main ones being codenamed H1, H2 and H3 after old pumping stations on the Haifa oil pipeline – Saddam Hussein had operational fighter aircraft capable of delivering chemical weapons. Thirdly, SF elements had to be in place to isolate and capture strategic oil wells, both on- and offshore as soon as any ground assault began. All of these operations were to be kept entirely separate from the political-military operations being run, mainly by the CIA and British foreign intelligence, inside Kurdish-controlled areas to co-opt Kurdish opposition groups, and in and around Baghdad and Basrah to gather intelligence from Iraqi opponents of Saddam Hussein's regime.

In late summer 2002, meetings were held in London, Washington and at the HQ of the US Military's Central Command (CENTCOM) at MacDill Air Force Base, led by the architect of the 2001 campaign in Afghanistan – Tommy Franks was at the helm again. The British SAS had one of their former commanding officers – Lieutenant-General Cedric Delves – at MacDill, working in situ as the British liaison officer to the director of Britain's Special Forces and the commanding officer of Britain's 22 SAS. Lieutenant-General Delves had commanded 'D' Squadron of 22 SAS in the Falklands, winning the Distinguished Service Order for his leadership in the attack against Argentinian aircraft at Pebble Island, during which the SAS destroyed eleven Argentinian Pucaras. He had then gone on to take command of the SAS in 1986, and had arrived in Tampa, Florida, as the British Special Forces liaison to CENTCOM at the beginning of January 2002. An excellent soldier, even Delves had not been immune to his share of embarrassing moments of failure, accident or tactical shortcoming in his distinguished career. In 1995, while visiting Sarajevo in his role as Director Special Forces, he and his bodyguards, all of them in civilian clothes, were stopped at a Serb roadblock in the Sarajevo suburb of Ilidza. The Serb troops disarmed Delves and his bodyguards – also from the SAS – stripped them of their clothes, weapons, Range Rover, computers and confidential documents and left them standing at the side of the road nearly naked. The lieutenant-general, reported SAS men who dealt with him afterwards, had not been amused.

The agenda at these meetings in Florida was to the point. President George Bush had asked sixty countries for their assistance in fighting a war to topple the regime of Saddam Hussein. Aside from the vital political allegiance of Tony Blair's government, President Bush wanted the

British SAS on board. He, the director-general of the CIA and General Franks were all too keenly aware of how close the British had come to capturing large segments of the al-Qaeda hierarchy in Afghanistan in late 2001, only to have their prizes slip away through lack of operational co-operation from overcautious US Special Forces. Bush, on the advice of Franks, also wanted the Australian SAS to join the Iraq operation, as well as Poland's Special Forces unit, GROM. Franks was well aware that the CO of the Australian Special Forces in Afghanistan, Lieutenant-Colonel Rowan Tink, had been awarded the Bronze Star by the Americans for his bravery in Afghanistan. Although the numbers of Special Forces troops provided collectively by the UK and its former colonial colleagues would be small – fewer than 1,000 soldiers – compared with the vast American SF deployment on Operation Iraqi Freedom – about 4,200 soldiers – the political allegiances and operational expertise were what counted.

The CIA immediately spotted in the Kurdish enclaves of Iraq another opportunity for their new political paramilitary operatives from the Special Operations Group to prove themselves. Teams of CIA staffers from Langley, Virginia, organised into 'proactive planning teams', had been highly successful in northern Afghanistan in 2001, along with US Special Forces, in co-opting the Northern Alliance into fighting alongside the US and coalition forces. It was decided that they should repeat their success in the harsh mountains and valleys of Kurdistan, bringing the Kurdish '*peshmerga*' guerrilla fighters from the rival Kurdish Democratic Party (KDP) and the Patriotic Union for Kurdistan (PUK) together in some semblance of a US-controlled allegiance against Saddam Hussein. By late autumn 2002, ten-man CIA teams backed up by small groups of US troops from the 5th Special Forces Group were infiltrating Kurdistan from Iran. They also went in by helicopter from the US air base at Incirlik in Turkey, and from Jordan. These ten-man teams and US troops based themselves in Kurdish enclaves in the Harir Valley outside Irbil, the *de facto* capital of Kurdistan, and around the north-western Iraqi town of Suleimaniya.

Their operational imperatives were simple: to train up to 30,000 Kurds in guerrilla warfare and to co-ordinate a psychological warfare campaign that would see up to 17 million leaflets distributed urging Iraqis to turn against their leader, as well as organising anti-Saddam and pro-American propaganda broadcasts on local radio stations. They were also desperately keen to impress upon the Kurds that were they to try to seize the two regional oil-producing centres of Kirkuk and Mosul, economically vital to all parties, Turkey would almost certainly respond by trying to invade northern Iraq in an attempt to prevent the formation of an independent Kurdish state, particularly one with access to oil reserves. The CIA teams, accompanied by Special Forces, would also be responsible for co-ordinating the seizure of the key airstrips at Bakra Jo near Suleimaniya, at Ainkawa, and at Bamarneh near the town of Dohuk, towards the Turkish border. Coalition control of these airfields would prove vital in the opening days of Operation Iraqi Freedom, allowing the Americans to open a second front in the assault against Baghdad.

Britain's Special Forces had, meanwhile, also been busy. By late February 2003, three operational 'Sabre' squadrons – 'B', 'D' and 'G' from 22 SAS numbering some 220 soldiers – along with fifty SF-trained signallers, plus medics, mechanics and pilots were deployed at forward operating bases in Jordan and Kuwait. More than 100 soldiers from the SBS were deployed with 3 Royal Marine Commando Brigade Group aboard the *Ark Royal* amphibious carrier group in the Persian Gulf. The British and Australian SAS were going in and out of Iraq from Jordan and Kuwait. Canada had, at the request of the United States, dispatched men from its specialist Joint Task Force Two to the Middle East. By early March 2003, the SAS headquarters at Credenhill was mostly quiet – the majority of its people were in the Middle East. Additional men had been drawn in from 'R' or Reserve Squadron, and from the more qualified, experienced members of the Regiment's two Territorial Army units, 21 and 23 SAS. 'A' Squadron had been left at home, on twenty-four-hour standby, to deal with any domestic terrorism situation arising within the UK, or involving British nationals abroad. As many personnel as possible from the Regiment's Training Wing, Revolutionary Warfare Wing and HQ Squadron had been detached to the Middle East as well. The 22 SAS CO was keenly aware that of all the units in his Regiment, 'A' Squadron had been in action most recently, in the most substantial way, when they had led the assault on the al-Qaeda position in Helmand Province during Operation Trent. 'C' Squadron, also involved in Operation Trent, reportedly rotated in a little after 'B' and 'D' Squadrons, as further assistance was required around Basrah and on the main thrust of the British advance, as well as in the western desert.

For the British, American, Australian, Polish and Canadian Special Forces teams, Operation Iraqi Freedom had begun long before Tomahawk Cruise missiles began slamming into Saddam Hussein's presidential palace, but they swung into an increasingly frenetic tempo of activity as the bombing campaign started. By 15 March 2003, US SF teams were in place south of Baghdad, British SBS, Royal Marine and US Navy SEAL teams were deployed to capture and secure oilfields in the desert near Basrah and offshore in the Gulf, while in north-western Kurdistan, CIA teams had been joined by US SF teams from Delta Force to prepare Kurdish guerrillas for initial assaults against Iraqi positions and against a small string of villages lying next to the Iranian border.

These villages were the operating base for Ansar al-Islam, a radical Islamic group believed by the Americans to be heavily linked to al-Qaeda. By the end of March 2003, these villages had been attacked in an operation involving 100 US Special Forces, including soldiers from Delta Force and the CIA, and up to 6,000 Kurdish '*peshmerga*' guerrillas. From 27–30 March 2003, this operation had taken place in the Beyara Valley, outside the town of Halabja. US SF teams had established an observation position in a mountain-top bunker on the peak known as Gilda Drozna. Flying over the Ansar al-Islam positions was a pilotless American UAV drone. Feeding back images from a video camera set into its nose-cone, the UAV allowed US personnel both in the Gilda Drozna observation post and at the HQ of Task Force Viking, as the US force was codenamed, at the top of the Beyara Valley, to monitor the battle in real time. Air strikes could be directed in as the progress of the battle was viewed on a video screen. A variety of ordnance was utilised, including Tomahawk Cruise missiles and aerial bombs from US fighter-bombers targeted in by laser designation systems operated by SF troops on the ground, in addition to more conventional artillery and mortar fire. A six-pronged attack was launched against the Islamic fighters by *'peshmerga'* guerrillas led by American troops. By the end of the action more than 150 enemy fundamentalist fighters had been killed, while some seventeen Kurds lost their lives. No US forces perished. Other SF teams from the US 5th Special Forces Group had meanwhile taken control of the airstrips of Bakra Jo, Bamarneh and Ainkawa. US paratroopers from the 173rd Airborne Brigade had parachuted into this area at the end of March to secure these airfields in preparation for establishing a second front for the coming fight against Baghdad.

In the suburbs of Baghdad, US forward air controllers – who had arrived in and around Baghdad as early as several weeks before the start of the bombing campaign right up to the beginning of it – were guiding in air strikes against Republican Guard targets, while in the centre of the capital the men from Delta Force were spotting targets for British and American air strikes. British SBS troops, operating with US amphibious specialists from SEAL Team 6 (DEVGRU) and Polish GROM Special Forces soldiers, had taken over oil platforms in the Persian Gulf and around the Al-Faw peninsula. The amphibious and marine operation to capture and secure the oil-production facilities of southern Iraq, particularly those around the port of Umm Qasr and on the Al-Faw peninsula, was the largest US Navy SEAL operation ever mounted. Led by officers from 3 Commando Brigade, the operation started tragically with the deaths of four US Marines and eight British soldiers and commandos when the CH-46 Sea Knight helicopter in which they were flying crashed a few kilometres south of Umm Qasr. On the British side, the operation involved Royal Marines from 40 Commando in addition to the SBS, with commando forward observation officers co-ordinating naval gunfire support as well as the fire from the Commando 105mm artillery batteries.

Out in the Gulf, the US Navy commandos stormed one platform, while the Poles were allocated the second. Both teams were dropped into the sea by helicopter at night and swam with full equipment to the base of the two oil platforms. The men were carrying ropes, explosives, fragmentation and stun grenades, Sig-Sauer handguns, MP5 Heckler & Koch sub-machine pistols, some of them in the MP5SD silenced version, and M4 Colt Commando assault carbines. Scaling the legs of the platform using ropes and magnetic pads that enabled them to climb hand-over-hand, the Poles reached the top of the platform's legs and consolidated. It was not known whether the rigs were manned or not, and if so, whether or not the occupants were armed or whether the oil platforms were booby-trapped. As the Polish teams made their way through the complex to the control room, an old telephone somewhere near them began to ring. The team froze, thinking that it had to be the tripping of the fusing and timer device of an explosive charge. After a few rings it went quiet. A GROM lieutenant who was on the rig that night commented that it was probably a wrong number.

When a photographer from Reuters news agency took some shots of the GROM operatives posing with DEVGRU men in the port of Umm Qasr – which the two different SF units had also taken – their superiors in Poland were concerned, to say the least. The men's supposedly covert presence had been drawn to the attention of the public. It did, however, do the GROM contingent nothing but good, and shortly afterwards they were asked to operate alongside Task Force 20, and to support the British Royal Marines' forthcoming attack on Basrah. Task Force 20, later to be renamed TF 21, then TF 121, was a composite multinational intelligence and Special Forces unit tasked with finding and arresting or killing senior figures from the former Iraqi regime, up to and including Saddam Hussein – basically the fifty-five most-wanted men whose faces appeared on the infamous US pack of cards.

At this time, US Special Forces were operating ahead of the US Marines

THE WAR THAT NEVER ENDED 191

on the road towards the capital, while 'psy-ops' specialists, SF teams, SIS and CIA agents were inside Basrah and other key cities trying to foment civil dissent between Ba'ath Party officials and anti-Hussein elements. Yet it was in the western desert of Iraq that one of the most salient and important operations was taking place.

In 2002, Brigadier-General Gary 'Shooter' Harrell, on the instructions of General Tommy Franks, had made a number of visits to Jordan. What Franks wanted from the Hashemite Kingdom was 'basing rights' – permission to base his Special Forces teams and aircraft inside Jordan for the forthcoming assault on western Iraq. Teams from 22 SAS had deployed to Jordan in autumn 2002 on exercises, during which the Americans claim that operations were conducted across the border inside Iraq, where, up until this point, only Israeli '*Sayeret*' teams were alleged to be operating. The main role for the special operations component of CENTCOM in western Iraq would be to deny Saddam Hussein the ground space from which to launch missile attacks against Israel or Egypt. By late autumn 2002, Jordanian 'basing rights' were in the bag and Harrell was able to set up a forward operating base (FOB) at Azraq Air Base in Jordan, towards the Iraqi border. By January and February 2003, the SF FOB was actively operational. At this Jordanian air base, alongside the American Rangers, US and British SF teams and the Australians who were shortly to arrive, there were two RAF Flights of four GR7 Harriers operating as 'designated' combat air support for the British SF teams. There were also ten US F-16 Fighting Falcons and an Air National Guard element of A-10 Warthog ground attack aircraft. The moment the war against Iraq started, the first objective for the British, Americans and Australians would be to seize a base inside Iraq from which they could operate. Their first targets would be the H1, H2 and H3 airfields in western Iraq.

On the night of 20 March, MH-6 'Little Bird' assault helicopters started attacking Iraqi border-defence positions. The small aircraft are armed with electronically operated 7.62mm miniguns and pods of multiple air-to-ground rockets. The Iraqi defences were quickly overcome and the coalition Special Forces deployment began. In Land Rovers and RAF Chinook helicopters, men from 'B' and 'D' Squadrons of the British SAS advanced in the dark on airfields H2 and H3. Iraqi resistance was light: the A-10 Warthog ground attack aircraft, with their nose-mounted 30mm Gatling guns capable of firing over 3,000 armour-piercing rounds a minute, backed up by Harriers and F-16s made short work of the ground defences. The coalition Special Forces called in combat air support and then simply drove their vehicles into the Iraqi air bases. The moment H2 and H3 were in allied hands, C-130 Hercules and Chinooks started deploying forward from Jordan, landing supplies, vehicles and the soldiers from the US 75th Airborne Rangers and Britain's 45 Commando who were to be responsible for the security of the air bases. Mobile Land Rover patrols of British and Australian SAS were operational almost immediately. On the night of 25 March, the American 75th Airborne Rangers dropped on to H1 airfield and captured it. The immediate operational objectives for the coalition SF teams would be to take control of the two main highways linking Baghdad with the Syrian border and Jordan, and to try to establish whether or not there were any Iraqi missile systems either already operational in western Iraq, or that could be brought into Iraqi territory from Syria.

While teams from the British and Australian SAS moved westwards during the following days in the direction of the Euphrates Valley, on 21 March a half-squadron of Australian SAS moved northwards, towards the Syrian border, tracking an intelligence report that Iraqi Scud launchers were attempting to deploy into Iraq's western desert from Syria. Behind them, air base H3 was feverishly busy: the airstrips were lined with American and British helicopters, and with the F-16s and A-10 Warthogs providing combat air support to the SF teams as they moved forward northwards and westwards. The intelligence that the Australians had received had confirmed that suspected Scud units were operating inside the Iraqi border: the two main dual carriageways to Syria and Jordan were being kept open by the Iraqis and protected by small groups of Iraqi commandos so that high-profile members of Saddam Hussein's regime could flee. As the SAS, both Australian and British, moved eastwards and north-eastwards, they were coming into contact with these groups, dispersing resistance along the two main road axes and carrying out 'area-denial' operations.

On 22 March, a troop of Australian SAS operating in six-wheel Land Rovers was tasked with destroying what they were reportedly told was the communications and headquarters element of an Iraqi missile battery that was to be deployed into the area from Syria. It had been repeatedly claimed by US intelligence assets that the Iraqis were trying to 'run' their Scud missile launchers across the border from Syria, fire them from Iraqi territory and then retreat back into Syria before they could be hit by coalition air strikes. Given that the volume of coalition air patrols over the Iraqi and Syrian borders was immense and that General 'Shooter' Harrell's entire Special Forces Task Force was looking for such an incursion, it would have been a tactically very difficult operation for the Iraqis to achieve, especially given the amount of satellite surveillance passing over the western desert area looking precisely for any images revealing telltale signs of such a Scud deployment. In spite of this, however, in the period immediately after the initial deployment into the 'H Bases', as they became known, in western Iraq, the Australians went into their first major contact.

The Iraqi command, control and communications facility was based on a small number of vehicles and some entrenched, well-dug-in positions. Up to fifty Iraqi soldiers were reported to be present in the area, along with five vehicles, yet the centre of the control facility appeared deserted when the Australians approached. A two-vehicle Australian patrol was, however, surprised by an unexpected Iraqi assault described in an Australian military report on the action as 'determined and aggressive', launched with a well-defined and well-aimed burst of automatic gunfire at the SAS men. The Australian patrol commander decided that an attack from a mobile patrol of two Land Rovers would take the Australians into the heart of the enemy position, and that the speed and surprise element of the attack would encourage the enemy to surrender. It did not quite work out that way. The Iraqis returned heavy fire as the Australian vehicles broke cover and approached them. An Australian SAS trooper, Bradley Vinnycombe, was manning a .50-calibre Browning heavy machine gun on one of the vehicles. The Australian Land Rovers were armed, like their British counterparts, with a variety of Brownings, 7.62mm GPMGs, 40mm M-19 grenade launchers and antitank rockets. As the Australian vehicles burst towards the Iraqis, Vinnycombe noticed that at least twenty Iraqi commandos and two vehicles had positioned themselves in such a way that they had the SAS patrol pinned down and were denying it freedom of movement. Swivelling the 'fifty-cal', he opened fire with the enormous 12.7mm rounds, scattering the Iraqi soldiers and hitting some of them. Moving to the Javelin missile system on the vehicle, he picked up a rocket and fired it from his shoulder at the first Iraqi vehicle, destroying it. The rest of his patrol and troop could now move forward, while he continued to fire with the Browning. His head and torso were exposed to Iraqi Kalashnikov rounds as he fired, the Browning cartridges juddering into the feed of the huge gun as he continued to engage the enemy. As his SAS colleagues moved forward towards the Iraqis, he continued his fire support, unleashing another Javelin missile into a second Iraqi vehicle, which promptly exploded. Iraqis near to Vinnycombe's vehicle were now setting up an 82mm mortar tube, so the SAS man grabbed his assault rifle and opened fire on the team, luckily succeeding with his first round in hitting the base of the mortar tube, in which a round was waiting to be fired. The mortar system exploded into the faces of the Iraqis operating it. The death toll of Iraqis from this action was judged to be around twelve out of a platoon strength of thirty or so. With two vehicles and six men, the Australians had accounted for a third of the enemy strength and forced the surrender of the rest without losing any of their own men.

By the end of March, more than two weeks after some of the Special Forces men had been deployed inside Iraq, an Australian half-squadron patrol in around fifteen vehicles were on the main highway, only 80km from Baghdad. Behind them in the dusty wake of their six-wheeled Land Rover patrol vehicles lay the smoking wreck of Al-Rutbah Prison, on to which Australian and American SF men had called combat air support a day earlier. By now the British and the Americans were approaching Baghdad, the entire western desert had been cut off to the Iraqis and on the southern outskirts of the capital, American Special Forces were waiting to link up with the US Marines. British SBS men, US Navy SEALs and Polish GROM Special Forces troops had seized the oil refineries on the Al-Faw peninsula, offshore in the Gulf and across the border from Kuwait. The SAS and SBS had supported the attacks on Basrah and, along with a US Delta Team, were deployed with Task Force 20 to assist in the tracking and arrests of senior figures in the former regime, and in the search for weapons of mass destruction. While 'B' and 'D' Squadrons of 22 SAS were operating in the western desert, it fell to 'G' Squadron, under Major Ivo Streeter – now with a Military Cross to his name after the fighting in Afghanistan – to be in charge of forthcoming SAS operations around Basrah.

The major land combat in Iraq was declared over by President Bush on 1 May 2003. Regardless of the fact that the guerrilla war in Iraq was, if anything, intensifying and US casualties were rising by the day, the US government had decided that once Baghdad had fallen, Saddam Hussein had vanished and coalition troops occupied the country, major conflict was at an end. George Bush was to be proved desperately, badly wrong. Throughout the blazing heat of the summer of 2003, Iraqi guerrilla fighters and foreign Islamic fundamentalists escalated their campaign against the Americans. There were sometimes up to thirty-six attacks on US servicemen and their installations in a single day. The Iraqis laid mines, placed explosive charges on bridges, in culverts and next to points on the roads where US vehicles would drive past. They ambushed the Americans again and again, with mines, explosives, RPG-7 rockets and Kalashnikov fire. They blew up their transport vehicles, machine-gunned their Humvees as they passed by, blasted antitank rockets from the ubiquitous RPG-7s at US foot and vehicle patrols, sniped at US positions at night, launched mortar strikes into their camps and fired missiles at their helicopters and aircraft.

Attacks tended to focus on the US-dominated sector in the centre and north of Iraq, where the majority of the population were Sunni, unlike the relatively pro-coalition Shi'ite population in the south. The British, based in the south in Basrah, were able to limit the spread of insurgency in their area of operations through superior military skills and a good track record in winning the hearts and minds of the local Iraqi population, skills they had perfected over the previous thirty years from Bosnia to Borneo and from Ulster to Aden. By late October and November 2003, there were some 9,000 UK troops in-theatre in Iraq, from the Light Infantry and the Green Jackets to the Parachute Regiment and the Queen's Royal Lancashire Regiment, from the Royal Tank Regiment and the Light Dragoons to medics, engineers, signallers and logisticians. At the helm was Major-General Graham Lamb, himself a former Director Special Forces. His nickname, depending on whom you talked to, was either 'Mad Dog' or 'Lambo'. During his time at the SF helm, he and the Regiment had been known as 'Mad Dog and his puppies'. The British took their casualties in Iraq, too, as on 24 June when six Royal Military Policemen were killed in southern Iraq, in the same town where eight paratroopers from the 1st Battalion had been wounded in an ambush on a patrol and a helicopter just days before.

In the scorching summer heat, the British patrolled on foot and in vehicles through the boiling streets and clamouring bazaars and along the dusty avenues of Basrah and the surrounding countryside. Their military aims were pacification, controlling crime and enabling the security situation to improve while the local infrastructure of schools, health clinics, hospitals, wells and local government was put into place. The Iraqis, both in Basrah and Baghdad, were quick to display that very common trait of a people liberated by a benign foreign force from an oppressing power: they took out their grievances against the former regime on the coalition forces. Like NATO in the Balkans, the white man was to blame for everything. Much of the local population was absolutely delighted to have the Americans and British in their country, but their appreciation was obscured by the declining security situation, the perpetrators responsible for which were those elements loyal to the former regime who were increasingly being aided by foreign Islamic fighters.

Nineteen people were killed on 7 August in a suicide bombing at the Jordanian Embassy in Baghdad; the UN headquarters in the capital was bombed on 19 August; and more than eighty-five Iraqis were killed in the Shi'ite Muslim holy city of Najaf by a bomb on 29 August. Bombings, shootings, ambushes, suicide bombings, sniper attacks, mortaring, roadside bombs, mines — the pro-Saddam Iraqi continued to unleash everything they had against the Americans in a series of daily attacks.

On 27 October, four suicide bombers targeted the headquarters of the International Committee for the Red Cross and four Iraqi police stations in Baghdad, killing forty people. The night before, the Al-Rashid Hotel in the centre of the capital, where many of the international administrators stayed, had been hit by a multiple-barrelled rocket-launcher strike during a visit by US Deputy Secretary of State for Defence Paul Wolfowitz. The hotel was situated in what had become known as the 'Green Zone', a heavily defended area of former-regime palaces, offices and hotels where the US military and coalition headquarters were based and where many of the international journalists, administrators, politicians, soldiers and aid workers had their offices. Part of the security for the 'Green Zone' was carried out by British Special Forces teams from the SAS and the SBS.

Throughout the summer and early autumn of 2003, the Americans had made a number of requests to the British government for a brigade of UK troops to be based in or around Baghdad. London, fearing that this would result in an increase in British casualties and would overextend the already severely overstretched British Army, had declined. But they had offered a compromise: the UK would deploy additional Special Forces teams outside of the British area of operations in the south, both to provide security assistance for the Americans, as they were already doing in the 'Green Zone', and to assist in providing 'security implementation' assets for the Iraq Survey Group. This team of scientists, intelligence officers and chemical experts was responsible for trying to track down any evidence of Saddam Hussein's alleged weapons of mass destruction (WMDs).

The additional SAS and MI6 men deployed on these operations would also be attached to the US–UK Special Forces and Intelligence group, known variously as Task Force 20. The British SF unit in Baghdad came under the command of a British lieutenant-colonel based at the American headquarters there, and was part of the small British advisory, training and operational co-ordination cell commanded by a major-general. There were from seventy-five to 120 British soldiers from the SAS, SBS and 14 Intelligence Company in Baghdad, with a smaller contingent – under a half-squadron of SAS and SBS – occasionally seconded in and around Basrah. Secondary to the intelligence and SF capabilities of the British and American Special Forces was a loosely defined Pentagon and CIA composite unit that had been put together to allow the coalition in Baghdad and the administration in the US access to ongoing intelligence operations without having to wait until they had been processed by the National Security Agency (NSA), the CIA or the Defence Intelligence Service (DIS). This unit, more accurately an intelligence-collating and -gathering unit drawing on the raw 'humint' or human intelligence flowing in from the covert SAS, SBS, Delta Force and US Navy operators in their hides out on the ground, was codenamed 'Grey Fox'. Like all covert intelligence units everywhere, Grey Fox also had more mundane appellations: in the rarefied world of Baghdad security circles it was referred to as 'the Group', 'the Collective' and even 'the Activity'.

The Iraqi capital had, by this point, also become the focal point for a roving 3,000-strong band of international security consultants made up of former members of the SAS, the SBS, Delta Force and every other imaginable US Special Forces unit, the German GSG-9, South African former 'Recce' and Special Forces soldiers plus former police, and lots and lots of staff from British private military companies (PMCs). Every hotel lobby, every building occupied by the coalition, every international headquarters, every meeting room and every checkpoint seemed to bristle and bulge with these ex-SF freelance security consultants and contractors, with their T-shirts, jeans, hand-held radio sets, holstered pistols, sunglasses, multi-pocketed waistcoats, several different types of Heckler & Koch sub-machine pistol, assault rifle or carbine and an all-consuming air of prioritised extreme urgency in their manner. On the up side, this meant that the serving members of the British SAS had a myriad number of unofficial intelligence gathering assets active in and around the capital in the form of their former colleagues.

Task Force 20 had been responsible for scoring the main coalition success against the Iraqi Sunni hardliners in the centre of the country on 22 July. An Iraqi businessman in Mosul had, on 21 July, made the last of a number of trips to a company base of the 101st Airborne Division in the northern city. His information was first-rate: Uday and Qusay Hussein, Saddam's two sons, were staying in his house in the affluent al-Falah neighbourhood of Mosul. The Iraqi building contractor finally persuaded the sceptical Americans to believe him. Claims of sightings of Uday and Qusay, respectively the ace of clubs and ace of hearts in the 'most-wanted' deck of cards, were relatively common. There was, after all, a $15 million bounty on each of their heads. The company commander from the 101st Airborne Division passed on the information to the Division's Special Forces liaison officer, who alerted the Delta Force and 22 SAS teams from Task Force 20.

There was a twelve-man team from 22 SAS operating with the Americans up in Mosul at that time, according to SAS sources familiar with the incident. One of the main advantages that the British had over the US Special Forces was they were much more adept at disguising themselves as members of the local population, their Arabic was sometimes superior and they were considerably less conspicuous than the large, rather obvious American Special Forces team members. The target of the operation was a two-storey building where the two brothers plus a bodyguard and Qusay's fourteen-year-old son were said to be hiding out. Uday Hussein, in particular, was no favourite of many mainstream Iraqis. He had been in command of Saddam Hussein's paramilitary *Fedayeen*. He also had a reputation for being a cruel, depraved playboy who cruised some of the more upmarket neighbourhoods of Baghdad at night; he would watch women walking along the streets and those who caught his eye and his profligate fancy were often kidnapped at gunpoint by Uday's henchmen and taken to one of the Hussein's palaces, where Uday and his friends would use them as sex-toys in multiple-rape sessions, often before killing them. His brother Qusay had been the senior Special Republican Guard commander and was also in charge of the notorious and feared State Security Sector detachment that had looked after Saddam Hussein. Both brothers had enemies, but realistically their betrayer had probably been lured by the vast sum of money on offer.

The 22 SAS soldiers estimated that their twelve men would be enough to storm the target, using the house-entry techniques that they had practiced so assiduously back at their close-quarters-battle training facilities at Pontrilas, 16km south of Hereford. The SAS plan was straightforward: their attack would take place that night, before either of the Hussein brothers became suspicious that their host had betrayed them.

The 22 SAS detachment in Mosul on the night of 21 July was commanded by a captain. He detached four men to perform a close target reconnaissance (CTR) to try to work out whether the house was in fact occupied, whether or not the Iraqi informant was trying to lure coalition forces into a trap – a common occurrence – and what defences, if any, were visible. When the CTR team reported back, their information was limited: the house was occupied; there were two entrances and, the team commander estimated, it would take some twelve men with explosives and entry equipment to storm the building and kill the four men thought to be inside. It was at this point that the 101st Airborne Division and the US coalition leaders intervened. The Americans were keen to show progress in the counterinsurgency campaign in Iraq and they also did not believe that twelve SAS men could storm the building safely and kill the occupants without taking heavy casualties themselves. Baghdad-based Lieutenant-General Ricardo Sanchez, commander of the US-led coalition ground forces in Iraq, wanted a definitive 'result' from this assault. Consequently, the operation was passed by the British to their American colleagues from Delta Force. The SAS men felt strongly, however, that they could have made the arrests in a different way, using practised close-quarters-battle and house-entry techniques rather than employing rockets to blow up the building.

The way in which the Americans went into the operation that day in Mosul was almost diametrically opposite to how the British would have handled it. It reminded observers, particularly the British, of another Task Force 20 action, again predominantly American, that had been carried out in Baghdad at the end of July that year. In the Baghdad suburb of Mansour, Task Force 20 had carried out a raid on a house belonging to an Iraqi prince, Rabiah Muhamed al-Habib, a man who by his own admission was respected and known by Saddam Hussein and was allegedly an associate of Ali, another of Saddam Hussein's sons. On Sunday 27 July, several cars containing members of Task Force 20 had arrived in the area to carry out reconnaissance. A local businessman, Ra'afet Saad, later described how the Americans had blown the gates off the compound and then, wearing gas masks, body armour and black T-shirts with brightly coloured identification lettering, had blasted their way into the building.

Prince Rabiah was 80km away at the time in Al-Kut, and only two of his bodyguards were inside the building, both of whom were arrested.

The outcome of the raid was a monumental public relations disaster – to put it mildly – for the Americans. Six Humvees and a variety of vehicles had been deployed at the major road intersections surrounding the prince's compound and a checkpoint set up, but unfortunately for the Americans, vehicles could also approach the area via unmonitored smaller back streets. At least two Iraqis were shot to death after approaching the palace along these back streets, reportedly indiscriminately by

Americans at the checkpoint, and another two were wounded. Casualties included a disabled man, a woman and her daughter. Another Iraqi who had not even been driving towards the US checkpoint was hit in the chest by two bullets as he slowed down 150m away simply to observe what was going on. A nearby restaurant was also hit by the Americans as they increased their volume of fire on and around the local civilian population. Given that US actions against the Iraqis were by this stage taking place dozens of times per day across the country, the subsequent loss of the 'hearts and minds' by the coalition as a result of incidents like these was staggering.

At the end of July, for the assault in Mosul against the Hussein sons, the Americans were going in heavily supported. In addition to the teams from Delta Force, they had on standby OH-58D Kiowa attack helicopters armed with 7.62mm miniguns and 2.75-inch rockets, Humvees armed with .50-calibre Brownings, TOW antitank missiles and M-19 automatic 40mm grenade launchers. The first Delta team through the door was fired on from the first and second floors with Kalashnikovs; they withdrew to the bottom of the stairs and then to the outside of the house, where grenades were dropped on to them from one of the balconies. As US negotiators used loudhailers and an interpreter to try to talk to Uday or Qusay Hussein – without success – Delta Force had another attempt at storming the building. It became apparent that there was a reinforced armoured door or some form of fortified position at the top of the staircase from behind which the defenders could fire down on their attackers. The second assault attempt was rebuffed as easily as the first. It was time for some fire support.

Antitank rockets and machine guns were fired at and into the building while a third assault was prepared, and when yet more fire was directed at the third team of Americans as they climbed the stairs, the company commander of the 101st Airborne Division outside, along with the Delta Force officer on site, took the decision to use heavier rockets. The third team was pulled back and ten TOW missiles were then fired into the building from the tops of the Humvees outside. A fourth team went in, this time to discover three dead people inside; a fourth, believed to be a body-guard, was shot and killed by the American troops. In the fortified room and on the stairs were the bloodied and bullet-struck bodies of three men and a fourteen-year-old boy. Two of them were, indeed, to be identified by DNA and dental records as Uday and Qusay Hussein, the second and third most-wanted men in Iraq.

At the end of October and the beginning of November in Iraq, three key things happened: the Americans lost the largest number of soldiers killed in one incident; the British lost their first SF soldier killed while serving with Task Force 20, and the first Polish soldier was killed in action. These three events were to highlight the ease with which the Iraqis could shoot down coalition helicopters; that British troops were no longer safe even in the predominantly Shi'ite southern region of the country; and that a main ally – the Polish – had also begun to take casualties.

On 2 November, in a wheatfield near the town of Fallujah some 48km west of Baghdad, the Iraqis scored their largest hit to date when they shot down an American Chinook helicopter with a guided missile. Just before 9.00 a.m. that morning, two CH-47 Chinook helicopters carrying American soldiers from the 10th Mountain Division based in Fallujah had taken off from the nearby Habbaniyah Air Base. With sixty troops and crew on board, the helicopters were heading for Baghdad International Airport, where the American soldiers were due to catch a flight back to the United States to go on leave. Many of them never got there. As the two Chinooks swooped fast and low over the small village of Hasai, south of Fallujah, there were two flashes from a clump of date palms set on the edge of a field of wheat. Two shoulder-launched ground-to-air missiles streaked into the sky. One missed the second helicopter, but the first Chinook was hit in the tail. It plunged to earth and burst into flames on landing, killing sixteen soldiers and injuring a further twenty-five. It was the most audacious and effective attack waged on the coalition forces since combat in Iraq had been declared over on 1 May, and it signalled to the Americans and the British that the counterinsurgency campaign in Iraq seemed still to be in its infancy.

Up until that day, the largest number of coalition troops or international humanitarian personnel that had been killed in one incident had been on 19 August, when twenty people were killed and a hundred injured when a suicide bomber driving a cement truck packed with explosives blew himself up outside the headquarters of the UN mission at the Canal Hotel in Baghdad. The attack not only killed the veteran UN chief in Iraq, Sergio Vieira de Mello — one of the lacklustre organisation's more talented bureaucrats — but also ripped the heart out of any reasonable hope for an effective humanitarian presence in the country.

By the end of the summer, fewer than thirty UN staff remained in the whole of Iraq. The UN secretary-general was Kofi Annan, the well-intentioned but ineffectual and essentially weak Ghanaian who, as head of UN Peacekeeping in the early 1990s, had been partially responsible for the disastrous debacle that had resulted in the failure of UN peacekeepers in Rwanda in April 1994 to take any effective action to halt the early stages of the Rwandan genocide. Nine years later, too little seemed to have improved in the ramshackle, inefficient and overfunded circus of international bureaucracy that the UN had become. Yes, there had been some effective missions in Africa run by the World Food Programme, the UN High Commission for Refugees had acquitted itself in a reasonably workable fashion in the Balkans in the early and late 1990s, and only those whose grasp of political economics was sketchy and character churlish would deny that the UN Interim Administration Mission in Kosovo had been groundbreaking in terms of an experiment in nation-state building.

Mr Annan wanted the UN to have a similarly fundamentally central role in the reconstruction and administration of Iraq. The problem was that the organisation was not up to confronting the security problems in Iraq and the Americans did not feel that the UN could handle the job. So when it came to simple matters of the security of its staff and peacekeepers and dealing with the awful possibility of actually having to earn the ludicrous levels of daily 'hazard' and 'danger' pay that slushed around the average foreign UN mission, it did what its critics had watched it do, sadly too often for its own good, in a dozen war zones over the preceding ten years. From the former Zaire, to Afghanistan, to Burundi, to Rwanda, to Liberia, to Iraq, to Kosovo, to Angola and to Somalia, when things got tough, too many of the UN's staff were evacuated – they packed their bags, turned off their laptops, got into their air-conditioned white Toyota Land Cruisers and drove as quickly as possible to the nearest airport for the first available flight out. They left behind not only their disenfranchised locally hired staff to face the music at the hands of their countrymen, but also the core international members of the mission who tended to be the ones who did all the work anyway. So it was in Iraq. The bombing in August left only the most capable international staff behind as a token skeleton presence, and even they were soon ordered to evacuate by Kofi Annan.

By September, almost every international organisation had left Iraq. A few of the more experienced, effective and die-hard veterans – *Médecins Sans Frontières*, for example – had stayed on, but when another suicide bomber blew himself and his vehicle up outside the Baghdad headquarters of the International Committee of the Red Cross on 27 October, hopes were almost non-existent for the continuing presence of a workable humanitarian presence in Iraq. By late summer 2003, the country was, in terms of foreigners, almost entirely run and administered by soldiers, or by the increasing number of private security contractors working for private military companies such as Olive Security, Erinys International, Rubicon, Kroll Associates and AKE. It was big boys' games, played to big boys' rules.

Even before the Iraqi attack on the Chinook on 2 November, the need for a change in the coalition's counterinsurgency methods had been recognised, and there is no place better to begin than with a name. Task Force 20 was renamed: the Americans had decided that the special operations and tactics teams searching for Saddam Hussein in Iraq, previously known as Task Force 20, and the team searching for Osama bin Laden in Afghanistan, known as Task Force 5, would now become one. From this point forward, Central Command's SF assets – British,

American, Australian and Polish – operating on the two high-profile manhunts became known as Task Force 121.

On 31 October, a Task Force 121 patrol made up of British and US Special Forces soldiers had been tasked with an attack on a compound of buildings in Mosul. A tip-off had suggested that there was a sizeable contingent of 'former regime loyalists' (FRLs) present there and a close target reconnaissance team was sent into the area. Task Force 121 was, by now, a fully developed anti-terrorist task force comprising Royal Marines from the SBS, elements of whichever squadron of 22 SAS was on rotation through Baghdad, US Delta Force teams and elements of the US Navy's Special Warfare Development Group or 'DEVGRU'. The intelligence received suggested that the compound was occupied by Hussein sympathisers and contained a stockpile of weapons, not just AK assault rifles, RPG-7 rocket launchers, mortars and grenades, but also shoulder-launched ground-to-air missiles. It was also suspected that the building might contain foreign fighters either from Syria, Yemen, Egypt or Saudi Arabia. Coalition intelligence officers had by this point, seven months after the end of land combat had been declared, divided their opposition into two distinct types. Firstly, there were the FRLs, who were all Iraqis – either hardline Ba'ath Party members, ex-*Fedayeen*, former members of the Special Republican Guard or former members of Saddam Hussein's intelligence services. Secondly, there were foreign fighters who were moving covertly across the border into Iraq from Jordan, Saudi and Syria.

On call for the Task Force 121 assault that night in Mosul were US Humvees armed with .50-calibre Browning heavy machine guns, M-19 40mm grenade launchers and TOW missiles, as well as OH-58D Kiowa attack helicopters. The British and American teams were taken into position in Mosul by MH-53 Pave Low helicopter, and then onwards by US Humvee. Many of the British SF soldiers working with the Task Force had taken to wearing US Army camouflage at this point. This had several benefits: it meant that they were indistinguishable from the Americans, which gave them an element of protection from exposure to the media, but most importantly it meant that the hostile Sunni Iraqis in the so-called 'Sunni Triangle' north of Baghdad did not know or suspect that they were in fact operating against British troops. For the Iraqis in the compound in Mosul that night, it was going to be far too late to do anything about it even if they were to realise who their attackers were. In the early days of the occupation of Baghdad, British Special Forces teams had been observed inside the capital wearing American camouflage; six months later, a group of ten to twelve SAS and SBS men standing at the Al-Jumhuriya Bridge entrance to the 'Green Zone' in Baghdad looked a little less uniform: gone was the US camouflage, in its place multi-pocketed waistcoats and chest webbing, M7 and C.8 Diemaco assault rifles with two magazines clipped together on each weapon, jeans and T-shirts on some men, khakis on others. By this point there were so many armed ex-pat civilians in Baghdad that the British could dispense with the 'uniform' and still blend in with everyone else. They were in place acting as a quick reaction force for the headquarters of the US 1st Armoured Division; in the event of an Iraqi attack on the headquarters they would deploy immediately, not only to counter the threat but also to arrest or kill the Iraqis who were physically firing RPGs or AKs at the HQ, or who were attempting to drive in vehicles loaded with explosives.

For the men of the SBS, the area around Mosul held some mixed memories. It had been in this part of northern Iraq in April that an SBS patrol had been forced to leave behind some of its equipment – Land Rovers, 'quad' bikes and motorbikes – after its position was compromised by an Iraqi patrol. The SBS unit had found itself in a sticky situation. Depending on whose reports are to be believed, be they those of US intelligence (furious), the British SAS (amused), Iraqis (delighted), MI6 (baffled) or the British *Mail on Sunday* newspaper (outraged and sensationalist), the incident was either relatively low-key, a lucky escape, an accident of war or a total disaster. In early November 2003, a number of senior British Special Forces officers appeared before the House of Commons Defence Select Committee and Secretary of State for Defence Geoffrey Hoon to complain that the SBS unit had been compromised because of poor intelligence received about the area in which they were going to be operating.

The facts appear to be that a convoy of SBS vehicles, including Land Rovers armed with 7.62mm GPMGs and .50-calibre Brownings, had been operating in an area near Mosul during the middle of April. Royal Marines on motorbikes and 'quad' bikes accompanied the Land Rovers. The number of Land Rovers reportedly on the patrol range from four to ten or more. At one point out on patrol, the unit is said to have driven past a vehicle-mounted Iraqi patrol, which was in fact the point reconnaissance unit of a much larger Iraqi force, including tanks, that was following behind. The SBS men and the Iraqis drove past each other without either side opening fire, and by the time the British troops realised what had happened, they were face to face with a much larger Iraqi force. A lot of equipment was abandoned at the scene, of which some items – including a Land Rover, a 'quad' bike and a motorbike – were filmed by the Iraqis and the tape passed to be broadcast on *Al-Jazeera* television, much to the embarrassment of the British. The SBS men escaped in a variety of remaining vehicles and almost all were exfiltrated by helicopter. The Americans claimed that among the abandoned British kit was a Stinger ground-to-air missile which the Iraqis not only removed and kept, but later used to shoot down a US F-16 fighter.

Six months later, the SBS – in the form of a part of Task Force 121 – were back in Mosul. 31 October had been a busy, hot, dusty, violent day of combat, bombings and rocket attacks in that northern city of 1.7 million people. The American forces were increasingly convinced that many of the attacks against the coalition were being directed by General Izzat Ibrahim al-Douri, a former commanding officer in the Iraqi Army in the northern region of the country and the former vice-chairman of the Revolutionary Command Council. Mosul was the city where Uday and Qusay Hussein had been killed by Delta Force in July and where hardline pro-regime loyalists had been fighting not only the Kurds but the American Special Forces who were training them, since months before the war had started in March 2003.

During the morning of 31 October, the US headquarters at Mosul Airport had been hit by three rockets fired from Russian-made '*Katyusha*' multiple-barrel rocket launchers – most probably, the Americans estimated, from the 122mm BM-21 'Grad' variant. The Iraqi police station at al-Majmua, staffed by officers of the newly formed Iraqi Police, had also been targeted in a drive-by shooting and a US vehicle travelling on a road in the Qasr al-Mutran district in the centre of Mosul had been hit by a bomb. US troops had cordoned off the area and had discovered another bomb hidden in rubbish near the first device. By late afternoon, local informants reconnaissance teams from the Special Forces and intelligence received from US helicopter pilots who had been overflying Mosul that day trying to spot the locations from which the Iraqis were firing and attacking had come back with a positive assessment. Armed men had been seen entering and exiting a compound, some carrying RPG-7s, and increasing levels of activity around the compound were being reported as the afternoon wore on. Mortars had been seen being moved; pickup trucks parked inside the compound were being loaded. The US military suspected that the Iraqis and possibly some foreign fighters who might also have been in the compound were going to mount an attack in force that evening or during the night against the coalition forces and the Iraqi police. The US commander on the ground, in consultation with Task Force 121, decided to attack it that night.

The teams that took part in the assault on the compound were made up of soldiers from the SAS and SBS, as well as American commandos from Delta Force. An outer cordon extending up to 1km around the compound was set up by US paratroopers from the 101st Airborne and the Iraqi police. Task Force members backed up by heavily armed Humvees took the British and Americans to within 500m of the target and dropped them off into the hot dust and night-time heat at six different street intersections, fearful that by approaching any closer to the compound, the noise of US vehicles would alert the occupants. The six teams of four men each were backed up by fire-support groups armed with 7.62mm and 40mm grenade launchers who, the moment the first shots were fired, would pour rifle grenades and machine-gun fire into the compound before the assault team itself was through its metal gates. Initial targets would include the four-wheel-drive pickups parked inside the compound, thought to contain 82mm mortars and ground-to-air missiles. The moment the front and back gates were blown off with explosive charges, the assault team would pour through and over the walls into the compound. By 10.00 p.m. it had become apparent that the Iraqis and foreign fighters inside were ready to make a move and possibly launch another attack. The order for the Task Force to go in was given.

The compound was hit from four different points by the multinational Special Forces teams. The main gate into the compound was strafed by bursts of machine-gun fire and a series of rifle grenades as startled sentries within began to return fire at the SF teams coming through the main gate and over the walls. A combination of Iraqi and foreign fighters inside the compound buildings streamed out of its front and rear doors, while others opened fire from windows and after climbing on the roof. A small joint team of SBS and SAS men managed, within the first two to three minutes, to get in through the front gate, firing their C7 and C8 Diemaco assault rifles straight at the opposition, changing their magazines with quick flicks of the wrist. The Iraqis and foreign fighters poured fire back on them. During the assault on the compound, there was a series of heavy exchanges of fire and an SBS man – Corporal Ian Plank – was killed and four soldiers from the SAS were injured. But the compound was eventually taken. Ten Iraqis were reported dead and an undisclosed number of foreign fighters, including Saudi Arabs, were captured.

The third incident of note that took place at the beginning of November, as the Americans began to fear that the Iraqi insurgency was moving northwards out of the 'Sunni Triangle' and into the north of the country around Mosul, was that the first Polish soldier serving on attachment to the coalition was killed. Forty-four-year-old Major Hieronim Kupczyk was killed in an ambush south of Baghdad. A 2,400-strong Polish contingent had been in charge of a sector south of the capital, around Al-Hilla, since September, but the Polish involvement, particularly at a Special Forces level, predated that by several months. Under the command of their US Ranger-trained colonel, Roman Polko, fifty-six GROM commandos were detached to serve on Operation Iraqi Freedom in 2003. The Polish were one of the 'new European' countries that most strongly supported the United States in their War on Terrorism. Historically sandwiched between, and repeatedly invaded by, Germany and Russia, the Poles had been moving closer towards the Americans in terms of forming tactical military and political allegiances since long before they joined NATO in 1999. [4]

By the time President Bush announced the end of major fighting in Iraq in May, many soldiers in the SF contingents, particularly the Australians, who were on their way home to Perth, must have thought that the major conflicts, combats and contacts in Iraq were over. They, however, like everybody else, had underestimated the strength of the oncoming Iraqi guerrilla onslaught, and the extent to which Special Forces units like Task Force 121 were going to continue to be in action in the new Iraq. The war may have been officially over, but the savage fight for peace was just beginning.

(4) The development of the Polish Special Forces capability is a microcosm of the country's relationship with the United States. The Russians had always been strongly opposed to the idea of their western satellite state developing any Special Forces capability, fearful that it could engender rebellious, partisan tendencies that the bulk of the Soviet-trained Polish military hierarchy would not be able to control. After the end of the Cold War, in the face of bull-necked, ex-communist, narrow-minded thinking from the upper echelons of the Polish military, a small group of officers began to develop a team of Special Forces whom they modelled on the British SAS, and on the US Delta Force and Navy SEALs.

A sharp-minded and independent thinker, Colonel Gromoslaw Czempinski was a former parachute colonel when he reportedly led a small group of Polish commandos on a mission into western Iraq in the First Gulf War, their target being a small group of CIA officials held by the Iraqis. The Polish Operational Mobile Reserve Group or *Grupa Reagowania Operacyjno Mobilnego* (GROM) contained a younger officer on that mission in 1991– Slawomir Petelicki – who went on to command the group, naming it GROM not only after its initials or because '*grom*' means 'thunder' in Polish, but also in honour of Colonel Gromoslaw. The group found the beginnings of its operational niche in 1990 during Operation Bridge, during which Poland helped Soviet Jews enter Israel. Mindful that

Hezbollah and the Popular Front for the Liberation of Palestine were reportedly operating inside Poland, GROM assured an anti-terrorist capability that brought it to the notice of some of the more militarily flexible officers in Warsaw. After their success in the First Gulf War, the unit began to instigate training exchanges with British and American Special Forces, and to emulate them operationally.

Their training and formation were familiar: operating in four- to six-man teams, trained in HALO techniques, mountain warfare, unarmed combat, a high degree of weapons skills, proficient in underwater warfare, long-range reconnaissance and long infiltrations by night, all culled during a gruelling selection process in the Carpathian Mountains in southern Poland that weeded out 90 per cent of applicants, their operational *modus operandi* was a composite of skills learned and cross-trained with Hereford, Fort Bragg and the Israelis. The Poles make excellent SF troops. There is something about the Polish character that lends itself to producing extremely competent, long-suffering and courageous soldiers. In 1997 the unit was responsible for arresting the Serb war criminal Slavko Dokmanovic, indicted by a Hague tribunal for his part in the deaths of some 200–260 Croats and other non-Serbs. As the President of Vukovar municipality, Dokmanovic was judged to have been responsible for allowing Yugoslav Army soldiers and Serb paramilitaries to remove more than 200 people from Vukovar Hospital in 1991, where they had been sheltering after the shelling of the city. The group was taken from the hospital to a nearby farm complex, where they were tortured and beaten. In groups of ten to twelve, they were then taken away to nearby Ovcara, where the group, mainly Croats, were shot to death. GROM arrested the former municipal president in 1997 in an operation during which several of his bodyguards were killed. Dokmanovic hanged himself in his Hague cell shortly before a verdict was passed in his case in 1999.

CHAPTER EIGHT

A World of Our Own

Iraq Onwards, 2004

With a pistol, a stash of cashew nuts and $750,000 in cash, Saddam Hussein was finally found in a hole in the ground at a farmhouse in Al-Dawr, south of his birthplace in Tikrit, on 14 December 2003. Almost from the moment he was hauled out of his 'spider hole' to face the glare of the Maglite torches and M4 assault rifles of the 1st Brigade Combat Team of the 4th Infantry Division, the unit that had actually found him, there was enormous speculation that his capture would lead to a significant drop in anti-coalition violence in Iraq. This was not to prove the case. Control over the foreign fighters and former Ba'ath Party members who were behind the attacks on coalition forces in Iraq was in the hands of a number of people, and it transpired that Saddam Hussein had actually had very little direct control over anti-coalition terrorism while he had been in hiding.

Attacks on the Americans continued. The British SAS and SBS teams based in Baghdad and Basrah had had no part in the capture of Saddam; their most high-profile success in December 2003 and January 2004 came when they were part of a composite unit that captured Watban al-Tikriti, number thirty-seven on the 'most-wanted' list. The British Special Forces took two high-profile losses themselves on the morning of New Year's Day 2004 when a major seconded to 22 SAS from the Welsh Guards and a sergeant seconded from the Cheshire Regiment died in Baghdad. Major James Stenner and Sergeant Norman Patterson were reportedly returning from a party where they had been celebrating with American Special Forces. The four-by-four vehicle they were driving crashed into a series of concrete bollards at the Assassins' Gate' entrance to the coalition-controlled 'Green Zone'. Both men died almost instantly. It was doubly tragic because Stenner, who was acting as the 22 SAS operations officer at the coalition headquarters in the 'Green Zone', had been awarded the Military Cross for gallantry the previous year in Iraq. However, Iraq was to prove more taxing to the Regiment in a different and rather more subtle way than as a result of men lost through combat or accidents.

There were a large number of private military companies (PMCs) operating in Iraq by early 2004, predominantly in Baghdad. Many of these, such as Rubicon, Erinys International, Global Risk Strategies, Kroll Associates and Control Risks, among others, employed large numbers of former British soldiers, predominantly from the Special Forces, the Royal Marines and the Parachute Regiment. These men – former officers, NCOs and other ranks – were employed in every sphere of the security industry in Iraq. They acted as bodyguards for international coalition officials, looked after television crews, protected buildings, provided corporate security, safeguarded oil interests and trained the Iraqi Police Force and the new Iraqi Army. In short, they were everywhere. They managed small private armies made up of Fijians and ex-Gurkhas; in the absence of UN peacekeepers and a UN peacekeeping mandate, this was the alternative. Former soldiers who knew how to soldier and how to provide the security services demanded of them, they were a military world-within-a-world, a workable, privatised, efficient, voluntary, corporate response to many of the security and peacekeeping demands of the new Iraq.

They got into their share of fire fights, saw their bit of action and were essentially in that place where many soldiers often prefer to be: in the thick of the action in the most dangerous, high-profile theatre of operations on earth, surrounded by and operating with friends and other like-minded professionals who understood them, all the while doing a job they felt to be worthwhile. The main difference between them and regular soldiers was that they got paid much, much more, particularly as they were working for large, cash-rich international contractors who had won vast multimillion-dollar projects from the coalition and the United States. Also, because Iraq was so dangerous, they could pretty much set their own rules and pay levels.

Like US and British troops, international expatriates and coalition officials, these PMC employees came under fire, too. And the former SAS soldiers, as well as those who had learned their skills with Delta Force or the Australian SAS, were rather good at firing back. In autumn 2003, a four-by-four containing two ex-22 SAS men came under ambush in Baghdad by three armed Iraqis in a saloon car. One ex-Hereford man was hit, but the pair managed to return fire effectively, killing two of the Iraqis. The third Iraqi, already wounded, died at the hands of one of the ex-SAS men who, having returned fire, walked across to the Iraqis' car and beat the wounded survivor to death. It was all the more extraordinary a feat because this ex-SAS man was reportedly nearly sixty years old. In another incident outside Tikrit in mid-April, towards the end of the coalition bombing campaign, a group of journalists from CNN were entering the town when they were fired upon by a group of Iraqis chasing them in a car. The Iraqis were sufficiently surprised and shocked to give up the chase when a lengthy burst of 9mm machine-pistol fire from a Heckler & Koch MP5 riddled their car. Driving the CNN vehicle, steering with one hand and firing with the other, was a former corporal from 'D' Squadron, 22 SAS.

This semi-military, semi-civilian lifestyle with its high levels of pay was immensely attractive to both serving and former Special Forces soldiers. A corporal serving in the SAS could make around £30,000 per annum, with parachute pay and various allowances thrown in; working in Iraq for a PMC, he could make that in four months. Why stay in the SAS when you stood a far greater chance of seeing some action outside of it and could end up being paid three times as much in the process? Consequently, the war in Iraq was beginning to present the British Special Forces with a problem. On the one hand it provided an operational forum where all of their skills could be put into practice; on the other, it had become an environment that was to prove extremely tempting to SAS men wondering whether or not to leave the Army. The Regiment suddenly found itself facing a massive personnel problem.

Any man serving within the Regiment can ask for an interview with the commanding officer, during which he can request premature voluntary release (PVR) from the unit. Up until fairly recently, very few soldiers wanted to leave the SAS, having fought so hard to get into it in the first place. But by the beginning of 2004, there was more money and more action to be had elsewhere. Forty men of all ranks had requested PVR to come into effect by the end of 2004. This meant that the Director Special Forces and the CO of 22 SAS were going to lose the equivalent of two-thirds of an operational squadron, many of them senior corporals and junior sergeants who would be extremely costly and difficult to replace. From mid-2003 onwards, the Regiment also changed the way in which its amphibious warfare assets were deployed, and at any given time up to twenty-four soldiers from the various squadrons' Boat Troops were to be attached to the SBS. The SAS was now confronted with the possibility of losing an entire squadron of its strength.

Faced with this problem of haemorrhaging men just when the operational demands being made of the SAS were higher than ever, the SF authorities were forced to consider how to address the problem. Lower the standards of unit selection? Allow direct entry into the SAS? Coming at the end of a tour of command which had seen the CO of 22 SAS take his men into action in Afghanistan and Iraq, this latest dilemma must have seemed desperately unfair. Yet it was the evolving nature of the international community's deployments and the nature of the way in which peacekeeping was becoming a semi-privatised affair that was responsible. It must have seemed ironic that having chafed at the bit to get his men into action in Afghanistan, he was only to find that Iraq threw up an unforeseen conundrum that left him very short-staffed just when he needed his men most.

The SAS was not alone in thinking that the world pre-11 September 2001 had been a simpler place. The events in New York had, for instance, also brought the conflict in Macedonia almost to a standstill. The line from the Americans to both the Macedonian government and the Albanian rebels was simple: we have another, very big war to fight. So behave. There was, however, to be a last gasp of conflict in the oak trees and cornfields of northern Macedonia in early September 2003. In the tiny village of Brest, on the slopes of the Crna Gora mountain range on the border with Kosovo, a handful of Albanian gunmen started the day with coffee and cigarettes, Kalashnikovs and handguns sliding around their feet as they sat in one of the village's cafés. The last remnants of the Albanian National Liberation Army (NLA) that had so nearly brought the government in Skopje to its knees two years before had now consolidated themselves into yet another nationalist grouping. This time it was called the Albanian National Army or *Armata Kombetare Shqiptare* (AKSH).

There weren't that many of them, and compared to the fully fledged guerrilla tactics employed so successfully by the NLA two years before, they had hardly had any operational experience worth the name. There had been a few half-hearted ambushes of NATO soldiers inside Kosovo, night-time affairs during which scared and inexperienced Spanish or French soldiers would be relieved of their weapons at gunpoint; a mortar bomb on a railway line in Macedonia; 100 rounds of RPK machine-gun ammunition loosed off at a Serb border post. Following such attacks, a press release burning with nationalist pride and the obligatory orange, red and black of the double-headed eagle and the AKSH rebel insignia would be faxed through to newspaper offices in Pristina and Tirana, or posted on the gaudy electronic pages of a web site maintained from a run-down sitting room somewhere on the Munich ring road. The tone would be the same as ever, promising the beginning of another campaign of liberation whereby all lands belonging to Albanian-speaking people would finally be united, from the Presevo Valley in southern Serbia, to the west of Montenegro, the north of Macedonia, Albania itself and, of course, the heartland, Kosovo. Armed liberation fighters would push the Serb and Slav occupiers out and the new dawn skies of the great victorious beginning would belong to the double-headed eagle. And in the newspaper offices of Pristina and Skopje, and elsewhere where such things were taken seriously, the loyal Albanian press would print the press releases word for word, and the Western diplomats and their analysts in Belgrade, Kosovo, Skopje and Macedonia would send the obligatory diplomatic cables to their Western capitals warning their governments not to take the threat seriously. Greater Albania meant one thing, quipped a Western analyst in late 2003 after five years of watching the KLA, the NLA, the AKSH and other rebel groups pontificate about it: 'Chaos that would stretch over half of Montenegro and Macedonia and northern Greece, rather than just over Kosovo and Albania itself.'

It was certainly true that by 2003 much criminal expansion had taken place – Albanian gangs controlled some 75 per cent of the European heroin trade, worth $15 billion a year – but in terms of a physical expansion of lands governed by or under the control of Albanians, little had changed. Kosovo was still struggling to come anywhere near to independence and low-key talks with the Serb authorities had been scheduled to start in Vienna, under heavy international supervision. Kosovo's political leaders were still daydreaming about fully autonomous status, their own army, a fully functioning economy, but the reality was that the political economy of Kosovo, like Bosnia's, was stagnating fast as the withdrawal of international funding left both places with political and financial status quos that barely worked. Kosovo's leaders were fantasising about their own airline when more than half of the population didn't have jobs. The takeover of the European crime scene by Albanians and Kosovars had finally lost them any sympathy on the European stage: the glory days of June 1999, when the streets of Prizren, Pristina and Peja were a sea of flowers, NATO troops and liberated Kosovars, were gone for ever.

So when Macedonian Special Forces troops from the 'Wolves', the best the army had to offer, accompanied by men from the 'Tigers', the Macedonian police's claim to SF fame, gathered in the pre-dawn chill outside the village of Brest one morning in early September 2003, nobody in the international community paid too much attention. An American soldier was dying daily in Iraq, Afghanistan was falling to pieces and North Korea was about to announce that it had nuclear missiles. Who cared about Macedonia anymore? The AKSH had pontificated, attitudinised and let off mortars and machine-gun rounds at a variety of targets during that long, hot Balkan summer. Now, they had decided, it was time for action. There had been a brief standoff in and around the village of Vaksince, one of the centres of the 1999 fighting, during the week preceding the events in Brest, but Macedonian forces had been held back from assaulting the village by the British brigadier liaising with their Ministry of Defence in Skopje. The fight that the Albanians wanted was not going to be theirs. A small 'thin red line' of senior British Army officers had been attached to the Macedonian MOD and the Interior Ministry since the Ohrid Peace Agreement had come into full force in November 2003. Theirs was to be a restraining hand when the more hot-headed senior Macedonian Army and police officers wanted to go and have another crack at the Albanians. As they were based in the operational centres of the two respective Macedonian government ministries, they were normally able to prevent incidents of rash Macedonian overkill. It was another small, undersung British military triumph.

The assault on Brest began with some rocket attacks by the Mi-24 helicopter gunships, flown by Ukrainians, that had been such a mainstay in the war two years before. Against the early morning sky the familiar *clat-clattering* of their rotors was heard, but this time their strikes were carefully targeted: a few Albanian machine-gun positions outside the village were hit, and then the troops went in. After a few hours of sporadic fire fights, a handful of Albanians were killed, some wounded and several captured. The Macedonians claimed not to have lost any men. The incident was briefly reported, and then the ripples the shooting had stirred on the tiny corner of the pond of international affairs that Macedonia had become edged gently outwards, and were calm.

To the west, in the forested mountains of eastern Bosnia, western Montenegro and Republika Srbska, the hunt for Radovan Karadzic was still ongoing. It had been a long, drawn-out affair. The former commander of the Bosnian Serb Army was still at large and, after Osama bin Laden, was still the most-wanted war criminal in the world. There had been several Special Forces operations mounted to snatch him since the Dayton Peace Accords had been signed and implemented in 1995. The main difficulty with apprehending Karadzic was that he was very well guarded by a floating team of loyal Serb soldiers, paramilitaries and bodyguards, whose numbers were estimated to have ebbed and flowed from some 500 to 150 between 1995 and 2003. He was highly mobile and changed hiding places constantly in an area of land where he was surrounded by his supporters, where he and his bodyguards would be tipped off the moment any NATO troops appeared, and which was well suited to defensive actions. By the time armoured personnel carriers full of German or American or French troops were spotted travelling on roads towards Foca or Prijedor or some other mountain village where he was thought to be hiding, he would have been warned off in plenty of time to flee.

One of the most recent operations that had failed to catch him had taken place in March 2002. On the first of that month, at 8.00 a.m., a squad of American Black Hawk helicopters thundered over the mountain passes and wooded ravines of the terrain south-west of Sarajevo. Just after 8.00 a.m., groups of US commandos from a joint Navy SEAL and Army Special Forces detachment exited the helicopters in the mountain hamlet of Celebici, where Karadzic had been spotted a day before. The US soldiers, faces covered with black masks, burst from their Black Hawks before they had had time to fully land. All roads leading in and out of the village had been sealed off by US Army Humvees and German armoured personnel carriers. A large group of children were immediately rounded up and centralised in one classroom of the local school building. The US Special Forces troops then went from house to house, blowing off the doors that wouldn't open or yield to rifle butt or booted foot, and looked for Karadzic. He was gone. A few shoulder-mounted ground-to-air missiles were found, some documents, a cache of weapons, but no war criminals. A thorough search of the village and the surrounding countryside over the following days produced nothing. Within hours, reports started filtering out of the headquarters of NATO's Stabilisation Force (S-FOR) in Sarajevo that the reason Karadzic had made good his escape was that he had been tipped off in advance by a mobile telephone call made to one of his bodyguards by a French officer in Sarajevo.

Three weeks later, if the local press in Montenegro was anything to go by, another snatch-attempt had been made either in the eastern Bosnian village of Srbinje or inside Montenegro itself. Ten Special Forces soldiers from the British SAS had been killed and two wounded, the Montenegrin press reported, and the failure of the operation had been covered up by the various Western governments involved. How *Dan* newspaper in Podgorica came by this information is unclear; while it is by no means impossible that the SAS would be involved in a deniable operation, the likelihood of ten SAS soldiers being killed without anybody in the British media discovering it is very unlikely. Had the SAS men been killed in a fire fight with Serbs, photographs of their bodies, equipment, identity cards and possessions would have been splashed in a triumphant manner all over the Serb nationalist media in Belgrade, Podgorica and Sarajevo within twenty-four hours.

The operations around Celebici were a long way from, and a complete vindication of, the British SAS operations such as 'Tango One' and 'Tango Two' around Banja Luka and Prijedor between 1997 and 1999. Between 1995 and December 1999, when twenty men from 22 SAS had seized Serb General Stanislav Galic from his car in Banja Luka without firing a shot, there had been fifteen international operations to arrest war

criminals in post-Dayton Bosnia. Fifteen people had been arrested, two
shot dead. Of these fifteen operations, eleven had taken place in the
British sector, involving British Special Forces assets.

By autumn 2003, there was little time left for the Hague-based International Criminal Tribunal for the Former Yugoslavia (ICTY) to process
the indictments and court cases of many more Balkan war criminals.
Scheduled to wind up its affairs by 2008, many of its original targets
were still at large. The trial of Slobodan Milosevic was still ongoing in
The Hague. There appeared to be precious little time left in which to
capture and have transferred to The Hague the individuals topping the
ICTY's most-wanted list. In Kosovo in March 2003, an operation carried
out by a snatch-squad of Italian *Carabinieri* from K-FOR's Multinational
Support Unit, backed up by Norwegian and British troops, had arrested
three Kosovo Albanian suspects on war-crimes charges. The nature of
their crimes was straightforward: in 1998 they were alleged to have participated in the killings, torture, beatings and maltreatment of Albanians
and Serbs held at a small KLA detention centre at Llapushnik in Kosovo's
Drenica Valley. The detention facility or mini-concentration camp had
been run and overseen by one Fatmir Limaj, an aggressive, capable and
single-minded KLA staff officer who ran much of the rebel organisation's operations in the Drenica. After the war ended and the KLA disbanded, Limaj joined the higher echelons of the Kosovan political
establishment, becoming vice-chairman of Hacim Thaci's Democratic
Party of Kosovo (PDK). Like all such political parties formed from the
relics of a successful guerrilla army, in reality there was startlingly little
that was democratic about Thaci's party. The PDK elbowed its way to
the top of the political system in Kosovo through the old Albanian tried
and trusted means of killing, terrorising and intimidating its opponents.
A hardcore of former KLA commanders sat at the centre of the PDK
and Limaj was one of them.

Good-looking, tough, youthful and energetic, he was in many ways
the kind of politician that Kosovars actually needed: a man of war and
action, a hero, somebody who had fought for Kosovo's liberation, a

person they could look up to. He was also a politician who was attentive to the needs of the population in his constituency. At political meetings in the poorer parts of Pristina he sat patiently, answering the questions of impoverished Kosovo Albanians who, by late summer 2002, had rather lost track of what it was exactly that the international community was doing in Kosovo. They wanted simple questions answered: when would they have a workable supply of hot water? When would the power stations outside Pristina deliver them a reliable supply of electricity? For many Kosovars, Fatmir Limaj's little business in Llapushnik, running his own detention centre, was of minor import. Who cared anyway? The inmates had all been collaborators or Serbs. Thus ran the Kosovo Albanian train of thought by mid-autumn 2002, when Fatmir Limaj, suited and groomed, was off on the stump campaigning for election as the new Mayor of Pristina. He didn't get elected, which was probably a loss for the people of Kosovo's capital.

One weekend in March 2003, he decided to take a skiing holiday in Slovenia with Hacim Thaci. The two former KLA commanders flew from Pristina Airport to Ljubljana on Adria Airlines, the Slovenian national carrier. As they passed through Slatina Airport, international border policemen from UNMIK made no attempt to stop them. Their names were not on any wanted list. They had left behind them a capital city a-buzz with rumours. Everybody was expecting there to be an imminent arrest, by NATO on behalf of the Hague Tribunal, of one or more leading Kosovo Albanians who had served in the KLA. Everybody, either from the international community or the Albanian population, had their list of favoured suspects. Word on the streets of Pristina, where winter snow had turned to grey mud and dust blown by the freezing wind, was that British and German Special Forces would be sent to Kosovo to arrest these suspects, in a replay of the seizure of the Albanian men who had bombed the Nis Express bus in February 2001. Up at Slim Lines, the barbed wire compound set on a hill overlooking Pristina that housed the headquarters of the Multinational Brigade Centre (MNBC), plans were being drawn up.

The chief prosecutor from The Hague, Carla del Ponte, had made no secret of the fact that she and her teams had been investigating Kosovo Albanian former rebel commanders since the end of 1999. Up until the fall of Milosevic in autumn 2000, the main resistance to arresting ex-KLA commanders had been from the Americans and the British, the two nationalities who had played the largest part in training the KLA and subsequently in facilitating their entry into mainstream Kosovo politics. As we have seen with the American involvement both with the UCPMB and the NLA in Macedonia, the US intelligence agenda was far from straightforward. The British position towards the ex-KLA men such as Hacim Thaci, Ramush Haradinaj, Agim Ceku and Fatmir Limaj was inclusive. All of them were on the British diplomatic cocktail party invitation list; all of them had stood, slightly ill at ease, at parties in the British diplomatic residences in Pristina, glasses of the ubiquitous red Macedonian Vranac wine getting warm in their palms. In private, these ex-rebels made no secret of the fact that when it came to dealing with former members of the KLA, they and everybody else in Kosovo knew that the British diplomatic establishment could be trusted about as far as it could be thrown. However, in the spirit of keeping their social and political bread buttered on both sides as well as on the crusts, all of them had picked at the burnished steel platters of cocktail-party food, nibbling at the cheese on sticks, the olives, the Ritz biscuits spread with fish paste and the indecently pink circles of sliced meat known in Kosovo, seemingly contradictorily, as 'beef ham'. They had all stood there listening to the endless speeches about democracy, about the importance of multi-ethnicity, of an end to the ethnic violence between Serbs and Albanians and how Kosovo could only find its way towards a modern Europe if it renounced such traditional Balkan pastimes as ethnic cleansing, violence and indulgence in organised crime.

By September 2002, a combination of British and American intelligence operatives, mainly from the SIS and the CIA, had decided that it was time for a 'gloves off' approach to arresting Kosovo Albanian war criminals. Paramount was the need to take to The Hague people against whom there was a case to answer, and sufficient witnesses to give the international prosecutors some chance of getting a conviction. Balanced against this was the importance of not upsetting the fragile apple cart of Kosovo Albanian politics: given that the most-wanted men in the province were also leaders of various political parties, it was going to be difficult to arrest them without sending possibly irreparable fracture lines down Kosovo's massively fragile political ecosystem. A massive level of pragmatic *realpolitik* was needed in dealing with the situation. On the one hand, Carla del Ponte and the ICTY were determined to bring in Ratko Mladic, Radovan Karadzic and other leading Serbs, and del Ponte's criticism of NATO's inability to arrest Mladic and Karadzic had been unceasing. On the other hand, she knew that in the interests of being ethnically fair she had to pay token attention to Macedonian and Kosovo Albanian suspects, in spite of the political disaster this might engender, partly because a demonstration of the will to arrest the latter made dealings with the new Serb government in Belgrade much easier when it came to persuading them to hand over Serb suspects to The Hague.

She knew that arresting Kosovars was not going to be conducive to the furtherance of political stability in the province. She knew that NATO and UNMIK wanted some sort of firm crackdown on those characters who occupied the central overlap of the three circles in the Venn diagram of Kosovo called 'organised criminals', 'ex-KLA commanders wanted for war crimes' and 'leaders of political parties'. UN police in Kosovo and the Judicial Affairs department of UNMIK were tasked with investigating and preparing cases against the majority of ex-KLA commanders, many of them members of the Kosovo Protection Corps, who were wanted for crimes committed before, during or after the bombing campaign. The Hague had primacy in deciding who was to be indicted by the ICTY, not the Kosovo judiciary, and Fatmir Limaj, Ramush Haradinaj and at least one other were among the ex-KLA commanders to be the subjects of 'sealed' indictments issued by The Hague. These indictments differed from 'public' ones inasmuch as those indicted did not know that they featured on any Hague arrest list. In the case of prior sealed indictments, the subject of it, once arrested, was read the charges against him while being transported to The Hague.

By late February 2003 it had been decided that Fatmir Limaj was to be the first Kosovo Albanian to be arrested. His 'lift', as it was called in security circles, would be timed to coincide with the arrests of three co-conspirators at the Llapushnik camp, all of whom were vital witnesses without whom it would be impossible to present a case against Limaj that stood any chance of resulting in a conviction. The British commander of the Multinational Brigade Centre (MNBC) was to be responsible for the arrest operation as the locations in which the suspects would be 'lifted' all lay within the MNBC's operational area. Limaj's primary residence was in Pristina itself. A combination of Italian *Carabinieri* from K-FOR's Multinational Support Unit, Norwegian soldiers and British infantrymen from the 1st Battalion of the Staffords would take part in the operation; in addition, Fatmir Limaj's apartment in Pristina had been under close observation by the British during the days running up to the operation. In an attempt to prevent details of the arrest operation leaking out to the Albanian community, the UN police detachment in Kosovo was not told about it; even Stefan Feller, the German UNMIK police commissioner, was to be kept in the dark about the arrests until after they had taken place. Between 3.00 a.m. and 5.00 a.m. on a typically freezing cold Kosovo spring morning in March 2003, two of Limaj's henchmen were picked up; a third, Agim Murtezi, had been arrested the week before.

Mr Limaj, however, was nowhere to be found in Kosovo.

There followed a day in which NATO's mission in Kosovo did itself no favours. K-FOR was, at that time, commanded by Italian Lieutenant-General Fabio Mini. Known by the British as 'Mini Me', after the character in the Austin Powers films, he was an affable, kindly man, but his ability to command a multinational operation in a post-conflict society had been described by a variety of critics as being somewhere between marginal and non-existent. Under Lieutenant-General Mini's direction, the British brigadier commanding the MNBC – a former CO of 2 Para – had been entrusted with the operation to arrest Limaj. The problem was that Limaj was not in Kosovo. He was skiing in Slovenia, and both Lieutenant-General Mini and Carla del Ponte knew it. So, unbeknown to them, did much of the media in Kosovo. K-FOR spent nearly two days feebly denying that Limaj had been the real target of the operation, despite the fact that Kosovo Albanian journalists from both Reuters and the Associated Press had been in touch with him by mobile phone on the slopes of Slovenia.

In the end, things moved fast: Limaj and Thaci were skiing together one afternoon in March, on a slope high up on the border between Austria and Slovenia. Fatmir Limaj had been in touch with Bajram Rexhepi, the Kosovo Albanian president of Kosovo, and had made an undertaking to turn himself in to UN police the moment he returned to Pristina. He and Thaci stood together on the snowy mountainside, then turned and skied slowly down to the hotel at which they were staying – Thaci skiing back to Kosovo, back to his leadership of a political party, and Fatmir Limaj sliding down the slopes towards arrest and a flight to The Hague. It must have been a strange moment for the two former colleagues-in-arms, who had fought their way across Kosovo against the Serbs and then swapped their camouflage uniforms for dark business suits and political power. At the end of things, Fatmir Limaj came out as the stronger, more impressive person: while NATO, the UN Mission in Kosovo and Carla del Ponte immediately indulged in a gratuitous and well-publicised round of mutual criticism for the failure to arrest Limaj and allowing him to leave Pristina for Slovenia without being apprehended, the man himself went to The Hague with good grace.

In all fairness, it should be mentioned that Carla del Ponte appeared to have enough appreciation of the successful missions carried out by NATO to give praise where it was due: in 1999 she is reported to have gone to Hereford to award the UN medal to a number of 22 SAS personnel who had been involved in operations to apprehend war criminals in the Balkans.

The ICTY arrest operations in March 2003 brought much of the story of Kosovo to an end. In itself, Kosovo had been a vital middle ground for the international community. It had stood between the agonies of the war in Bosnia and the birthing pains of the international community, and the military operations carried out during the War on Terrorism and by those establishing illiberal democracies. Earlier we posed the question of whether perhaps NATO, the UN and the international community had found their best (though very flawed) expression in those days in Kosovo and Macedonia, and that everything thereafter would smack of US-tainted anti-climax. The events in Rwanda and Somalia in the early 1990s had become the two fundamental absolutes by which the necessity for international intervention was to be judged thereafter. While the loss of American lives in Somalia led to its reluctance to deploy troops to assist in halting the Rwandan genocide in 1994, so again much of the responsibility for the launching of NATO air strikes in 1995 against the Serbs in Bosnia – and the subsequent signing of the Dayton Peace Accords – lay with the Americans. If Rwanda and Somalia demonstrated what happened if there was no intervention, or if it went wrong, then the operations of the international community in the former Yugoslavia between 1991 and the signature of the Dayton Peace Accords in 1995 showed what happened if there *was* an intervention which then fluctuated between the successful and disastrous. The interventionist experiments in Bosnia led in no small part to the decision by NATO to bomb Kosovo without a UN mandate. In turn, the chaotic nation-state-building exercise in Kosovo showed the Americans the difficulties of implementing a joint UN and NATO mandate while trying to carry out successful peace-support, peacekeeping and counterinsurgency operations in a post-conflict environment. In Kosovo and Macedonia, Europe and the US were not necessarily in harmony, but perhaps, for once, in some sort of balance that would not be repeated in the foreseeable future.

After the attacks of 11 September 2001, the Americans were firmly decided that any coalition would effectively have to work unilaterally under US command. Afghanistan was the initial implementation of this train of thought, and Operation Iraqi Freedom its natural progression. By the winter of 2003, the focus of international military intervention operations was firmly on Iraq, with its hunt for Saddam Hussein, its daily US military deaths and its scorching suicide bombings in the dust of post-intervention Baghdad. Yet there was to be one possible closing chapter yet to be played out by the SAS in the Balkans. The chaotic, contradictory, impulsively violent, often charming, physically striking former Yugoslavia was to provide the backdrop to one more mission for the Regiment, the last in a decade of operations that had involved the SAS's 'band of brothers' from 1993 onwards. This was to be a final operation to attempt to catch Radovan Karadžić.

After their limited and frustrating role in the war in Afghanistan, which, apart from the strike by 'A' and 'G' Squadrons against the supposed opium-processing plant and al-Qaeda headquarters in southern Helmand, had merely consisted of interdiction patrols on the Afghan–Pakistani border and two small actions in the mountains around Tora Bora, Iraq had been a mixed blessing for the Regiment. The operations to capture Basrah were short in duration, the missions in the west of Iraq were shared predominantly with Australians and in the north of the country and around Baghdad, the Regiment was competing for targets and areas of operations with the Americans. Excellent though they unquestionably were at Special Forces soldiering, the SAS was discovering that while small may be beautiful, size did ultimately matter. When it came to operating on the ground in competition with the Americans, there were often too few of them, with too few and limited assets, to be able to make a huge tactical difference when faced with the sheer numerical and technological superiority of the United States. Task Force 121 operations saw the SAS operating at their best with other nationalities, where their clear superiority in tactical reconnaissance, surveillance, intelligence gathering and close-quarters battle were to the fore.

Operation Trent was a perfect example of what happened when they were handed targets by the Americans. SOCOM had, some said, effectively passed 22 SAS a target just to keep them in the war, allowing them to attack an objective that the Americans perceived as bordering on the marginal side of risky. A well-planned, executed and successful operation 'Trent' had been: a night-time HALO assault into al-Qaeda territory with full kit to mark a tactical landing zone deep in enemy territory, followed by a mobile approach and an attack put in on target without time to carry out detailed advance observation or surveillance. Then had come the assault, with its heavy AQT casualties, some SAS men wounded and intelligence gathered. All in all, it had been a very successful demonstration of the SAS's tactical skills.

However, it could be argued that the operation was completely superfluous to tactical requirements and was excessively risky in terms of manpower and equipment. The Americans could have blown the Helmand opium factory to pieces without the al-Qaeda operatives even knowing that aircraft were passing overhead. The operational imperative for the British was supposedly the capture of intelligence information from the headquarters – two laptop computers and an amount of paperwork were recovered from the central building – but it is worth questioning whether the derived information was worth the cost of Operation Trent. A small US team could have been inserted by HALO to call in an air strike: a couple of bomb runs from an FA-18 followed by some ground-attack runs by a pair of A-10 Warthogs would have happily taken care of the facility. The problem with Afghanistan, from the British SF point of view, was that the Americans had shown that although they needed the SAS, and there was much for them to do, the men from Hereford risked being tactically diverted into carrying out assignments that were not strictly in keeping with their SF remit.

However, it can be argued that an operation to capture Radovan Karadzic would see the Regiment return to the kind of small, contained close-quarters-battle scenario in which it excelled, where its superior skills in weapons drills, surveillance capabilities, tactical fieldcraft and concealment would be at a premium. If a squadron or half-squadron of 22 SAS, backed up by the surveillance assets of 14 Intelligence Company, were able to get a decent fix on Karadzic's whereabouts, conceal that information from the other nationalities of S-FOR in Bosnia-Herzegovina and thus retain a level of secrecy, they would have a decent chance of catching him without taking an unacceptable level of casualties. A successful snatch of Karadzic would firmly cement the SAS's reputation as the lead unit in the world's SF community when it came to complex, high-profile covert operations in hostile territory against a well-armed and numerically superior enemy, with the aim of snatching one high-profile target. The additional tactical skills required to get a team to target would be of the highest order. Lastly, the message such a successful raid would give would be simple: the British would have demonstrated that they could succeed where American, German, French and Dutch SF teams had failed.

An additional benefit of a successful snatch of a high-profile target such as Karadzic would be that the British Special Forces hierarchy would have yet another unique 'battle honour' that would contribute to the unit's worldwide reputation and which would in turn decrease the extent to which 22 would be reliant on the SAS myth to 'sell' the Regiment. They would not have to worry about members of the unit unofficially disclosing information that presented an operational and tactical reality of 22 SAS that somehow fell rather short of the mythical status that has both grown up around the unit and been encouraged to do so. There is a very real danger with a unit like 22 SAS, which has a knife-edge reputation to uphold, that the 'content' of the unit will be exceeded by its 'style'. SAS men are very highly trained soldiers, some infantry, some from support arms, with additional skills in such fields as HALO parachuting, communications, combat medicine, languages, close-quarters battle and vehicle mobility skills. Their officers are picked from the brightest, fittest and best tactical military thinkers and commanders in the British Army, which places them squarely among the highest level of military aptitude in the world. The SAS 'band of brothers' is probably unequalled in its collective expertise. But the Regiment suffers from several flaws. One of them is its occasional tendency towards reliance upon myth to sustain its collective self-image and external perception.

Despite the increased demands put upon the unit by the War on Terrorism, it still does not see nearly as much pure active service as most of its members would like. There will never be enough opium factories or Iranian Embassies, Rokel Creeks or Tora Boras, desert airfields or Kosovos to absorb its hunger for a satisfactory level of event, action and activity to fulfil its perception of itself.

When the Ministry of Defence announced, at the end of October 2003, the list of awards for gallantry, good service, commendable conduct and suchlike from Operation Telic, as the operations during the war in Iraq had been codenamed, there was a very high-profile piece of understatement at the end of it. At the bottom of the list of seven Distinguished Service Orders, twenty Military Crosses, two Conspicuous Gallantry Crosses and one George Cross – all awarded to named recipients – a small, anonymous collection of medals was announced. These included a brace of Distinguished Flying Crosses, plus a bar thereto, and six Military Crosses. It did not take much for anybody inside or outside the Special Forces community to realise that these were MCs awarded to SAS and possibly SBS men, and that the DFCs were probably awarded for flying them in and out of action. The covert message was clear: twenty Military Crosses were awarded for gallantry to named recipients out of a total of some 40,000 British personnel involved in the whole of Operation Iraqi Freedom, but almost a third as many again went to British Special Forces. The message emanating from this couple of lines at the end of the honours list was simple: we saw a good chunk of action, we were brave and gallant, but we will certainly not dream of letting on where, how and to what extent. Yet.

Were the medals awarded for raiding airstrips in western Iraq or shooting up enemy convoys on the main supply routes to Syria and Jordan? Were they for covert insertions into Baghdad dressed as US soldiers? For operating with US Navy SEALs in raids on oil installations on the Al-Faw peninsula? Or for assisting with Secret Intelligence Service information-gathering missions around Basrah before the start of the land conflict? Almost nobody will ever know, for certain, the full details.

This writer certainly will not. Even within the 'Regiment' itself, many members of the unit keep their operational activities as secret from members of other squadrons and troops as the intimate, self-regarding and self-mythologising nature of an elite military unit allows. Serving members are cautioned sometimes from having excessive – or indeed any – contact with former members of the unit. The much-publicised 'disclosure' contract that each man now signs on passing Selection means that the flow of SAS books has been largely curtailed.

Back in Hereford, away from the newspaper shelves and the book stores, among the troops and squadrons that have been in premium 'contacts' – i.e. have exchanged fire with an enemy and perhaps killed people – every man guards jealously as personal, psychologically self-defining trophies those moments of highest risk and achievement, the participation in combat and the shots he has fired at, and perhaps into, the enemy. Whether at the Helmand opium plant, up against the MUP in Kosovo's Drenica Valley or 'slotting' the West Side Niggaz in Sierra Leone, every single SAS man, like every soldier everywhere, knows that the shots he fires in combat and his performance in 'contact' may only comprise, at best, a few hours or days in fifteen to twenty years of service. Yet they are the moments that will define his place among his peers, in the barracks, in front of his superiors, on his official record, at the shining mahogany of every bar worldwide and, most importantly, will fulfil, exceed or fall short of his expectations of self. And most soldiers, like most human beings everywhere, are only really content with themselves when what they do, have done or achieved equals their own expectations of themselves.

Unfortunately, many SAS men may feel that there isn't enough 'contact' to go around, which is why some choose to leave the Regiment to find high-paying employment with private military companies. Hundreds of men have passed through Hereford since the First Gulf War, and since then the number of active service operations in which the unit has participated have been relatively limited. Two Gulf Wars, Bosnia, Kosovo, some war-criminal arrest operations, Sierra Leone, Northern

Ireland and Afghanistan have been – officially – almost it. There are, of course, those operations that have never been officially or unofficially publicised, in places that may or may not include, among others, Yemen, Chechnya, Congo, Pakistan, Ecuador and various parts of Africa. The shock value, the implied threat of an SAS deployment, is often most effective when the full capacities, achievements and shortcomings of the unit remain purposely opaque and obscure. The most powerful cards in the hand are often those that are never laid on the table.

Regardless of the atmosphere of necessary secrecy surrounding the unit's operations, any military analyst, pundit or SF-watcher with a reasonable capacity for military prediction and some technical imagination and knowledge can predict or guess with a reasonable amount of accuracy how some of the unit's operations are carried out. There are, after all, only so many ways to storm a building, rescue hostages from a plane, call in an air strike, mount an assault against a variety of positions, or drive, swim, fly, climb, parachute, walk or run to a particular location. A would-be analyst would not have to be a rocket scientist to imagine the basic format of how an SF operation would be carried out. Part of the argument the British SF community uses to support the concept of total lack of disclosure of information regarding missions is that prior knowledge of SF operating techniques would prove advantageous to those against whom those troops may one day find themselves in opposition. However, in terms of this knowledge, any would-be terrorist, al-Qaeda, IRA or otherwise, is presumably experienced enough to have a good idea of how the SAS, US Delta Force, German GSG-9, the CIA or the British SIS operates.

The internet is too available, specialist defence and electronic publications far too advanced in their knowledge and inside information, the world simply too small for many SF technical operating procedures to remain secret. The enemy nowadays is not some omnipotent criminal mastermind that James Bond might encounter, stroking an albino cat on a swivel chair deep inside his headquarters hidden inside a mountain, where armed lackeys of some indeterminate south-east Asian nationality dressed in orange boiler suits spin around on golf buggies, armed with Uzis, waiting for the order to launch the dastardly missile. Nor are British Special Forces the secret agents of popular imagination, creeping black-suited up to the enemy, poised to strike him down with a lethal combination of cheese-wire garrottes, matt-black crossbows and syringes filled with a killer cocktail of truth serum and tranquilliser. An absence of disclosure to the media does not mean that operational details of SF deployments can be prevented from reaching the amoeba-like organisation of Islamic fundamentalist terrorism, for instance. What should reasonably be kept secret is the locations and deployments of SF teams. The techniques, the equipment, the *modus operandi*, are either partially known, or can sometimes be imagined.

Let's imagine, for instance, how an operation to arrest Radovan Karadzic would be carried out. How would it work? Let us speculate that the operation would take place in the snowy winterscape of western Bosnia-Herzegovina, or across the border in Republika Srbska. Winter is the best time of year to mount such an operation in the Balkans: Serbs, Slavs, Albanians and Croats all prefer to reduce their lives in winter to the absolutes of keeping warm indoors and, where possible, reducing contact with the outside world to a minimum. People in the Balkans prefer to psychologically tunnel away from winter, to hibernate, to try to avoid it rather than confront it. A 'lift' or arrest in winter is also best because Serb four-wheel-drive vehicles would find it almost impossible to navigate on narrow, steep mountain roads covered in ice and snow, thus minimising the possibility of flight. Enemy reinforcements hurrying to the area are thus easier to ambush; it makes a helicopter extraction of the suspect the only possibility. Surveillance and assault assets trained in mountain and arctic warfare will also have an enormous advantage in the snow over any forces defending the target, and the fact that snowy conditions make movement and transport more difficult on every single front leans the advantage towards the attackers.

The location of any assault would obviously be crucial: to be able to hide effectively, Karadzic would rely upon the loyalty of the local Serb population in parts of western Bosnia, Montenegro and Republika Srbska where his bodyguards can operate. It is thus likely that the arrest operation would take place in a remote rural area. One advantage for British Special Forces would be that the insertion of British military assets in the areas named above would be much easier than other potential 'lift' locations because no permission would have to be obtained to allow them to infiltrate a second sovereign country. The NATO troops – British and otherwise – deployed on the S-FOR mission in Bosnia-Herzegovina are present under an international mandate, and the men from the SAS, SBS and 14 Intelligence Company could enter the area unrestricted by the necessity to request permission from a host government.

A secondary consideration would be that of secrecy. Given the fact that past operations to arrest Karadzic have been compromised by tip-offs passed from NATO headquarters to his security apparatus, allegedly by elements of the French military, among others, it would be of paramount importance to restrict operational awareness of any arrest attempt to British and US circles. If the deployment of a full SAS squadron, along with requisite attachments and detachments of intelligence and surveillance personnel, could be effected while keeping the information as covert as possible, it is conceivable that Karadzic could be taken by surprise. Strangers approaching any location where he was even remotely suspected of being in hiding, or where members of his family live, have over the last few years been strongly suspected of being hostile forces masquerading as journalists or humanitarian workers. Given that sightings of Radovan Karadzic in parts of the Balkans are as frequent as the dozens of claimed sightings of Saddam Hussein and Osama bin Laden in Iraq and Afghanistan, speed would be of the essence.

An operational breakdown might look something like this. It should be borne in mind that everything in the subsequent scenario is entirely fictionalised, despite being based upon known Special Forces operating procedures, past operational plans, local conditions and information received from S-FOR, ICTY and other NATO officials involved in planning arrest operations.

The arrest operation will be codenamed 'Operation Otter', while the diversionary operation will be known as 'Dilemma'.

British military assets: thirty-four men from a squadron of 22 SAS – whichever Sabre Squadron is on standby – would be allocated the task. Up to ten two-man teams from 14 Intelligence Company (14 Int) plus, as necessary, one troop of Royal Marine Mountain Leaders from the Mountain and Arctic Warfare (M&AW) Cadre.

Intelligence assets: British SIS, US CIA and requisite UN personnel from the International War Crimes Tribunal for the Former Yugoslavia (ICTY), based in The Hague.

Air assets: helicopter strike capability, as well as helicopter-lift capability for British assets. The former would probably have to be US Apaches or Cobras, the latter Pumas and Chinooks from the RAF's Special Forces Flight.

Weaponry: personal assault weapons for the SAS teams, including a variety of Heckler & Koch options, US M4 carbines, Barratt .50-calibre sniper rifles, PM Accuracy International sniper rifles, 7.62mm GPMGs and M-203 40mm grenade launchers. Fire support will also be provided by Apaches if necessary.

Exfiltration of suspect: by helicopter to Eagle US Air Force Base, Tuzla, thence by aircraft to The Hague.

Posing as a combination of humanitarian assessment officials from the UN Development Programme, the British Department for International Development, the US Agency for International Development and an American NGO, eighteen men and women – British, American, Bosnian, Polish, Albanian and Croat – from the CIA's Special Operations Group, the British Secret Intelligence Service, the British Army's 14 Int and the Royal Marines Mountain and Arctic Warfare Cadre, have had Radovan Karadzic and his entourage under intermittent surveillance for seven weeks. Karadzic travels in a combination of Toyota Land Cruisers, unmarked saloon cars, Nissan Patrol four-by-fours and police vehicles. Twelve of these individuals from the CIA, the Royal Marines and 14 Int are now dug in around the village where Karadzic is hiding;

the remainder are in Sarajevo and hidden in and around the towns of Foca and Pale, and observing three other villages.

Between thirty and fifty-five bodyguards accompany Karadzic on major moves between villages and towns; he sometimes travels accompanied by fewer than five companions. All are heavily and permanently armed. They are in touch with each other and with loyal colleagues in Sarajevo, Banja Luka, Belgrade and elsewhere by satellite phone, Thuraya satellite mobile, mobile phone and Codan radio system. French and Russian officers and officials in Kosovo, Bosnia-Herzegovina, Republika Srbska and Zagreb, as well as Paris, Moscow and at the UN, along with a network of loyal Serbs, are in touch with them frequently. In addition, a German intelligence official from the BND (the *Bundesnachrichten-dienst*, the German Intelligence Service) stationed in Sarajevo is also a Serb double agent, and two French military intelligence officials from the *Direction Générale de la Sécurité Extérieure* (DGSE), a man and a woman, are both tasked to protect Karadzic from arrest at all costs. The female member of the team is fascinated by and partly in love with a Polish paratroop colonel who is posing as a freelance photographer, while actually free-lancing for MI6. The ICTY investigators, American and British, are also passing information to their respective governments. The Polish colonel has guessed what the French woman does. An Israeli woman working on secondment from her foreign ministry to the European Agency for Reconstruction, essentially a forestry expert but in fact working for MOSSAD, is sleeping with both the British Foreign Office's liaison officer to S-FOR (who is ignorant of her true identity) and a lieutenant-colonel from the French Army who is working as a military attaché to the EU. He in turn is sleeping with his Serb interpreter and knows who the Israeli woman is and is thus passing information accordingly both to the inter-preter, who he knows is passing it on in turn, and to the DGSE. This small group of people are intricately connected, via the vast, sprawling network of the international community, to S-FOR, the Office of the Higher Representative, the UN, the EU and every humanitarian organisation represented in the region. All is as normal in the Balkans.

By early December snow is thick on the ground in Krastovac, the mountain village above Foca where Karadzic has spent three nights. The night-time temperature drops to -15°C. The population of the small village is 490 people. Three families lost male members in the war, killed by Bosnian Muslims and Croats. Another family's eldest son disappeared after his vehicle was ambushed in 1993 by a unit of *mujahideen* fighters in northern Bosnia. The only trace of information they have heard about him has come from Karadzic's entourage of paramilitaries, who tell them that a photo exists of some foreign Islamic fighters playing football with his head. A fifth family has no head of the household after he was arrested by the British in Prijedor in 1997. There are three roads and tracks into the village that are negotiable by vehicle in this weather, all being watched by members of the 'lift' team. From the village there is a clear view across both sides of the valley. Behind the houses the forested slopes rise up to a small mountain plateau, only a day or two's trek from Montenegro. Karadzic is here with thirty-one bodyguards. In the neighbouring three villages, from which he has come and to which he will go, are another seventy-three bodyguards. All of them have killed before, frequently, in Kosovo, Croatia, the Krajina and Bosnia. They are former members of Franko 'Frenki' Simatovic's paramilitary gang – 'Frenki's Boys' – and ex-members of the former special-operations troops of the Serbian State Security Service – *Jedinica za Specijalne Operacije*, or JSO. The remainder are a combination of former MUP anti-terrorist policemen, members of Karadzic's extended clan and Serb soldiers. When Karadzic moves, the retinue of 104 men will move with him through a network of towns and villages, providing a mobile, fluid protection unit alert to the comings and goings across 32km of mountain and valley.

Dug into snow-hides on the side of the opposite valley, in the tree-line above and behind the village and in a clump of scrub oak just next to one of the three routes in and out of the village, are three teams of watchers. Down the mountain in Foca and in Pale, two of the British and American teams are working in mobile clinics run by *Médecins sans Frontières* and recently taken over by an American aid agency. In the last two days, a Serb man whom the team has identified as being wanted by the ICTY for a minor role in the fighting and subsequent killing of Albanian refugees around the Kosovan town of Pec in 1999 has been to the clinic in Foca twice. He was asking for insulin supplies and a particular injectable medicine for a liver disorder common among Serbs and Albanians who have been exposed to a particularly high level of lead in their drinking and washing water. Karadzic and his entourage, the team know, are somewhere in the hills. That night it snows again. The two footpaths into the village of Krastovac, where Karadzic is hiding, become impassable. Only the main road is accessible, and even that is covered with iced mud. Karadzic stays put but warns his sentries and bodyguards to be on the alert, particularly during the night, and to be ready for an immediate move across the frozen plateau to Montenegro. Later that night it snows again, much more heavily. While Karadzic sleeps, neither he nor his bodyguards – not even those on guard – can hear the rumble of the engines of a C-130 Hercules aircraft flying at 7,315m above the clouds. They certainly cannot hear the *smack* and *flap* of the Ram-Air parachutes belonging to the sixteen members of Air Troop of 'D' Squadron of 22 SAS, who have made a night-time HALO parachute jump off the back of the Hercules' ramp, with oxygen, from 6,400m up in the snowbound sky. Nor can anybody hear the soft *crump* as the men land with their equipment in a snow-drifted field 2km below the village, swiftly burying the parachutes and vanishing into the tree-line, guided in by two of the 14 Int recce patrol in liaison with four Marines from the M&AW Cadre.

Simultaneously, another eight-man half-troop from 'D' Squadron's Mountain Troop, led by a captain, are climbing up the mountainside from the road that threads through the valley towards Foca, and another twelve SAS men from Mountain and Mobility Troops along with the squadron OC have been dropped by helicopter on the deserted plateau 4.8km from the village. A Royal Marine team has marked a helicopter landing zone and secured it just out of the tree-line between the plateau and the village. The three watching teams leave their observation posts and all six members – four British, two American – move towards the village. The sixteen soldiers from Air Troop, along with four Royal Marines, four 14 Int personnel and two American CIA Special Operations Group operators will make up the cut-off-and-ambush group along the road, on the edge of the valley and on the southern flank of the village as the assault team of twenty SAS troops enters the village from behind and to the right just before 4 a.m. Minutes before midnight, Karadzic will get a phone call from the French colonel, the German BDR double agent and a Russian intelligence co-ordinator in Sarajevo and from Serbs in Banja Luka. All will warn him that the following day, at dawn, an operation to arrest him will take place some 40km from his location in another village. Shortly after this information has been received, Karadzic's men will take a flurry of other mobile phone calls, mostly from their Serb paramilitary bodyguard colleagues in and around the location of Operation Dilemma, where, in a diversionary assault, a convoy of American, French and German Humvees and armoured personnel carriers have just arrived, accompanied by a noisy helicopter assault. Shortly before 4 a.m., the assault in Krastovac will begin.

Within an hour of the start of the operation, Radovan Karadzic will be on board an American Black Hawk helicopter, escorted by three Apache helicopter gunships, heading for Tuzla, plasticuffed, sedated, his charges having been read to him by a UN staffer from The Hague. Behind him, 'D' Squadron and their various attachments and detachments will be fighting back from the village with air cover from two Apaches as they make their way to the helicopter landing zone on the edge of the plateau and the tree-line. Behind them are twenty-four dead Serbs, five very seriously wounded and six more lying injured or dying somewhere out in the snow as they were caught trying to flee. Eight have been taken prisoner. The British and American forces have taken seven wounded, two badly, and two dead. Back in Sarajevo, the CO 22 SAS signals a successful operation . . .

Some of the Regiment's detractors would argue that a company of the Duke of Wellington's Regiment, the Scots Guards or the Princess of

Wales's Royal Regiment, for instance, could have fought and won the battle at the opium plant in Helmand Province, or at Tora Bora, or, sufficiently well mounted, some of the Regiment's other operations in Iraq. Casualties would no doubt have been higher. However, lifting Radovan Karadzic – alive – from inside hostile western Bosnia, against extremely well-armed, numerically superior close protection, would be an operation requiring tactical speed and complete flexibility, enormous skill at arms and CQB skills of the SAS. It would be subject to massive, critical media scrutiny in the case of collateral damage to civilians or if the operation failed with significant loss of British life, or with SAS men taken prisoner. Essentially, therefore, it was a job tailor-made for the SAS.

By September 2003, as the hunts for Saddam Hussein, Osama bin Laden and Radovan Karadzic continued apace in Iraq, Afghanistan and the former Yugoslavia, and as the global war on terrorism struggled manfully onwards, the British SAS found itself engaged on active service almost continuously. Many of the theatres of operations in which they had worked for the preceding ten years were now quiet, while several, like Iraq, were busier than ever. Another fundamental way in which the Regiment had changed operationally since the attacks in New York on 11 September two years before was that the nature, number and geographical locations of its deployments had increased enormously. Prior to 11 September 2001, the Regiment had maintained a necessary balance between training and operations that had proved impossible to sustain post-11 September.

For a unit with a 'bayonet strength' of some three hundred men at most, they had become extremely overstretched, and despite calling on 'R' Squadron and the two Territorial Regiments, 23 and 21 SAS, for extra manpower, there was no shortage of worldwide operational commitments. There was a feeling among the higher echelons of the British Special Forces that the SAS risked being deployed operationally on tasks which did not allow them to maximise their potential. Put bluntly, the then Director Special Forces – a Parachute Regiment brigadier, and the CO of the Regiment – a lieutenant-colonel from the Irish Guards, felt that many of the operational missions being carried out by the unit could just as easily be assigned to infantry units, or to the Parachute Regiment or Royal Marines. If the existing 16 Air Assault Brigade was split into two, to allow the British forces' helicopter assets to remain in one brigade and their airborne and parachute assets to be consolidated in another, then a company of paratroopers – or indeed a battalion – could be earmarked to be on standby to support SF operations in an infantry capacity. This proposal for two effective brigades would see the re-instatement of 5 Airborne Brigade, a unit to which at least two battalions of the Parachute Regiment would be attached.

Secondly, there was concern that the preponderance of Parachute Regiment soldiers serving in the SAS and the subsequent 'Para-isation' of the unit should be addressed. Although highly trained, aggressive and well-motivated airborne infantry, part of the concept of Parachute Regiment élitism does not really fit into the world of the SAS. The idea of a 'badged' SAS man from a non-airborne parent unit being discriminated against or criticised by a former member of the Parachute Regiment for belonging to a 'craphat' or non-airborne unit displays a remarkable lack of judgement. One of many ways in which the SAS has become what it is today is through the homogenisation of soldiers with vastly differing backgrounds from many different units. If a newly relaunched 5 Airborne Brigade, with its predominance of paratroopers, can be established as a temple to the airborne spirit, then the SAS can surely continue to uphold its original values as a multidisciplinary, truly special force. In several accounts of SAS operations that have taken place from the First Gulf War to the Second, written by SAS men, defence analysts and journalists, there is a suggestion that the SAS Regimental Headquarters believes that the 'blooding' of troops untried under fire is sufficiently important that it can become an operational imperative in itself. The attack on the Iraqi radio facility codenamed 'Victor Two' carried out by a patrol from 'A' Squadron during the First Gulf War is an example of this. Yet the need for the Regiment to undertake operations is paramount: the only way that soldiers who have never been in combat can become good soldiers in combat is by being in it. The only way to learn how to react to effective enemy fire, to shoot straight and keep your weapon clean and prevent stoppages while under fire and to master the physically exhausting techniques of fire and manoeuvre is to perfect them on exercise and then transfer this capacity into combat. 'Train hard, fight easy,' as the Russian military tactician Victor Suvorov would say. This is an operational given understood by the SAS. Self-evident though this truth is, it is a difficult one to implement in reality. In fire fights from Angola to Macedonia, from Somalia to Serbia via way of Burundi, Chechnya and Afghanistan, there is no substitute for the direct experience of being shot at or being in a live battlefield situation. Some armies – the upper echelons of the French military being a good example – prefer to claim tactical efficiency and operational know-how through mastery of technical 'stages' or courses, rather than of basic fighting skills. Thus a French paratroop corporal with a couple of years' service may have passed a sniper course or a commando course, or been trained as a reconnaissance swimmer, yet be incapable of digging a trench, camouflaging himself properly or of understanding why smoking at night in an ambush position is a tactical no-no.

However, tempting though it is to give men operational experience, it is preferable that the SAS should avoid operations such as 'Trent'. The intelligence gained from the al-Qaeda laptop computers and paperwork obtained in the raid may have been marginally useful, but very unlikely to have justified the enormous cost of the operation and the risk of losing many highly trained SAS soldiers. Operation Trent, were it to have been deemed an operational necessity, should perhaps have been carried out in the following manner. A battalion of paratroopers, Marines or infantry could have been in position to support the SAS operation, and could even have carried out the assault themselves. SAS troops or troops from 5 Airborne Brigade's Pathfinder Platoon could have used freefall parachute techniques to prepare a tactical landing zone for Hercules transport aircraft, as the SAS did in the actual operation. Sufficient vehicles could have been brought in to transport a company of infantry or more to the target, which would then have been assaulted in exactly the same manner as it was by the SAS, except by Paras or Marines or another line infantry unit. However, it is debatable whether another unit would have taken such low casualties as the SAS, and it is also questionable whether or not the training levels of another less specialised unit would have been sufficient to let them win the day. What is not in question is that if such operations are going to be carried out for the foreseeable future purely by Special Forces, then it is unlikely that the Regiment will ever have a chance to revert to its true, original identity the cross between the Long-Range Desert Group, the Special Operations Executive and a counterinsurgency combat and training team, the role for which it was originally created.

In summary, it is, perhaps, time for the SAS to revert a little in terms of its role. It should remain elliptically distant from the public eye and robustly independent from being tainted by any political and socio-intellectual mediocrity from the political sphere. It should seek to understand, yet maintain a cautious distance from, the proto-humanitarianism of some military interventions and from the attitudinising of the experienced, able yet ultimately closeted civilian echelons of the international community. It is overdue and necessary that the British SF operational family should become slightly bigger, better funded and have more equipment. It is equally important that more operational opportunities be given to infantry units outside the SF and 'nearly SF' wagon circle.

But the British Special Forces community does not need to fret: there is still plenty for them to do. The bar of world geopolitics and Special Forces operations has, as it were, been granted a late licence. The phone will always ring, and somebody important will always want to ask the Regiment to dance. And when it does, among its contemporaries, its colleagues and competitors from America, Australia, Poland and wherever else, it will always look good under the midnight lights.

Postscript

On a quiet Wednesday in March 2004 Kosovo exploded into the worst inter-ethnic violence the province had seen since NATO's arrival in June 1999 and the days of the old Serb regime. At the time all international eyes were focused on Iraq and on the renewed hunt for Osama bin Laden on the border with Pakistan and Afghanistan. SAS men from 22 and from the two Territorial Regiments, 21 and 23, were reported to be operating with Taskforce 121 and the Pakistani army on both sides of the isolated frontier: word was that bin Laden or one of his senior deputies was holed up in some lost mountain hideaway in Waziristan, where the Pakistan border meets Afghanistan. The air was filled with helicopter clatter; sporadic and intense fire fights erupted from valley to valley. Islamic fundamentalist prisoners were being taken, and the net, once again, was said to be closing in.

In Iraq the first anniversary of the war was heralded by a round of bombings as the former regime loyalists tried to terrorise the internationals into quitting; they, in turn, were triumphant in their announcements of the number of schools rebuilt, wells dug, local councils installed, and the number of Iraqis delighted to see the coalition in power rather than Saddam Hussein. Seven countries away, the scene on the edge of the railway lines at three stations in Madrid gave no cause for celebration: 200 people were killed and hundreds wounded by the simultaneous blasts of seven al-Qaeda explosions. Reacting immediately, the newly elected Spanish Prime Minister Jose Luis Rodriguez Zapatero swore to pull Spanish troops out of Iraq. Some quarters saw that terrorism was a winning card to play.

So when on 17 March Kosovo exploded overnight into a wave of ethnic cleansing unparalleled since Milosevic's days, everybody from K-FOR and the UN was taken completely by surprise. In a co-ordinated and planned series of attacks on the province's remaining Serb ghettos – from Mitrovica in the north to Gnjilane in the east and from Peja in the west to Pristina itself – gangs of Albanians hundreds strong fought running battles with K-FOR and UNMIK police as they tried to storm into the Serb enclaves. The embattled Serbs were evacuated by NATO armoured vehicles under hails of rocks, hand grenades and, in some cases, bullets. Even American troops, up until now the saviours of the Albanians, were not immune to attack. By the time the tear gas cleared and the flames died down on the dozens of burning Serb houses across Kosovo, twenty-eight people lay dead and 600 had been injured, while twenty-five Serb churches and seven villages had been torched.

It took this Albanian race to cleanse Kosovo of Serbs once and for all before the international community realised that perhaps partition of the province along ethnic lines was the only answer. The international community had tried to impose democracy where there had never been democratic standards; multiculturalism where there had mostly only been intolerance, and multi-ethnicity in places where recent history said that only mono-ethnic societies could flourish. While it was understood that Kosovo had a long way to go, it was imperative that the efforts of 1999 should not be wasted, and that the international community make something work before leaving this, their most dramatic experiment in building the foundations of a nation state.

'We must make sure that we never come back here again,' Britain's astute Brigadier Simon Mayall had said in autumn 2002 in Pristina. 'It is incumbent on us to make sure that we get this one right.'

Index